"'Sustainability' is an elusive concep[t] requires us to envision what cannot [...] it persuasively is one of the most urg[ent ...]ing *Sustainability*, Margaret Robertson take[s] a very solid step toward achieving that lofty goal."

—*Sam H. Ham, Professor Emeritus, University of Idaho, USA*

"Communicating anything effectively requires understanding not only the content you want to convey, but also your target audience: how they perceive, learn, and think, as well as what motivates them. *Communicating Sustainability* provides, in one easy-to-read resource, the knowledge you need to enable you to explain sustainable practices to your audience, and to motivate them to follow through with action."

—*Jeffrey Johnson, Assistant Professor, University of San Francisco, USA*

"Margaret Robertson's book provides an in-depth examination of the many methods used to present sustainability and contains a new and relevant perspective on how sustainability is explained. This comprehensive and thoughtful work engages all readers and describes a range of tools used to effectively explain sustainability. The reader leaves with a new-found understanding of the subject."

—*Michael Meister, Director Of Exhibition Design,*
American Museum Of Natural History, USA

"If sustainability is the major concern for people in the 21st century, then communicating sustainability is one of our biggest challenges. This book is not only timely, but critical in generating the level of public involvement necessary to move towards a more sustainable future. The book integrates and then applies existing communication theory and practice to the complex situations that underpin sustainability and should be required reading for all sustainability practitioners."

—*Gianna Moscardo, Professor, James Cook University, Australia*

"Margaret Robertson has synthesized an impressive amount of interdisciplinary research into a fascinating and readable book. To achieve sustainability, we need to understand how complex ecosystems and organizations work. But to communicate beyond the bubble of the converted, we also need to know how people work. Importantly, *Communicating Sustainability* draws on state-of-the-art research in human cognition to suggest methods of communication between communities with widely divergent values. Such a comprehensive and scientifically grounded approach to a multifaceted problem makes this a truly exceptional text."

—*Rebecca Todd, Assistant Professor, University of British Columbia, Canada*

COMMUNICATING SUSTAINABILITY

Communicating Sustainability is a book of evidence-based strategies for making sustainability vivid, accessible, and comprehensible. To do this, it brings together research from a range of specialties including cognitive psychology, visual perception, communication studies, environmental design, interpretive exhibit design, interpretive signage, wayfinding, storytelling, courtroom litigation, information graphics, and graphic design to illustrate not only what approaches are effective but why they work as they do.

The topic of sustainability is vast and complex. It interconnects multiple dimensions of human culture and the biosphere and involves a myriad of systems and processes, many of which are too large, too small, too fast, or too slow to see. Many people find verbal explanations about all of this too abstract or too complicated to understand, and for most people the concepts of sustainability are regarded as quirky, peripheral, and not essential to everyday life. Yet the challenges of sustainability concern the very survival of most species of life on Earth, including the human species. In order for life as we know it to survive and thrive into the future, sustainability must become broadly understood—by everyone, not just activists or specialists. This book offers tools to help make complex systems and nuanced, abstract ideas concrete and comprehensible to the broadest range of people. The goal of communication, and of this book, is to build understanding.

Margaret Robertson is a member of the American Society of Landscape Architects (ASLA) and teaches at Lane Community College in Eugene, Oregon, USA, where she coordinates the Sustainability degree program. She is the author of *Sustainability Principles and Practice* (second edition) and *Dictionary of Sustainability*.

COMMUNICATING SUSTAINABILITY

Margaret Robertson

Routledge
Taylor & Francis Group

LONDON AND NEW YORK

earthscan
from Routledge

First published 2019
by Routledge
2 Park Square, Milton Park, Abingdon, Oxon OX14 4RN

and by Routledge
711 Third Avenue, New York, NY 10017

Routledge is an imprint of the Taylor & Francis Group, an informa business

© 2019 Margaret Robertson

The right of Margaret Robertson to be identified as author of this work has been asserted by her in accordance with sections 77 and 78 of the Copyright, Designs and Patents Act 1988.

British Library Cataloguing-in-Publication Data
A catalogue record for this book is available from the British Library

Library of Congress Cataloguing-in-Publication Data
Names: Robertson, Margaret, 1950– author.
Title: Communicating sustainability / Margaret Robertson.
Description: Abingdon, Oxon; New York, NY: Routledge, 2018. | Includes bibliographical references and index.
Identifiers: LCCN 2018009976 (print) | LCCN 2018026502 (ebook) | ISBN 9781315659015 (eBook) | ISBN 9781138963054 (hbk) | ISBN 9781138963061 (pbk) | ISBN 9781315659015 (ebook)
Subjects: LCSH: Sustainability—Social aspects. | Communication in the environmental sciences. | Communication in economic development.
Classification: LCC HC79.E5 (ebook) | LCC HC79.E5 R62425 2015 (print) | DDC 338.9/27014—dc23
LC record available at https://lccn.loc.gov/2018009976

ISBN: 978-1-138-96305-4 (hbk)
ISBN: 978-1-138-96306-1 (pbk)
ISBN: 978-1-315-65901-5 (ebk)

Typeset in Bembo
by codeMantra

CONTENTS

Abbreviations   *xi*

PART I
Perception and Communication   **1**

1 Context: Why It Matters   3
   About This Book 3
   Sustainability: Life in the Anthropocene 4
   Information Overload 6
   Positive Messages: Beyond the Deficit Model 7
   Social Factors 8

2 Perception and Cognition   12
   Visual Perception 12
   Emotion   17
   Cognition 18

3 Communication Principles   23
   Guidelines for Clear Communication 24
   Visual Communication 27

PART II
Making Sustainability Visible   **31**

4 Metaphor   33

5 Stories 37
The Significance of Stories 37
Narrative Principles 38
Narrative Structure 40
Some Examples 41

6 Interpretive Exhibits and Signs 44
Interpretation 44
Exhibit Design 55
Personal Interpretation 59
Interpretive Signage 60
Art 64
Planning for Interpretation 65

7 Wayfinding 71
Wayfinding and the Ancient Human Brain 71
The Wayfinding Process 72
Wayfinding Planning and Design 77
Signage 78
Maps 81

8 Visible Processes 84
Models 84
Concrete Representation 85
Frames 90
Infrastructure 90
Green Infrastructure 91
Buildings and Sites 92

PART III
Practical Details **95**

9 Graphic Design 101 97
Shapes 97
Color 98
Typography 101
Composition and Design 104
Grids and Other Layouts 107
The Golden Section 108
Doing Design 109

10 Images   110
    Images Have Impact 110
    Comparing Photographs and Drawings 112
    Choosing Images 113
    Composing Photographs 115
    Digital Images: Rasters, Vectors, and Resolution 116
    Finding and Using Images 117

11 Graphs and Diagrams   119
    Information Graphics Help Us Understand
        Systems 119
    Tables 120
    Graphs 121
    Other Charts 122
    Diagrams 123
    Maps 124
    Design 125
    Information Visualization 126

12 Reporting Tools   128
    Indicators 128
    Frameworks 131
    Footprints 132
    Labels 132
    Menus 134
    Information Dashboards 135

13 Digital Media   136
    Websites 136
    Video 142
    Multimedia 144
    Interactive Digital Media 144
    Simulations 146
    Animations 149
    Social Media 150

14 Meetings   153
    How to Have a Good Meeting 153
    Public Participation 161
    Conferences and Workshops 162
    Planning Tools 166

15 Communication Tools   169
   Written Documents 169
   Policies 175
   News Media 177
   Personal Communication Tools 179
   Presentations 182
   Communication Plans 188

Bibliography   193
Index   205

ABBREVIATIONS

ADA   Americans with Disabilities Act
BIM   building information modeling
CAD   computer-aided design
CMYK   cyan, magenta, yellow, black
CPM   critical path method
dpi   dots per inch
DWG   drawing
EGD   environmental graphic design
EMS   environmental management system
FAQ   frequently asked question
FSC   Forest Stewardship Council
GIS   geographic information systems
GRI   Global Reporting Initiative
HTML   Hypertext Markup Language
ISO   International Organization for Standardization
JPEG   Joint Photographic Experts Group
LEED   Leadership in Energy and Environmental Design
LIDAR   Light Detection and Ranging
NCS   Natural Color System
PARK   preserve, add, remove, keep
PDF   Portable Document Format
PERT   program evaluation review technique
PNG   Portable Network Graphics
ppi   pixels per inch
RFP   request for proposal
RGB   red, green, blue
SEGD   Society for Experiential Graphic Design

SEO	search engine optimization
SPI	Society of Plastics Industries
STARS	Sustainability Tracking, Assessment and Rating System
SWOT	strengths, weaknesses, opportunities, threats
TBL	triple bottom line
TIFF	Targeted Image File Format
TORE	theme, organized, relevant, enjoyable
URL	Uniform Resource Locator
VNR	video news releases

PART I

Perception and Communication

1

CONTEXT: WHY IT MATTERS

About This Book

This book is not about how to motivate behavior change, which many others cover in detail. This book focuses on the role of communication in building understanding. It is about how understanding can be nurtured and ideas can be made more clear. Effective communication begins with an understanding of how the human brain works, then uses practical skills grounded in this understanding. After we build some knowledge of cognitive psychology and perception, we can learn practical approaches to good communication from a range of specialties, including how storytellers reach audiences, how interpreters design museum exhibits, how environmental designers facilitate wayfinding, how graphic designers lay out pages, how information designers make graphs and diagrams, how trial lawyers communicate to juries, how web designers make useful websites, and how writers and speakers of all sorts communicate clearly. In the course of this book we will try to understand not only what approaches are effective but why they work as they do.

You will find the same themes appearing repeatedly across these specialties: figure/ground, landmarks, chunking, pattern-seeking, association, contrast, and story. We will consider how our goal is not only to increase our audience's knowledge of facts, but to help them to think their own thoughts and to make their own connections based on better understanding. As an interpreter with the US National Park Service said, "Interpretation... facilitates democracy. It allows for and stimulates a conversation of multiple meanings and points of view" (Larsen 2003, 73). It is true not only of interpretation, but of communication in its many forms. There are multiple scales at which to work, there are multiple arenas in which to work, there are all kinds of people living all kinds of lives with all kinds of worldviews, and in this time of consequential planetary changes, we need them all. Effective communication will be essential in navigating the challenges and opportunities of life in the Anthropocene Epoch (Folke 2013, 27).

Sustainability: Life in the Anthropocene

Sustainability is about systems. They operate at every scale, from the microscopic to the planetary. Human society and economies are connected to and intimately dependent upon these systems. Yet our brains are not wired to process interconnectedness and systems thinking; we are wired to see primarily simple cause and effect (Makower 2009, 269). And so a significant part of our goal in communicating sustainability is to make the work of the biosphere visible, including the ways ecosystems are intertwined in all the dimensions of life on Earth: environmental, economic, and social (Folke 2013, 27).

Sustainability means enduring into the long-term future. It refers to systems and processes that are able to operate and persist on their own over long periods of time.

In the modern era, however, the planet faces many problems that are connected, including poverty, impaired health, overpopulation, resource depletion, food and water scarcity, political instability, and the destruction of the life support systems on which we all depend. We live on a planet that is changing fast. Since 1960 the human population has more than doubled, global consumption of water has more than tripled, and the use of fossil fuels has quadrupled (Foley 2010, 54). Synthetic pesticides and heavy metals are found in the tissues of every animal on earth. The end of cheap fossil fuels is looming. The planet's sixth mass extinction is underway, with 50 percent of species alive today predicted to be gone by the year 2100 (Wilson 2002, 102). Ninety percent of large fish have disappeared from many ocean fisheries, victims of overfishing. Where rivers empty into oceans, runoff laden with synthetic fertilizers has pulled oxygen out of coastal waters and left dead zones devoid of animal life. Coral reefs are dying and mollusk populations shrinking as carbon dioxide concentrations make ocean waters increasingly acidic. Mountain glaciers are melting, deserts are growing, sea level is rising, and waves of climate refugees are likely in the near future.

Collectively our consumption currently exceeds Earth's carrying capacity by 40 percent (Ewing et al. 2010, 18), and we are on track to exceed it by 100 percent by the 2030s (Gilding 2011, 52). That is, we are already in overshoot, the condition in which human demands exceed the regenerative capacities of the biosphere by depleting its natural capital and overfilling its waste sinks.

Humans have become a geological force on a planetary scale. We live at the beginning of a new geological epoch known as the Anthropocene, an unprecedented period in which human activity has become such a powerful force that it has major, planet-scale impact on climate and on every living system. A proposal to formalize the Anthropocene as a geological epoch, that is, at the same hierarchical level as the earlier Pleistocene and Holocene epochs, is currently being considered by the International Commission on Stratigraphy

(ICS), the official scientific body which formally establishes the geological time scale (Anthropocene Working Group 2016). The Anthropocene epoch is generally understood to have begun around 1800 CE at the start of the Industrial Revolution (Crutzen 2002, 23). Beginning in 1945, the Anthropocene entered a second stage researchers identify as the "Great Acceleration," when multiple aspects of human impact including population, resource use and environmental deterioration began expanding exponentially (Steffen, Crutzen, and McNeill 2007, 617).

The Holocene has apparently come to an end, and humanity faces novel conditions it has not encountered before. We face multiple, global-scale issues including food scarcity, aquifer depletion, pollution, habitat destruction, extinction, depletion of renewable and nonrenewable resources, climate destabilization, social inequity, failing states, growing control by powerful corporate interests, and widening gaps between rich and poor. Many of these issues are what are known as wicked problems, problems that are difficult to solve because they are complex, interconnected, and continually evolving (Steffen 2014, 1). Behind them all lie two fundamental drivers: consumption, built on the economic growth model, and human population growth.

The question is not whether we will change, but how, and what form the transition will take. Navigating the shifting conditions, fostering transformations in the sociocultural realm while we strive to avoid crossing planetary-scale thresholds into an undesirable state-shift in the biospheric realm, will require that we find ways to live better and to work together like never before.

We will need to shift rapidly away from fossil fuels, power our lives with renewable energy sources, and use energy more efficiently whatever the source. We'll need to reduce per-capita resource consumption, provision ourselves from zero-waste circular economies, reduce population growth, and provide food to increasing numbers of people without converting new areas of land or destroying habitat. We will need to use renewable resources no faster than they can regenerate. We will need to live within the planet's capacity to support us and our fellow creatures into the long-term future.

We will need not just technological adaptations, but social and political ones as well. Sustainability will depend on having informed, ecologically literate citizens working toward healthy ecosystems, genuine social inclusion, and equitable distribution of resources. We will need strong communities, networks of all kinds, and participatory governance at multiple scales, as we build the foundations for a thriving, sustainable human civilization and biosphere (Engelman 2013, 17).

Humans have gone through several major transitions in their history: the discovery of fire, the development of language, the development of agriculture and civilization, and the Industrial Revolution. Today we live on the threshold of what has been called the "fifth great turning" (Heinberg 2011, 284), a turn away from a fossil fuel-powered, climate-destabilizing, growth-based industrial economy and toward a sustainable, regenerative society.

Better communication is a missing piece. Thanks to decades of scientific research, we have ample information to understand the severity and causes of the global problems that face us, and projections of future trajectories of these problems are remarkably consistent (Groffman et al. 2010, 284). We have enough understanding to be able to halt and even reverse these trends. Yet year after year surveys find that the level of concern over climate change and other environmental issues remains relatively unchanged despite increased public debate and media coverage (Gallup 2017; Makower 2015). Apparently, pure facts are not enough. A fundamental goal for all people who work to educate or to foster positive change is to make the issues and potential solutions of sustainability visible.

Why are the realities of the threats to sustainability so hard to acknowledge and understand? For one thing, because they are invisible to us; they are very large, very small, and very slow. We think of many of the impacts of climate change, for example, as in another time in the long-term future, or in a distant place, such as the melting of glaciers on faraway mountaintops. The primary cause of climate change, greenhouse gas emissions from burning fossil fuels, is an invisible clear gas that acts slowly over time and does not lead directly to immediate or noticeable impacts (Kunkle and Monroe 2015, 150). The changes seem undetectable and not immediate, and so we don't think of them as relevant to us and our individual lives.

Our brains did not evolve to look generations into the future (Marshall 2014, 46). We are descendants of hunters and gatherers whose lives were short and dangerous, and who stayed alive longer by watching for immediate threats. So human brains evolved to focus primarily on the present, which is where danger lurked. Today our brains still react sensitively to sudden, short-term changes such as movement or loud noise, but we hardly notice slow changes, and we tend not to notice slow-moving threats (Ehmann, Bohle, and Klanten 2012, 6). Threats that catch our attention are concrete and immediate, such as a charging lion or an approaching car. Threats such as pollution or climate change, by contrast, are abstract, distant, and invisible (Marshall 2014, 56).

Our brains are wired to scan masses of incoming stimuli for clues that tell us whether we should pay attention. The issues that demand our attention are in front of us, now, with a clearly visible threat from an identifiable danger (Marshall 2014, 97). Our brains evolved to look for immediate benefits, too: shelter, a mate, water, or something good to eat. We who face short-term needs in our daily lives do not easily recognize incentives toward delayed or intangible benefits (Jacobson 2009, 30).

Information Overload

In addition to all that, we are awash in information. Communicators must compete with voluminous quantities of information and visual pollution. Our perception is selective, as it has to be; we would be overwhelmed if we were aware of everything around us. We are wired to see what we expect to see. In order to deal with floods of multiple stimuli and to prevent information overload, people use selective attention to filter out information that doesn't match what they are looking for. Attention is a valuable commodity (Ehmann et al. 2012, 6). A speaking coach for presenters at TED Talks says, "In a society with too many choices and too little time, our natural inclination is to ignore most of it" (Gallo 2014, 126). In this era of information overload, finding ways to make information visible is essential.

We have instant access to information, if we can notice it or find it. Unlike earlier in history, when information sources were limited to a few books, or a single news journal, or one television channel which constrained our attention, audiences can now move constantly from source to source (Gallant, Solomon, and Esser 2008, 21).

There is a vast and growing gap between the entire body of recorded knowledge and our limited capacity to make sense of it all. Inherent in that trend is increasing specialization and the resulting fragmentation of knowledge. The more the quantity of information multiplies, the more specialties divide into more narrowly focused subspecialties, each of which may be unaware of valuable knowledge in the others (Chen 2002, 230). We often don't see the connections between them, and we often miss the bigger picture.

Information is not useful in and of itself. We need to make sense of it somehow and understand what is meaningful. This is the goal of good communication. The challenge for communicators is to present information clearly and succinctly and to help audiences make sense of it (Few 2012, xv).

Positive Messages: Beyond the Deficit Model

Communicators must deal with the problem of confirmation bias, the human tendency to pay attention to evidence that confirms our beliefs, and to ignore information that does not. Search engines and social media intensify confirmation bias by filtering out information with which we disagree. Confirmation bias means that we will not change our ideas about an issue just because we are given new facts (Wijkman and Rockström 2012, 6).

We have been hammered for decades by facts about the threats of climate change and environmental degradation, across a range of media types. We have enough facts, yet as a species we continue to move in destructive directions. Scientists and activists often operate within what is known as a "deficit model," the idea that communication is a one-way delivery of information to people who don't have enough knowledge. It holds that if people simply have more facts about what is wrong, they will become engaged (Groffman et al. 2010, 284). It turns out that the opposite is true.

The "deficit model" approach to communication says that people's perceptions of issues are rooted in ignorance. This approach overlooks the reality that knowledge is only one of several factors in how people make judgments and reach conclusions. In fact, social identity and ideology often have stronger impacts.

Research tells us that scaring people is not likely to make them feel engaged. On the contrary, fearful messages often result in apathy from a feeling that nothing can be done about the situation. People do not like feeling incompetent or helpless. Once they are aware of threats, continued negative inputs cause most people to tune out the messages and move on to other, more pleasant concerns (Robertson 2017, 330).

You can use fear sparingly to get someone's initial attention, but then you are more likely to reach them with positive opportunities and solutions (UNEP 2005, 13). Once they know that problems are real, then what they need to understand is that there is hope and there are things they can do. People become engaged by a positive vision of how life could be different. The alternatives are more economically secure, ecologically stable, and socially equitable than the status quo; we just need to make them visible (Rees 2014, 198).

Mental frameworks can help audiences make connections between what appear to be isolated events, issues, and solutions, and between those issues and solutions and their personal lives (Groffman et al. 2010, 286). A United Nations communication initiative suggests you think like a modern storyteller, using challenges to provide drama and solutions to provide excitement and story resolution (UNEP 2005, 15). As a storyteller you can present a problem, then complete the story by pointing toward how to fix it (Baron 2010, 223).

Social Factors

Good communication is not only about presenting ideas in ways that are clear. It is also a process of understanding your specific audience so that you can connect with them on their terms and in ways that are relevant for them (Smith et al. 2013). Even though a message may be sent and received successfully, receiving is not the same as understanding. A message passes through personal contexts, belief systems, and social frameworks (Corbett 2006, 289). People will be more engaged and more motivated to change their behavior when they recognize connections between their individual values and their group identities, and the environment and society on a larger scale (Kunkle and Monroe 2015, 161).

Fragmentation among social groups is a challenge in communicating topics such as ecological restoration, social equity, or climate change. Each of us has a belief system about the biosphere and our relationship to the rest of the nonhuman world (Corbett 2006, 12). If we think of this relationship as a spectrum, some are on the anthropocentric end of the spectrum, believing that humans are the most important life form and that resources exist entirely for human benefit and use. Others are on the ecocentric end of the spectrum, and believe that nonhuman beings and even land itself have intrinsic value regardless of their usefulness to humans. Most people's worldviews fit somewhere in the middle (Corbett 2006, 37).

Our level of economic and social opportunity affects how we receive communication in various forms. People with ample personal opportunity can be powerfully motivated by information about environmental problems and planetary crises. People with ample personal crises of their own are less likely to respond to environmental crisis, and will be more engaged with reports about environmental opportunities that connect to jobs or other economic opportunities (Jones 2009, 110). In one study on environmental attitudes and knowledge, affluent students were more concerned about recycling and destruction of rainforests, while low-income students were more concerned about lead poisoning, lack of good drinking water, and energy shortages (Roper-Starch 1996, 25). In a number of polls, including Gallup, Pew, and others, a larger percentage of the general public give a rank of higher significance to immediate concerns including clean air and clean water, while many of the issues that scientists recognize as of the most grave concern including climate change, biodiversity loss, and species extinction, which are abstract, long-term, and distant, are ranked as less important for most people (Makower 2015).

Segmentation in social science is the process of subdividing human populations into groups based upon social, cultural, or other attributes. Various segments of the public have differing worldviews and respond in different ways to the same issues.

Various studies have looked at how human cultures divide into segments. A large-scale 2007 segmentation study, the Ecological Roadmap by the nonprofit environmental law organization Earthjustice, found that people in the US could be grouped into 10 distinct environmental worldviews, of whom about 12 percent could be considered 'environmentalists,' while other segments were motivated by other concerns (Earthjustice 2008, 5). A study in the European Union found that the majority of citizens consider the state of the environment to be as relevant to their quality of life as economic and social factors, while other studies in various other cultures around the world found levels of knowledge and engagement that ranged from very low to very high (Groffman et al. 2010, 286).

Large-scale, ongoing studies by Yale and George Mason Universities identify six unique audiences in the US who each perceive and respond to the issue of global warming in distinct ways. These audiences, known as the Six Americas, differ markedly from each other in attitudes, beliefs about climate change, perception of risk, motivations, values, policy preferences, behaviors, underlying barriers to action, and levels of engagement (Leiserowitz, Maibach, and Roser-Renouf 2009, 1). The audience segments in the Six Americas range from the Dismissive, who do not believe climate change is real or is a problem, to the Alarmed, who are very concerned and support aggressive response to deal with it. Between these two ends of the spectrum are four other groups constituting about 70 percent of the US population: the Doubtful, the Disengaged, the Cautious, and the Concerned, who vary in level of concern, certainty, behavior, and policy support.

These studies tell us that different communication strategies are required for different segments of the public (Makower 2009, 273). Communication is not likely to be effective if diverse populations are treated as a homogeneous mass, with uniform messages delivered in the form of plain facts (Roser-Renouf et al. 2015, 368). The findings imply that there are differences between the types of information various groups will be interested in learning, types of media most likely to reach them, and the communication strategies that will be most effective (ibid., 370). Segmentation studies underscore the importance of a basic principle of effective communication: Identify your audience; think about who they are and what they want to know, then communicate in ways that are relevant to them and that resonate with them.

People in the Dismissive and Doubtful segments of the Six Americas feel certain of their ideas. They develop their understanding of issues within the framework of their existing cultural values, which are conservative (ibid., 383). They are not convinced by recitations of facts and logic, which in fact can trigger feelings of opposition and cause them to become more deeply entrenched in their positions.

People in the Disengaged and Cautious segments are generally less involved, give little thought to the topic of climate change, and think it is a problem for people in the future (ibid., 376). Study authors believe that strong, logically sound arguments are more important for these two groups (ibid., 375).

People in the Disengaged segment have the lowest incomes, lowest rate of college education, and lowest percentage of voters. A higher percentage than the general population believes the bible is literal fact, rejects the theory of evolution, and rejects climate science. They pay less attention to politics and public affairs, watch less news, and watch more entertainment television than any other group (ibid., 377). Study authors believe that the most effective communication strategies for this group are entertaining and require minimal information processing, and could include humor, attractive and credible sources, examples that illustrate constructive behaviors that are popular and respected, use of stories, and showing rather than telling (ibid., 378). These strategies are effective in all segments, but are particularly needed in the Disengaged and Cautious segments, who are less willing to pay attention (ibid.). Stories are effective because people become involved with the story line and the characters, and when people have become absorbed in a story, they tend to remember its content (ibid., 379).

Demographics in the Concerned segment are similar to national averages. People in the Alarmed segment are more likely to be liberal, interested in social equity, and more educated. People in both Concerned and Alarmed segments already feel certain of the reality of climate change, so are most interested in learning about effective, feasible solutions (ibid., 373). They accept messages in print media, which can be effective; print requires greater processing effort and therefore is more likely to be remembered and acted upon, according to the study (ibid., 374). People in the Alarmed segment have the potential to act as opinion leaders, which is a way to reach people in the less-involved middle segments who are more likely to be influenced by social connections than by mass media (ibid., 375).

Efficacy, the belief that one is able to act and make a difference, is a factor which varies by segment. Research indicates that people who feel threatened, but also feel capable of taking action that is effective, are more likely to act. Threatening information only results in behavior change when people feel capable of taking action that will be effective, which is generally only true within the Alarmed and Concerned audience segments, and counterproductive among the other segments (ibid., 375).

Segmentation studies point to differences between groups in terms of environmental attitudes, income, and education. They also underscore differences in social equity including access to communication. Some scholars point out that marginalized communities not only bear greater burdens from environmental degradation and climate-change impacts, they face communication barriers that weaken their ability to speak and act on their own behalf. Approaches which use social marketing to focus on behavior changes also obscure power inequities, and approaches which focus on media advocacy do recognize inequities but encourage experts to retain control while minimizing critical roles of community members themselves (Ryan and Brown 2015, 132). In addition, a digital divide persists in which campaigns and communications which rely on the internet are effective in reaching some groups of people, but are invisible and inaccessible to marginalized people. Without access to specialized knowledge, skills, and communication infrastructure, marginalized groups have limited ability to gain standing as credible participants in decision making that affects their lives (ibid., 134). Strengthening community connections and social capital is essential to addressing this gap.

2

PERCEPTION AND COGNITION

Research on how the human brain works tells us a lot about how messages in words and images get from one person to another. When we understand how our brains perceive patterns and process information, we can do a more effective job of communicating.

Visual Perception

The human visual system is a pattern-seeking instrument that has evolved to enable us to perceive and act in the physical world. When patterns are presented in certain ways we see them easily, and when they are presented in other ways they are invisible to us (Ware 2013, 30).

Perception and cognition are profoundly connected (Chen 2002, 35). Perception is a cognitive process in which our senses take in stimulus and our brain makes sense of it. The structure of our perceptual system plays a fundamental role in shaping how we see the world. We are a visually oriented species, and our language reflects this. We use the word "see" when we mean "understand," we say "reflect" to mean "think," we say "vision" and "insight" to indicate knowing, we say "darkness" to refer to ignorance, and we use words related to light—bright, brilliant, illuminate, enlighten, clear, lucid—to refer to knowledge.

About 40 percent of the human brain is involved with seeing and interpreting what we see (Werner, Pinna, and Spillmann 2007, 92). We do not see physical objects directly; we receive reflected light, which is processed by the brain and synthesized with our own experience to form a mental image which we perceive as reality. A percept is the mental concept that forms as a result of perception (Dobbs 2005, 36). A percept of a thing we have seen consists mostly of a range of associations stored in memory, activated by a small amount of visual information from the outside world (Ware 2013, 324).

Light comes to us as waves of energy.[1] Electromagnetic radiation travels throughout the universe in various wavelengths. Waves with shorter wavelength have a shorter distance between waves; more waves pass by in one second, so they also have a higher frequency. Electromagnetic radiation with shorter wavelengths and higher frequency includes gamma rays, X-rays, and ultraviolet rays. Some electromagnetic radiation has longer wavelengths and lower frequency, including infrared, microwaves, radar, and radio waves. Visible light is electromagnetic radiation that has waves within a particular range of wavelengths that lie between the shorter and longer ends of the wavelength spectrum.[2]

Our visual system begins with the retina. Light reflected from the surfaces of objects enters the eye through the pupil and is focused on cells of the retina at the back of the eye. Specialized neurons in the retina extract a dozen distinct representations, including motion, edges, shadows, and light (Werblin and Roska 2007, 73). From here, the eye sends signals along the optic nerve to multiple regions in the brain within the visual cortex, and the brain interprets the signals.

Our eyes send signals along three separate channels: color, form, and motion (Ware 2013, 145). Because color, shape and size, and movement are processed separately, they are visually distinct and easy for our brains to separate. Information from one visual property, such as color, does not interfere with that of another property, such as shape, and we can pick out contrasts or changes in any one of them. In our evolutionary past, the ability to see differences in our surroundings allowed us to spot potential dangers; shifting our attention to anything that moved or was a different color or different shape or texture offered a survival advantage (Arnheim 1969, 20).

The retina is filled by two types of receptor cells, rods and cones. The rods detect light levels in black and white and are used for seeing in dim light, especially useful in conditions in which our ancestors lived for most of human history. Rods are overloaded in daylight and artificial light and essentially shut down.

The cones detect colors. Most of the time our vision depends entirely on input from cones (Ware 2013, 49). There are three types of cones, each specializing in detecting a different segment of the color spectrum. Low-frequency cones are most sensitive to red and yellow frequencies, but are sensitive to colors across the range of visible light. Medium-frequency cones respond to frequencies of blue through yellow and orange, and are less sensitive. High-frequency cones are sensitive to blue and violet frequencies, and are the least sensitive of the three types. As a result, our eyes are more sensitive to reds and less sensitive to blues than to other colors (Johnson 2014, 38). This comes from a time earlier in human evolution when the ability to see edible berries and other fruits, often red, was an aid to survival (Lester 2011, 6). Our sensitivity to red remains, and in modern life, the color red attracts attention and is used for signal lights, warnings, and other attention-getting purposes.

In the center of the retina is the fovea, which makes up about 1 percent of the retina's area. Cones are densely packed here, so images from the center of the visual field are in high resolution. About 50 percent of the brain's visual cortex is devoted to input from the fovea; the other 50 percent processes input from 99 percent of the retina (Johnson 2014, 50). Most of the cones are packed into the fovea. Most of the rods are spread over the rest of the retina (ibid.). Cones become less concentrated as we move from the center to the edges of the retina, which means that peripheral vision has a lower resolution than the center of the visual field. When we look at a page or an image, our eye focuses sharply on a small area in the center, with our vision becoming more blurry and faded toward the periphery (Barnes 2011, 36). The parts of the retina beyond the fovea, our peripheral vision, often do not notice stationary objects that are not brightly colored, although they are good at detecting movement and other changes (Card, Mackinlay, and Shneiderman 1999, 24). In addition to detecting motion, our peripheral vision gives us low-resolution images to help guide our eye movements and it allows us to see better in the dark (Johnson 2014, 53). In our evolutionary past, a moving shape could be food or could be a predator, and detecting moving objects in low-light conditions was important to survival (Barnes 2011, 49).

Our eyes are constantly in motion. The high-resolution field at the center of the retina moves around two to five times a second, sampling the visual field to build up a percept or to direct the focus to something of interest, while the non-foveal parts of the retina survey the full field of vision to selection the next point of focus (Few 2012, 64). These constant automatic movements, called saccades, produce a rapid series of images that give us the impression that we are seeing our surroundings sharply and clearly. Each of these movements can be thought of as a discrete visual search. For compact displays, eye movements can be shorter and faster, so visual searching is considerably more efficient (Ware 2013, 140). This is one reason that when we design visual communication, we try to compose elements that can be noticed in a single glance.

Gestalt Principles

In the early twentieth century a group of German psychologists studying pattern perception found that people tend to perceive organized, coherent patterns from visual cues and that in perception, the whole is greater than the sum of its parts. They called this pattern-seeking behavior Gestalt (Chen 2002, 27). The word *Gestalt* means "form" or "shape" in German.

The psychologists proposed a set of principles to describe how humans perceive visual wholes. Researchers no longer think that Gestalt theory explains how perception works, but Gestalt psychology principles are still considered a valid framework for describing perceptual phenomena (Ware 2013, 181). Humans seek patterns and when looking at a set of details, our brains automatically impose a structure and perceive an overall, coherent pattern first (Chen 2002, 28). We are wired to see whole objects rather than disconnected lines and areas.

The Gestalt laws of pattern perception are proximity, similarity, connectedness, common fate, continuity, closure, symmetry, and figure/ground. Designers use these Gestalt principles to help make words and images more visible.

Proximity is the principle which says that things that are near each other appear to be part of the same group. We assume things that are close together belong together.

The principle of similarity says that objects which are similar in size, shape, color, or texture appear to be part of the same group. We assume things that are like each other belong together.

Connectedness is the principle which says that we are wired to see continuous forms rather than disconnected segments. Connecting objects with straight or curving lines indicates to our minds that there is a relationship between them.

The principle of common fate concerns moving objects. Elements that point in the same direction or move together appear to be grouped together.

Continuity is the principle which says that when we see separate segments that might be related, we are biased to see them as continuous forms leading the eye across space from one element to another, rather than as disconnected lines.

Closure is the tendency to unite contours that are close together (Card et al. 1999, 30). This ancient survival mechanism happens when the brain fills in missing gaps and imagines a complete shape when presented with an unfinished shape. Closure is related to the principle of continuity (Johnson 2014, 19).

The principle of symmetry says that once we have seen half a symmetric shape, our mind predicts the other half (Sussman and Hollander 2015, 122). Objects which are symmetric can be processed more quickly by our brains, and we perceive them as parts of a whole. We most readily perceive symmetries around vertical and horizontal axes (Ware 2013, 185).

The principle known as figure/ground is probably the strongest perceptual tendency (Chen 2002, 41). Our brains separate visual patterns into figure and background. Figures are objects which are perceived as being in the foreground; they stand out as the focus of our attention. Background is everything else; it appears to lie behind the figure. We apply this principle when we use contrast in graphic design to make certain information stand out, or when we use landmarks that are distinct from their surroundings as part of a wayfinding strategy.

Perceiving Shape, Size, and Distance

Graphic designers say that whenever you present a quantity, your display should answer the question, "compared to what?" (Tufte 1990, 67). Our perceptual system does this, too. Every visual attribute is influenced by context, so that we see it in terms that are relative, not absolute (Few 2012, 74). Our visual receptors are much more sensitive to differences in color and brightness than to absolute color or amount of light. For example, a candle burning in a dark cellar appears quite bright, while the same candle burning in outdoor sunlight appears dim. You could say that our retinas and visual cortex do not function as light meters; they function as change meters (Ware 2013, 69). Early humans needed to be able to recognize food or predators whether they were hidden in shade, or under cloudy skies, or out in full, bright sunlight. Thus we perceive a red berry as the same color of red regardless of its lighting conditions, a property known as color constancy. We tend to perceive the size of an object as constant regardless how distant it is. Our brains process these size and color cues and stabilize our environment (Zettl 1998, 6).

Since early humans looked for food and watched for danger, our brains have depended on strategies for perceiving distance and spatial depth. One cue we use is overlap: When one object is partially covered by another, we know that the one being covered must be farther away than the one doing the covering. Another cue is relative size: When we look at a set of objects we believe to be similar in size, those which appear to be smaller are perceived as farther away.

These are examples of perspective: visual cues about size, location, and distance. Linear perspective, created by differences in size and texture, is a powerful depth cue. Objects at a distance appear smaller than the same objects which are nearby. Parallel lines such as railroad tracks, roads, or building edges appear to converge at a point in the distance, known as the vanishing point, while vertical edges become lower in height and spaced closer together as they move into the distance. Elements of texture appear smaller, textures of surfaces become finer, and density of texture increases as distance increases.

Atmospheric or aerial perspective is the phenomenon in which distant objects appear lighter in value, bluer in color, and with reduced contrast, while objects which are nearby appear darker and with sharper contrast. It occurs because the farther away an object, the more dust and moisture are in the atmosphere between it and our eyes.

Our perceptual systems evolved to notice contrast and thus edges. Objects which are bright, larger, or more distinct in some way are more likely to be noticed. This is useful when searching for food and avoiding danger, and it is a key attribute of design. We detect contours and edges by perceiving differences in color and brightness. Abrupt differences in texture and abrupt differences in brightness are interpreted as edges; gradual transitions in texture or brightness are interpreted as round surfaces.

Getting Noticed: Preattentive Processing

When we read or examine an image, we consciously process information in a detailed, linear way. But at the same time, an automatic recognition known as preattentive processing occurs unconsciously and at very high speed before the conscious mind is involved. It is an ancient survival mechanism that allows an organism to determine within milliseconds whether to move forward or flee (Sussman and Hollander 2015, 107). Features that are preattentively processed are form, position, motion, and color including contrast. Designers use preattentive attributes to help people interpret words and images more readily. We do this by making a target object distinct from its background and by ensuring that background objects are not too distinct from each other, so that the target object stands out. Taking advantage of preattentive factors, we can outline a target, add color, make the target a different shape than background objects, and make the target larger relative to smaller background objects. Using more than one preattentive factor increases distinctiveness so that an object is more likely to be noticed (Ware 2013, 159).

Emotion

We can think of the history of the brain in three general parts: The oldest and most primitive structure, the brainstem and cerebellum, is sometimes called the reptilian brain. The reptilian brain controls automatic functions such as respiration and heartbeat, and roughly classifies everything as food, sex, or danger. The limbic brain emerged later in the first mammals and is responsible for what we call emotions. The most recent to develop is the neocortex or rational brain (Johnson 2014, 132).

Thus, our brains have two parallel processing systems, in addition to the automatic processes of the reptilian brain. The newest system of the brain operates through the cortex and is analytical and logical; it can collect and interpret facts and is capable of abstract reasoning and planning. The other is older, operates through the limbic system including the amygdala, and is emotional. That system developed as a tool for assessing benefits and threats. It presents us with immediate information about the world and is capable of responding rapidly. Neuroscientists call these two systems cognitive and affective, or analytic and experiential, or rational and emotional, or System 1 and System 2 (Marshall 2014, 49).

The parts of our brain where memories are stored need to be able to distinguish between events that are significant and those that are less important so that they can transform significant events into long-term memory. One way the brain does this is by priming nerve cells, or neurons, to remember events. A heightened state of emotion such as joy, surprise, fear, or anger causes the brain to release the hormone norepinephrine. This hormone increases the chemical sensitivity of neurons at synapses, the sites where neurons make electro-chemical connections and new memory circuits form. It primes them to form new memories by making many more nerve receptors available so that new connections can lock a memory into place (Johns Hopkins 2007).

Emotion enhances our ability to form vivid memories (Hu et al. 2007, 160). Events which arouse emotions—including looking at images—are known as emotionally charged events, and unlike more mundane events, they are remembered vividly. The amygdala tags the emotional importance of things. It communicates with the visual cortex and stimulates its activity so that we perceive events more actively (Todd 2013, 142). The amygdala, in the older limbic brain, is full of the neurotransmitter dopamine. When an event arouses our emotions, the amygdala releases dopamine which helps us to process information more easily and to store it in long-term memory (Ham 2013, 12). We see things that are emotionally arousing more clearly than those that are more mundane, and we are more likely to remember events that arouse our emotions (Todd et al. 2012, 11201).

We remember vivid events and forget mundane ones. When you are emotionally aroused, you perceive an event more vividly at the time it occurs, and that increases the likelihood that you will remember it. You can probably remember where you were when the attacks of 9/11 happened, but you probably do not remember where you were on 9/10 (Johns Hopkins 2007). How vividly we perceive something in the first place determines how vividly we will remember it later (Todd et al. 2012, 11201).

The emotional brain, with its ancient ability to assess threats rapidly, continues to play a dominant role in decision making. It draws on personal experience and responds to stories. We use our rational brain to interpret facts and evaluate evidence, but it is our emotional brain that causes us to care and spurs us to action. Communication, to be effective, needs to go beyond analytical facts and must be expressed in forms that can reach our affective system: social meaning, metaphors, and stories.

Cognition

Cognition is the acquisition, storage, and use of knowledge (Arnheim 1997, 13). Research into how we receive, store, and process information is the field of study known as cognitive psychology (Ham 2002, 161).

We use our senses to gather information about the world. Our brains process, analyze, and look for patterns, and much of this processing takes place unconsciously (Lakoff 2010, 72). Our perception is selective, as it has to be; we would be overwhelmed if we were aware of everything around us.

We all filter information as it comes at us. We tend to seek out and pay attention to evidence that confirms our beliefs, and we ignore information that does not (Marshall 2014, 14; Morgan and Welton 1992, 59; Weinschenk 2011, 98). This pattern of seeing what you expect to see and discounting evidence to the contrary is known as confirmation bias. Confirmation bias means that we will not change our ideas about an issue just because we are given new facts (Wijkman and Rockström 2012, 6).

We are wired to see what we expect to see, which means we have selective attention. Our goals focus our attention, and as a result we may fail to notice objects or events around us, a behavior known as inattention blindness (McNall and Basile 2013, 299). In the famous "invisible gorilla" study, subjects watched a black-clad and a white-clad team of basketball players passing a ball to each other and were told to count the number of times the players in white suits passed the ball. As they watched, a person in a black gorilla suit walked onto the court, thumped his chest, and walked off. When asked later what they remembered, about half the subjects had not noticed the gorilla (Simons and Chabris 1999, 1059).

One of the most consistent findings from cognitive psychology research is the fundamental role associations play in our thinking and learning (Chen 2002, 69). How we store information involves an intricate network of associations, links, and cross-references in our brains that allows us to find and retrieve information (Few 2012, 67). For new information to be meaningful, it must relate to something that is already encoded in our brains (Jacobson 2009, 349). We take in new information by connecting it to what we already know or think we know (Moscardo 1999, 33). This has implications for how we communicate new information to audiences.

Here is an example of association at work. Look at this series of nine letters, and see how many you can remember: FB … IPH … DIB … M. You might or might not be able to remember all nine. Now try the same series of letters, this time grouped so that you can connect associations from long-term memory: FBI … PHD … IBM. Notice how they are now easier to remember (Ham 2002, 167).

Another significant finding from cognitive psychology research is that we can acquire and remember more information if we consolidate the diverse pieces into chunks, a process known as cognitive chunking (Ham 2002, 166). For many years, common wisdom among communicators was that we can make sense out of no more than five to seven separate ideas at once, a number based on a well-known study by George Miller (1956, 81). Later studies have found that our memory capacity is typically a number closer to three or four items, depending on how much prior experience we have with the topic (Ham 2013, 28). Try glancing at the two groups below for no more than one second; which is easier to count, A or B?

A	B
★★★★	★★★★★★★★

Group A was probably easier to count because it contained only four items. Now try counting the number of items in each of the two groups shown below. Which one is easier to count?

A	B
★★★★★★★★	++++★★★★

This time both groups contain the same amount of information, but you probably found the items in B were easier to count because they have been chunked into two groups of four so that B contains only two pieces of information, while A contains eight (ibid., 29).

The human brain is a pattern-seeking machine. It receives millions of sensory inputs every second, and it makes sense of the enormous quantity of stimuli it receives by detecting patterns (Weinschenk 2011, 2). Pattern recognition was an evolutionary strategy for survival in early humans that allowed them to detect threats and find resources in a noisy world (Shermer 2005, 37). By bringing together complex details into simpler groups, this strategy reduces the quantity of information to be processed (Chen 2002, 28).

While there are broad principles of cognition, based upon the structure of the brain and its neural networks, there are also variations in how people acquire information. Research by psychologist Howard Gardner suggested that humans exhibit at least seven ways of learning which they have in varying degrees, a theory he called the theory of multiple intelligences (Jacobson 2009, 354). Some people are more visual, some more auditory, some more kinesthetic; some cognitive styles for understanding the world are more logical or mathematical, some more verbal (Falk, Dierking, and Foutz 2007, 52). Gardner argued that there are seven separate intelligences, including linguistic, logical-mathematical, musical, bodily-kinesthetic, spatial, interpersonal, and intrapersonal, and that all these ways of acquiring and representing knowledge are equally important (Barnes 2011, 6).

When we learn, we retain not just facts, but experiences. Research by Canadian psychologist Endel Tulving demonstrated that many standard memory tests were actually measuring not people's memory of factual information but their memory of an experience in which they were exposed to that information (Tulving 1972, 381). Psychologists call this episodic memory, in contrast to semantic or factual memory. It turns out that simply having factual information in short-term memory is a poor predictor of long-term learning. Rather, ideas tend to be stored in long-term memory when they are connected to experience and personal meaning. That is, cues that enable us to retrieve memories are those that were stored along with the memory of the experience itself (Ham 2007, 10). Images, feelings, and other details related to a past event come together to produce episodic memory. Episodic memory and then actual knowledge, or semantic memory, are strengthened by repetition and by relevance to the individual who is having the experience (ibid., 11).

Frames

Frames are mental structures that shape the way we see the world. Just as a picture frame or the edges of a television screen provide a boundary for an image, or a house frame organizes the contents inside, a frame organizes the content of an article or presentation. It focuses and organizes our perception. We make meaning from what is within the frame, and we ignore what is outside the frame. Frames are sometimes also called schemata (the plural of schema).

We encounter a seemingly infinite number of concrete details. A framework allows us to locate and organize these details defined within its terms (Goffman 1986, 21). We are often unaware that such a framework exists. Framing, by giving greater weight to certain elements over others, is a way to trim masses of information while remaining accurate about what is known about a complex topic (Nisbet and Newman 2015, 325). Policymakers and planners use frames to help to organize information for public debate. Types of frames include economic development, social progress, ethics, scientific uncertainty, risks, conflict, governance and transparency, and strategy (ibid., 328).

Humans are social animals, and most of us relate to two types of frames: those which are relevant to our individual mental model and those which resonate with our social and cultural identity (Monroe and Krasny 2015, 162). Our cultures are organized around the primary frameworks of our social groups (Goffman 1986, 27). Each of us is more likely to pay attention to some frames than others, depending on our own mental models, so that frames can reinforce our existing opinions. When you select a frame, you encourage your audience to see an issue one way and not another way.

Many advocates think that if we just tell people the facts, they will automatically reach the correct conclusion. However, facts are synthesized through frames; if a set of facts does not make sense in terms of an audience's frames, they will be ignored. Particularly in the case of complex facts, like those connected to sustainability issues, an audience needs a frame or system of frames in order to make sense of the facts (Lakoff 2010, 73).

Many frames connect directly to the emotional or limbic system in the brain (ibid., 72). That means that lack of agreement on sustainability issues is not just rooted in ignorance and people would not change their minds if they simply had more facts, the belief known as the "deficit model." Simply delivering scientific facts to an audience is not convincing to most people. You need to frame issues in ways that resonate with your audiences.

In journalistic writing, a frame determines in what order to arrange facts. News writing uses an inverted pyramid structure, with the most important information at the beginning of an article and less important information at the end. For example, quoting an assertion by an environmental group near the beginning of an article gives it significance; quoting it in the last paragraph indicates it is less important than other claims in the article (Corbett 2006, 239).

In a news story, a journalist must make sense of a vast quantity of information, and so they must select and emphasize some facts and omit or downplay others. Frames are a kind of mental shortcut, allowing us to comprehend a situation without needing to analyze every detail (Johnson 2014, 3). A frame is an interpretive story line (Nisbet and Newman 2015, 325).

One way to categorize frames, particularly with environmental issues, is as status quo frames and challenger frames (Corbett 2006, 239). Another approach is framing that stresses positive outcomes, or a promotion focus, versus negative outcomes, or a prevention focus (Kahle and Gurel-Atay 2013, 160). An issue like climate change can be communicated through a problem frame or a solution-based frame. Research indicates that audiences are more likely to respond and care about a subject when it is communicated through a solution-based frame (Monroe and Krasny 2015, 162).

A single word can activate a frame (Lakoff 2010, 72). In the debate over genetically modified organisms, "Frankenfood" triggers a different frame than "farmer's crop." Consider a community group working on transportation issues. Following the entrenched habit of calling preventable crashes "accidents" frames them as unavoidable side effects of the transportation system, when in reality they are not inevitable; the word choice limits how people think about solutions. Think about the frame which is activated by the phrase "protecting the environment." These words mean that the environment is separate from humans, and that there is an external threat to this external environment, overlooking the fact that the threat is us (Butler 2004, 54). How we frame a message can affect the cognitive and emotional processing of the message, and thus the listener's decisions about actions (Kahle and Gurel-Atay 2013, 160).

Every message is framed in one way or another (Monroe and Krasny 2015, 162). You build a frame based on which facts and ideas you select, what you exclude, which ones you emphasize, and in what order you arrange them. Words are not frames, but your choice of words can activate particular frames (Lakoff 2010, 73).

Of course, you do not overtly state what frame you are using. Instead, you use word choice, metaphors, stories, symbols, examples, and images to frame a message. The elements you choose tell stories that connect to the emotions in a way that a list of dry facts cannot do.

Know your audience, and select frames that resonate with them, with their particular social segment or group identity. Look to the social structure or culture within which you are communicating for cues about selecting frames (Corbett 2006, 238). For example, in one study people were more willing to pay a greenhouse gas surcharge when it was described as a "carbon offset" rather than a "carbon tax." In a similar case, in preparation for a climate-change bill in the US Senate, lobbyists replaced the word "tax" with the term "fee on polluters" (Marshall 2014, 109).

Find frames that are appropriate to your audience. Scientists want technical details; policymakers want legal and policy options; disadvantaged groups may want to see an issue through the frame of costs and risks, ethical considerations, or potential benefits; other groups may want appealing story lines. Redundancy improves the likelihood of effective communication. If you communicate through multiple frames, you will be able to speak to a variety of perspectives.

The challenge of framing is the way it can limit thinking. Just as a picture frame excludes some of the scene of a photograph, so a frame excludes some ideas from communication, usually outside of our conscious awareness that it is happening. When a frame becomes firmly established, ideas and social structure can become entrenched and social change can be difficult to achieve (Corbett 2006, 309). A frame can cause us to see things that are not there, or to miss things that are there.

Notes

1 Light also travels in energy packets called photons, but that is a discussion for a physics text.
2 We call it visible light because it happens to be the range of wavelengths that our species' optical system is designed to perceive. The eyes of some other animals perceive light in different ranges of the spectrum.

3

COMMUNICATION PRINCIPLES

Communication, from a Latin word meaning "to share," refers to sharing information. It is about making connections and creating understanding. It involves participation by at least two parties: a sender and a receiver.

The sender, or source, selects an idea or develops content for a message, then encodes or translates the message, perhaps in the form of written words or pictures or dramatization. The encoded message is sent through a channel or medium, such as a document, an interpretive sign, a website, or a television program. The medium or channel is how the message is presented. The receiver or audience then decodes or interprets the message based on their own experience and values, then decides what action to take or what changes in opinion to make. Action on the part of the receiver is a kind of feedback which gives the sender information for adjusting the message (Jacobson 2009, 11).

Theories about effective communication often trace back to Aristotle. His treatise, *Rhetoric,* which means the art of speaking or writing effectively, says that there are three elements of persuasion. In Greek, they are *ethos,* the nature of the information source, or the credibility of the speaker; *logos,* the nature of the message itself and the type of evidence offered; and *pathos,* the emotion of the audience who receives the message (Barnes 2011, 150).

The audience is not a passive receiver; they can choose which parts of a message to attend to or ignore (Moscardo 1999, 33). The sender, the content of the message, its medium, and the experience of the receiver all influence how the message is perceived. In order to communicate, the sender and receiver must share the same language or symbols and use them in the same way, and they must have at least some attitudes in common (Morgan and Welton 1992, 10).

Noise can cause some of the signal to be distorted. Noise, which is usually random and unpredictable, is anything which affects the signal so that what is received is different from what was sent.

The constructivist theory of communication says that we cannot deposit knowledge into other people's heads; audiences must construct their own knowledge. This was the essence of the idea behind Socrates' method. As communicators, our role is not to deposit information but to stimulate audiences to wrestle with ideas themselves and to do their own thinking. The more a communication provokes an audience to think their own thoughts, the stronger and more resilient are the attitudes which result (Ham 2013, 66).

Guidelines for Clear Communication

Your goal should be to communicate clearly. Stendhal captured the goal in a letter he wrote to a fellow French writer, Balzac: "I see but one rule: to be clear" (Stendhal 1840, 146). The general approaches are the same, whatever medium you choose.

Empathy for Your Audience

When you want to communicate to an audience, the first thing you must do is to define your goal. Your purpose in sharing information may be to build trust and credibility, to build partnerships, to raise awareness, or to help make decisions (ISO 2006, v). If you were a scholar and your goal were to increase your stature among fellow academics within your specialized field, then you would choose a particular communication style to fit that situation, using technical jargon and sophisticated syntax. But usually your goal is simply to convey information. And that means you should do everything you possibly can to help your audience receive that information. The best communicators have one quality in common: an empathy for their audiences (Garner 2013, 171).

Write for your audience. After defining your goal, the next step is to identify your audience. Think about what they know about your subject now, what they need to know, and what questions they might have (Garner 2013, 112). Then you can think about how to guide them from what they already know to what you want them to know. People are most interested in what applies to them, so the best way to capture someone's attention is to figure out who they are and what they want to know (PLAIN 2011, 2). Tell them how what you are saying is important to them. For example, if you were writing a blog about individual efforts toward climate mitigation you might say, "If you want to figure out how to reduce your carbon impact, here is what you need to know."

Think about your audience. Think about their values and interests, and ask yourself why they should care about what you are saying. This is sometimes known as the "So what?" question. Make your communication relevant and meaningful to them. Match your style of writing or speaking with that of your audience. Frame the ideas within a context that will resonate with people in your particular audience. Your ability to see things through their eyes will determine whether your message gets through or not (Hart 2006a, 110).

People learn through association. Use associations to help audiences make connections. Make your communication meaningful to your audience by connecting new information to associations already in their long-term memory.

Plain Language

Use plain language, in as few words as possible. Messages in plain, clear language are the most easily understood, and by the most people. The quality that distinguishes good writing from bad is that it is built on empathy for the reader (Garner 2013, 171). Good writing makes the reader's job easy. The more language and message structures are similar to the verbal style of an audience, the more meaningful they are (Ham 2002, 162).

Using plain language also forces you to understand the content yourself before you can express it. Anyone can be unclear; one hallmark of intellect is the ability to express complex ideas simply (LaRocque 2003, 16). The renowned theoretical physicist Richard Feynman, who was known for using clear, simple language, once told a colleague, "I couldn't reduce it to the freshman level. That means we really don't understand it" (Goodstein 1989, 70).

Avoid jargon. Jargon is specialized, insider language used within a particular discipline and is often unfamiliar to people outside the group. Assume that your audience may not know anything about your subject. For technical terms, find synonyms that are more familiar. For example, instead of talking about "infrastructure," talk about power grids and water systems.

Chunking

Design your document to be accessible and easy to read. Limit the number of conceptual units to five or fewer (Weinschenk 2011, 48). Research shows that human working memory is capable of handling only three to five items at one time, so focus your message on a few core ideas (Baddeley 1994, 353). Consolidate information into three to five chunks and group related items together. Make chunks visible by using white space. Try replacing some blocks of text with headings, lists, and tables (PLAIN 2011, 88).

Make the key points readily apparent with attention-getters such as bullets to guide the reader's eye from one point to the next (Garner 2013, 148). A bulleted list gives the reader an orderly procession of ideas along with white space and visual interest (LaRocque 2003, 8). When you use lists, put the most important items at the beginning of lists if it seems logical to do so. Items at the beginning of a list are held longer in working memory, and so tend to be easier to recall and to have more impact on our thinking (Hall 2007, 104). Use parallel structure: for example, begin every item with a verb, or begin every item with a noun.

Structure

Provide structure. Giving your audience a conceptual framework of some kind allows them to process information by chunking. Break the material into sections, break large sections into subsections, and use headings to make sections visible.

Some non-profit communication consultants offer the brownie-mix analogy: If you are in a market choosing a box of brownie mix, you notice that the front of every box on the shelf has a simple picture of finished brownies. There are no technical details about formulas for ingredient proportions or the chemistry of leavening agents. You just see a picture of your goal: brownies. On the back of the box are simple instructions in plain language with few words and probably some pictures. You can find details if you want them, but they are on the side panel of the box, in small type, and they are not the focal point (Fahey 2015).

If your document is longer than about six pages, give your readers a table of contents. A table of contents has a similar function to an outline in helping your readers to form a mental construct. It gives your readers an overview of what is in the document, helping them to understand the structure and the big ideas. It also allows readers who will not read the entire document to find the information that concerns them (Garner 2013, 152).

Reaching Your Audience

Support the message. Illustrate your idea with specific examples. Make it engaging by using metaphors and stories.

Use redundancy: deliver each idea in more than one way. Deliver your message using multiple channels and a variety of media to increase the chances of reaching more people. Present your ideas through the perspective of more than one frame so that you are more likely to speak to a variety of audiences.

Focus on solutions rather than problems. Scaring audiences is unlikely to engage them and is more likely to result in apathy. It often takes only a small obstacle to cause a person to give up doing something (Ritter 2004, 117). People are more likely to connect with what you are saying if they believe they can make a difference and contribute to solutions. Since many problems seem vast and far away, give local examples of positive actions, if you can, to help audiences feel connected and motivated to act.

Harmonize. Avoid approaches that trigger what martial artists call "fighting mind." Your aim is not to win fights; your aim is to promote understanding. If we try to tell an audience how to think, we risk a boomerang effect in which listeners entrench themselves more deeply in an oppositional stance. Your goal is to provoke your audiences to make their own connections, however different from yours those may seem. The only way a person can care about something is when they make the thoughts about it their own.

If your goal is to communicate, then simple is almost always better than com-plicated (Ham 2013, 30). Two ideas will help to get you there: make it organized, and keep it brief. Organizing your communication means that your audience can recognize the main points quickly. That means using some kind of structure that lets them distinguish between your main points and subordinate information that goes with those points, and it means chunking the information into no more than five main points, preferably three or four (Weinschenk 2011, 48).

Aim for brevity. Freeman Tilden, whose work laid the foundation for the pro-fession of interpretation, said that the critical component of good composition is brevity (Tilden 1957, 62). People sometimes ascribe to Mark Twain, Ludwig von Beethoven, and various other figures an apology for writing a long letter because they didn't have time to write a short one. The idea comes from French math-ematician Blaise Pascal, who ended a letter he wrote in 1656, "I only made this letter longer because I had not the leisure to make it shorter" (Pascal 1982, 232).

Visual Communication

We take in a great deal of information about the world through our eyes: 40 percent of our brain's processing resources are dedicated to visual processing (Werner et al. 2007, 92). Our language is full of visual metaphors. We refer to an opinion as a "point of view," and when we understand something, we say "I see."

We process images differently than we do words. We decode language in a linear way; when we read or hear a story, we process the words one after another. Images, however, are presented to us all at once, and we are free to look at their elements in any order (Lester 2011, 59). Images enter our brains immediately and they affect us quickly, both cognitively and emotionally. We have seen a major cultural shift, from a culture dominated by written and spoken words to a cul-ture increasingly built on visual images and graphic displays (Gallant et al. 2008, 14). A hundred years ago visual images were used primarily as art; as culture has shifted, the majority of images created today are used in the process of commu-nication (Barnes 2011, 245).

When images are used in journalism, their purpose is to communicate in-formation. When images are used in advertising, their purpose is different: it is to persuade. Visual journalism is the practice of telling stories with words and pictures (Barnes 2011, 139). Often, many different stories could be told from a single photograph, so the accompanying words help guide the reader toward a particular story.

When we put words and images together, the combination has a power to communicate that neither has by itself. When we include visual representa-tions, we amplify cognition, extending the capacity of our working memory and greatly enhancing our ability to perceive patterns (Card et al. 1999, 7). The power of visual images comes not from their exact reproduction of the natural world; it comes from their ability to clarify relationships (On the Cutting Edge 2004). Visual images have a powerful effect on people, reaching not just the frontal cortex of the rational brain but touching the more ancient part of the brain, the seat of the emotions in the limbic system, in a deep way.

In the fourteenth century the Italian poet Petrarch did something that was unheard of at that time: He climbed Mont Ventoux. Petrarch claimed to be the first person since antiquity to climb a mountain in order to see a view from above (Weiss 1998, 11). Although others did not actually see what he saw, some scholars believe that his reports had a profound impact on people's understanding of the world. He brought back a dramatic perspective of Earth as the human home to people who until then had been focused only inward and heavenward (Rogers 2001, 125).

In the twentieth century, humans went to the moon and ended up discovering the Earth. In 1968, Paul Ehrlich published *The Population Bomb,* protests over the Vietnam War raged in the streets, and the Apollo 8 mission sent astronauts around the moon. On December 24 the astronauts entered the lunar orbit planning to take photos of the moon's surface. They looked up to see the Earth rising over the moon's horizon; amazed, they grabbed a camera and took an unplanned picture (Poole 2010, 1). When the photograph of "Earthrise" reached Earth in a live broadcast, people saw a tiny blue-and-white planet floating in the black void of space. The impact of that image was significant. People began to use the term "spaceship Earth" as a reminder that this world on which we live is finite and the only home we have. Galen Rowell, a photographer for *Life* and *National Geographic* magazines, called Earthrise "the most influential environmental photograph ever taken" (Hosein 2012).

An even more dramatic photograph was sent back to Earth by the crew of Apollo 17 on their way to the moon in 1972. The sun was behind them, the Earth was fully illuminated, and this time the camera captured the entire planet floating in blackness. The crew dubbed the photograph the "Blue Marble." The picture captured people's imaginations during a surge in environmental awareness (Miller 2009, S35). DDT had just been banned, a series of environmental laws had just been passed, and memories of the first Earth Day were still fresh. The "Blue Marble" vividly reinforced, in an immediate and inescapable way, the vulnerability and isolation of the planet in the vast expanse of space. These two photographs, "Earthrise" and "Blue Marble," enabled ordinary people to conceive of their world on an unprecedentedly global scale.

Images can take various forms. Visual communication can use photographs, drawings, digital graphics, or other illustrations. It can also use symbols.

A symbol is something that stands for or represents something else. It is abstract rather than representational (Lannon and Gurak 2017, 265). Symbols are an economical way to communicate, incorporating a lot of information into a small space. So, for example, a triangle with arrows communicates ideas related to recycling. The recycling icon, however, illustrates the limitations of using a symbol as shorthand: Often this triangle is used simply to identify the type of plastic from which a product is made; it does not necessarily mean that the product will be or can be recycled. In the *OECD Environmental Outlook to 2050,* the intergovernmental organization of nations uses red, yellow, and green traffic light symbols as a communication device alongside written text to highlight the relative urgency of issues and pressures on which it reports (OECD 2012, 36).

Symbols are not universally understood and must be learned, and so they are influenced by social and cultural context (Lester 2011, 56). For example, on signs that help people find their way, an arrow pointing down might mean "downstairs" in the US and "straight ahead" in the UK; an arrow pointing up in the US means "straight ahead," and never means "upstairs" even though a down arrow can mean "downstairs" (Arthur and Passini 1992, 35).

An icon is a representative pictorial image. Icons acquire rich connotations and stable meanings after frequent repetition (Morgan and Welton 1992, 109). So, for example, a padlock indicates security on a computer screen, even though a physical lock is not used, a simplified airplane silhouette on a sign indicates an airport, and the Eiffel Tower indicates the city of Paris (Barnes 2011, 68).

A logo is an abstract symbol that typically has no visual resemblance to an actual object. Logos are created by designers to represent organizations and are usually the result of a rigorous design process. The best ones are simple, recognizable, and reproducible in a variety of media (Caputo, Lewis, and Brochu 2008, 71).

Is a picture worth a thousand words? When we communicate, we should generally avoid clichés and use them only when our purpose calls for them. One cliché we often hear repeated is that a picture is worth a thousand words. According to scholars, this phrase originated with a 1920s advertisement for Royal Baking Powder (Card et al. 1999, 1). The ad manager for a streetcar advertising company, Frederick R. Barnard, was trying to convince clients to include pictures in their streetcar ads. He claimed in a 1921 ad in *Printer's Ink* that the phrase came from a Japanese philosopher (Lester 2011, 404). In a 1927 issue of the same trade journal, he decided Chinese would be a more compelling source and switched to an illustration of a "Chinese proverb" he invented. And he changed "a thousand" to "ten thousand" so that his new caption read, "One picture is worth ten thousand words" (Stevenson 1965).

There are times when an image can communicate as much information as a page filled with words. This is especially true of photographs that tell a story, diagrams that explain a scientific process, and graphs that reveal trends contained in many numbers. There are other times when "one word can take care of a situation that would require a whole sheet of drawings to depict it" (Langer 1979, 74). Words and images work together and should be treated with equal respect (Lester 2011, 405). Wilson Hicks, the influential picture editor for *Life* magazine, wrote in his book *Words and Pictures* that "It is not correct to say that either medium supplements the other. The right verb is 'complements'" (Hicks 1952).

PART II
Making Sustainability Visible

4

METAPHOR

We learn new ideas by connecting them to what we already know (Moscardo, Ballantyne, and Hughes 2007, 70). As cognitive research shows, these associations play a fundamental role in thinking and learning (Chen 2002, 69). You can promote this mental connection by pairing two things. A symbol is something that stands for or represents something else. A comparison shows how two or more things are alike. A contrast shows how they are different.

When we want to integrate new information, we relate it to something that is already encoded in our brains (Jacobson 2009, 349). We do this by working from the familiar to the unfamiliar, from the known to the unknown. Communicators facilitate this by using analogies, metaphors, and similar devices to enable people to create links between past and new experiences. Like visual symbols, these devices convey not literal meaning but conceptual understanding by using non-literal, more resonant meanings. Figures of speech in this category include metonym, synecdoche, analogy, simile, and metaphor.

Metonym and synecdoche are two related figures of speech and image. Metonymy is the use of one thing to refer to another thing that is related to it (Lakoff and Johnson 2003, 35). A photograph of slippers, a fireplace, and a soft armchair are used as a metonym for the feeling of comfort (Barnes 2011, 67). Saying that "the *Times* reported from the press conference" is a metonym meaning the reporter from the *Times* reported (Lakoff and Johnson 2003, 35). In the US, the White House is a metonym for the President. In the West, non-Soviet news media used the Berlin Wall as a metonym for the division of Germany into two states. Metonyms often depend upon extensive cultural knowledge (Hall 2007, 40).

Synecdoche is a special case of metonymy in which a part represents the whole (Lakoff and Johnson 2003, 36). For example, if you say we need new blood in our organization, what you mean is that we need some new people. In the Shakespeare play *Julius Caesar,* when Mark Antony begins a speech by saying, "friends, Romans, countrymen, lend me your ears," he means that the audience members should listen. We can use visual synecdoche, as well. For example, we often use an image of the Eiffel Tower to represent Paris.

Synecdoche is a communication device that allows people to move from a specific case to a general concept. For example, if you are communicating about the need for sustainable development in a low-income region, presenting a story about a particular person in a population who was malnourished, and using them to represent the group, would be more vivid and personal than presenting abstract statistics about malnourishment in that group (Hall 2007, 42).

An analogy is a technique for bridging the familiar and the unfamiliar which compares two different things that have some characteristics in common. Often it makes connections between something complicated and something simple, or between something abstract and something concrete (LaRocque 2003, 152). Analogies make connections easier to see. When we call streets and roads arteries, we are making an analogy between a highway system and the circulatory system of a living organism (Millward 1980, 320). An analogy compares something familiar and something new. It can provide an effective introduction to a story or presentation when you first introduce a new concept.

A simile is a technique for bridging the familiar and the unfamiliar which compares two unlike things, usually using the prepositions "like" or "as." For example, you might say "busy as a bee" or "as welcome as water in your shoes." A simile can also be visual, such as an image of a light bulb above someone's head to represent an idea. Both similes and metaphors compare two unlike things that have something in common. When we use a simile, we say that x is like y. When we use a metaphor, we say that x *is* y (Hall 2007, 38).

A metaphor describes one thing in terms of another (LaRocque 2003, 149). It is a technique for bridging the familiar and the unfamiliar which describes one thing using language usually used to describe something very different, a way of understanding one thing in terms of another thing (Lakoff and Johnson 2003, 5). Aristotle characterized metaphor as a process of "giving the thing a name that belongs to something else," writing that "ordinary words convey only what we know already; it is from metaphor that we can best get hold of something fresh" (quoted in Lakoff and Johnson 2003, 190). William Shakespeare used metaphor often; in a famous scene from *As You Like It* he wrote, "All the world's a stage and all the men and women merely players."

Not only do metaphors help us make sense of new information by connecting it to previous experience, these colorful figures of speech are a good way to attract and hold attention (Moscardo et al. 2007, 72). A metaphor draws attention to ways in which an unfamiliar thing can be conceived in terms of a familiar thing. Good metaphors are vivid, they invoke images, and they allow us to see things in new and different ways.

Metaphors are cognitive tools for helping us understand abstract concepts by means of other, more concrete concepts which are more familiar to us (Lakoff and Johnson 2003, 115). It is easier to describe objects or ideas by comparing them with others than to describe them by themselves. With metaphors, the pairing of two images highlights a quality they have in common; seeing the common quality allows the audience to conceive a perceptual abstraction while still retaining the single qualities of each element of the metaphor (Arnheim 1997, 62).

When we say "great oaks from little acorns grow," or when we help people understand the challenges of getting nutritious food in some inner city neighborhoods by calling them "food deserts," we are using a metaphor. The term "greenhouse effect," while not technically accurate, is a metaphor which helps nonscientists understand the process of global warming. Researchers on planetary boundaries describe economic development as a straight highway into the future with no guardrails, and humanity as a vehicle rushing ahead with an oversized engine and no headlights; in this metaphor, the planetary boundaries could provide guardrails (Wijkman and Rockström 2012, 45).

We can use visual metaphors, too. For example, computer designers use a desktop and objects found in offices, including file folders and recycle bins, as a metaphor for computer organization. An anti-drug campaign shows an image of an egg frying in a pan, with the caption "this is your brain on drugs." A flyer about the importance of wearing gloves when working with chemicals shows an image of a sponge cut into the shape of a hand, combined with a caption which says, "this is what your hand looks like to most toxic chemicals" (Barnes 2011, 66). A discussion of albedo and urban heat islands shows an image of a stream of water pouring from a hose, striking a wall, and deflecting into soil; it compares solar radiation striking a light surface to a jet of water hitting a smooth, impermeable surface, and compares radiation on a dark surface to a jet of water hitting a porous sponge (Brown 2010, 66).

Designer and visionary R. Buckminster Fuller (1895–1983) used a trimtab as a metaphor for effecting change. A large ship moving through the water has great momentum in a particular direction, impossible to turn using just a rudder. A trimtab is a small flap on the edge of the main rudder; turning the trimtab allows the rudder to turn, which then allows the ship to turn. Airplane wings use trimtabs as well. Fuller suggested the words "Call me Trimtab" as his epitaph; they are engraved on his tombstone (Robertson 2017, 300).

Metaphors shape our worldviews, for better or worse. When we talk about "protecting the environment," some listeners form an inaccurate image of the environment as a category separate from themselves, with humans as the powerful protectors (Butler 2004, 54). When we talk about ourselves as "stewards," we imply incorrectly that humans are separate from, and perhaps superior to, other living things.

Natural capital is a metaphor that compares ecosystem services[1] and natural resources to a planetary equivalent of a finite savings account (Folke 2013, 19). Designers of closed-loop systems within a circular economy[2] use healthy ecosystems as a metaphor for sustainable human economic systems (Ehrenfeld 2008, 10). Robertson (2017, 26) refers to these natural systems as our "instruction manual."

Metaphors and the associations and meanings on which they draw are culturally based (Marshall 2014, 113). What something means to one person is based on the experiences they have had; another person may not have had those same experiences. On the other hand, metaphors provide a bridge, a way of communicating at least partially about experiences we have not shared (Lakoff and Johnson 2003, 225).

The story of three blind men describing an elephant, each based on what he can feel in one spot on the elephant, is a metaphor in a folk tale from China probably dating to the Han dynasty. The story later expanded to six blind men in India. There is also an African version (Chen 2002, 32).

Metaphors have been part of human culture for millennia. We see them in constellations, invented as memory aids to help us divide the sky into more manageable regions. The symbolic patterns typically bear little resemblance to the beings they represent, but ancient farmers knew that when they saw certain constellations, it would be time to plant or to reap (Chen 2002, 47).

Constellations as precise visual calendars coexisted with a very real sense of mystery and transcendence expressed through metaphors as humans sought to imbue meaning within the natural world. In ancient societies, the realms of myth-based religion and scientific knowledge were fused. Spatial forms of the axis, pyramid, and grotto were physical metaphors that have occurred almost universally in various ancient cultures, expressing cosmic concepts rooted in human cognition and perception (Rogers 2001, 26). The concept of the *axis mundi,* the "axis of the world" connecting physical substance and the sacred, was a metaphor that acted as a center pole which touched both heaven and Earth and united them; it could be expressed by a pole, the center space of a kiva, or the vertical dimension of a temple (ibid., 30). In ancient cultures, structures and spaces were understood as figurative representations of the sacred, cosmic world. They were visible embodiments of invisible ideas. The immediacy of physical elements gave people access to the eternal.

The centrality and symmetry of *axis mundi* structures and spaces was understood as a metaphoric gesture that represented the unity of the cosmos (Corner 1998, 63). The fundamental nature of symmetry is rooted in the physiological bilateral symmetry of all mammals and the processes of human cognition, and is reflected in later principles of Gestalt psychology.

Metaphors and similar figures of speech or image are powerful communication tools. They have the ability to convey a complex idea in a way that is easy to understand. In the world of science, they are considered essential to the development of new theories, used whenever new situations are being investigated. Perhaps most significant, we use metaphors to craft stories.

Notes

1 Ecosystem services are essential benefits that come from ecosystem processes. They are the biological functions that support life including provision of food, assimilation of wastes, nutrient recycling, and climate regulation.
2 In a closed-loop system, matter circulates within the system but does not flow through it, and so there is no waste. In a circular economy, output from one process becomes input for another.

5

STORIES

The Significance of Stories

We share many psychological traits with other animals but no other species, as far as we know, has our narrative ability. Storytelling capacity is a characteristic which distinguishes our species, the result of a unique arrangement of complex neural circuitry. The fact that the need to tell stories is ubiquitous across all cultures, both ancient and modern, indicates that stories have a function (Hall 2007, 153). Biologists consider the human capacity to create stories and multiple scenarios in any situation, and not necessarily act upon them, to be a highly adaptive trait (Sussman and Hollander 2015, 133). This drive to put information into story form is apparently hard-wired into our brains; it is an adaptation that helps us learn, build relationships in social groups, work and create together (McKenna-Cress and Kamien 2010, 113).

A story is not like a report. A report conveys information and organizes facts by topic. A story, on the other hand, is dramatic, experiential, and emotional; it is organized by story arc, and the results are associations and memories (Duarte 2010, 26). A story produces an experience.

To see an example, look at a story in a top news journal: journalists are professional storytellers. Not everyone is interested in the facts of climate science, for example, but people are interested in other people. Science stories often use the drama of challenges and the excitement of solutions.

Stories are containers of information, a way our brains organize information into memorable form. A story creates a mental structure that helps an audience remember the main ideas (Duarte 2010, 52). Stories present information in a way that people can remember; and because stories are memorable, they are easy to repeat. They are a way that humans make sense of the world, learn values, and shape cultures. Consider Aesop's fables, which have been transmitting lessons and cultural values since the sixth century BCE.

Stories perform a fundamental cognitive function: they are how the emotional or affective brain makes sense of information collected by the rational brain (Marshall 2014, 105). Storytelling combines intellect and emotion, facts and feelings (Makower 2009, 123). People want to know facts, but they also want a story. The story charges the information emotionally; it tells us what the facts mean. Factual explanations are about transmitting knowledge, but storytelling is about generating understanding and making personal meaning (McKenna-Cress and Kamien 2010, 114). While information may be static, stories are dynamic. A story weaves information into its telling, but it also arouses our emotions and energy (McKee 1997, 12). A story gives an audience a reason to care.

Stories help us learn by allowing us to join in and become part of them. We become the heroes of the story. This goes beyond visualization. Neurological imaging has shown that when we imagine events, we are using the same parts of our brains that are evoked for real events (James 2010, 5). By imagining the stories, we are practicing the knowledge and skills contained in them.

Narrative Principles

What makes an effective story? A compelling story has simple cause and effect, a focus on people, either individually or in distinct groups, and a positive outcome (Marshall 2014, 107). Every narrative has two key ingredients: characters and conflict (LaRocque 2003, 100). A good story stirs up emotion or passion. A story provides the audience with a setting in which it takes place, it has engaging characters relevant to the audience, it has an evolving story line (Gallant et al. 2008, 15). It contains the unexpected, something surprising. It offers mystery: Who are the characters? What are the plot twists? What will happen next? This sense of adventure gets an audience interested in the details. A good story has a conflict to be resolved. If Odysseus had sailed around the Mediterranean without problems, we might not still be reading Homer's stories today.

A story can be told orally, in writing, or with pictures; the most powerful impact results from a combination of words and images. Images enhance memory and deliver emotional impact (ibid., 26).

There are several types of stories that make for effective communication. There are stories where two or more people communicate across a divide and form a connection, such as Romeo and Juliet, or affect the thinking of a climate skeptic. There are stories where someone makes a surprising discovery, such as Newton and the apple, or a college student's invention of a bicycle-powered generator. There are stories where a hero overcomes challenges, such as Odysseus, or a community group in the South Bronx bringing affordable housing, job opportunities, parks, and transportation to a formerly polluted, low-income neighborhood.

A good story has certain characteristics: First, it is about people. What engages the emotional brain are stories about other humans. A story with people in it will grab and hold our attention (Weinschenk 2011, 159). Events are caused by people or happen to them. An event means change; in a story, it creates meaningful change in the life situation of a person (McKee 1997, 33).

Our brains are hard-wired for imitation and empathy, including a special class of nerve cells called mirror neurons. These neurons fire not only when we perform an action, but when we watch someone else perform the action. By running a simulation of their actions using a visualization of our own bodies, these mirror neurons allow us to empathize and to read someone else's intentions (Ramachandran 2012, 22). The mirror-neuron system is thought to be an evolutionary development which has been central to social learning and the transmission of culture (ibid., 23). Because of this neural system, a vivid story allows us to enjoy a vicarious experience in which we become engaged.

A good story has a hero with a problem, a person who has a goal and something they want to achieve. The story contains risk: The goal is threatened in some way, and the audience must believe that something significant will be lost if the hero does not accomplish their goal (McKee 1997, 303). The story must present a problem with obstacles to be overcome in order to sustain our interest. If someone has a goal, we can identify with them. If they also have an obstacle, we root for them; we become engaged in the story. It is this tension that keeps the story interesting.

A good story has surprise. When you create a story, offer your audience something novel or unexpected. Help them learn something new. Interrupt the ordinary. We all build mental structures based on our experiences. When something unexpected happens these schemata are challenged. We then pay greater attention so that we can correct our cognitive frames (James 2010, 4).

Good articles, presentations, and exhibits use mystery as a way to attract and hold people's attention, often done by posing a question. "Who is killing the polar bears?" "How many hours do you think you could power this light bulb with the energy saved by recycling that aluminum can?" The answers can then unfold like the plot of a mystery story, where people pursue leads, chase clues, hit obstacles, and eventually break through to a resolution (Heath 2007, 80). Make it a mystery the audience needs to solve.

Behavioral economists say that curiosity arises when we discover a gap in our knowledge, a theory known as the information-gap perspective (Loewenstein 2007, 152). Posing a question or a puzzle allows people to notice a contrast between what they know and what they may not know. The initial clue allows us to imagine what we do not know and this information gap generates a desire for knowledge. The more we learn about a topic, the more likely we are to focus on what we do not know, a necessary condition for curiosity (ibid., 157). Curiosity is an intellectual urge to answer open questions. Movie scripts engage audiences by posing questions and creating knowledge gaps. They cause us to ask, What will happen? How will it turn out? Because we will not learn the answer until the climax, we are held by curiosity until the end (McKee 1997, 346).

Environmental psychology research on people's perception of outdoor spaces reveals a parallel process at work related to mystery. First, people want coherence;

they want to understand where they are. That understanding is a foundation which then frees them for exploration, something people also desire. A mystery suggests that there is potential for exploration; physical cues imply that there may be more to be seen, and people feel compelled to find out more (Kaplan, Kaplan, and Ryan 1998, 13). In outdoor spaces, a coherent image is based on a two-dimensional picture plane. Mystery, suggested by an enticing curved path or vegetation that partially obscures what lies behind, requires that people infer a third dimension. And in this process of inferring a third dimension, people imagine themselves in the scene. Mystery arises from having a partial view of things to come. A view which is completely blocked lacks a sense of mystery; a view which hints that there is more to see compels a person to explore and find out more (ibid., 39). This same mechanism is at work in interpretive design, where audiences become intrigued by a theme and want to know more (Ham 2013, 122).

A good story engages the senses. When you create a story, strive to move the story from the abstract realm to the concrete and make it real. Help your audience to feel, touch, and experience what you are talking about. Give them details so that they envision themselves in that story.

Writing teachers often tell their students: show, don't tell. A good story shows, rather than tells. That is, it recreates reality for the audience through description (LaRocque 2003, 134). Words can introduce an idea, but it takes experiencing something to transform you. The idea of showing prompts us to use the five senses with images, visualization, and metaphor to build a story and create an experience. In the show-don't-tell approach you don't tell an audience what to think but allow them to think their own thoughts and reach their own conclusions.

A story exists when something happens. If nothing has happened, then there is no story. If you say, "the cat sat on a mat," that is not a story. But if you say, "The cat sat on the dog's mat," now you have some kind of tension that could lead to something happening (Hall 2007, 168). A story can be only one sentence long, it can fill a 30-second advertisement, or it can cover an entire book, presentation, or movie.

Narrative Structure

Good stories have structure. At its most basic, a story has a beginning, a middle, and an end, a structure first proposed by Aristotle. You could summarize the structure as situation, complication, and resolution (Duarte 2010, 29). The narrative structure presents a problem or conflict, launched by some disturbance or "inciting incident" that leads to disequilibrium (McKee 1997, 181). This is followed by a turning point, and then resolution.

The beginning introduces the characters and the situation or conflict. Your audience needs a reason to care. Introduce the main character and their challenge.

The middle section involves complication. This section is the longest, and is where the main character overcomes challenges. Give the audience more information about the nature of the obstacles or conflicts, which will often add novel or unexpected details. At the height of the tension there is a turning point, where things will either get a lot better or a lot worse.

A story may take a turn that surprises the audience. And because the audience is surprised, they are more engaged. As a story arc builds, the characters go through progressive complications. Some stories have more than one turn; these turns are called plot points in screenwriting. A plot point is a turning point, an incident or event that "hooks into the action" and spins it around in another direction. In the process of hooking into the action, a turning point hooks our curiosity (McKee 1997, 346). A plot point sets up the story for a change; its function is to move the story forward (Field 2005, 143).

At the end of the story, the conflict is resolved. Audiences enjoy experiencing a conflict and resolution. A story creates an imbalance, one which the audience wants to see resolved.

The Hero's Journey

The hero's journey is a category of narrative structure, popularized by Joseph Campbell's 1949 survey of comparative mythology *The Hero with a Thousand Faces* (Campbell 1949), and found in many stories and myths including Jason and the Argonauts in Greek mythology, Odysseus in Homer's *The Odyssey,* Dorothy in Baum's *The Wonderful Wizard of Oz,* Bilbo Baggins in Tolkien's *The Hobbit,* Luke Skywalker in the movie *Star Wars,* and transformation stories from indigenous cultures in North and South America, Africa, Asia, Europe, and Australia. The hero's journey is a story of transformation, in which the hero accomplishes difficult tasks on behalf of a group or culture. The hero or central figure is an ordinary person who is presented with a problem. The audience can identify with them and their dilemma. The hero is at first reluctant, but through the advice of a mentor or through personal introspection overcomes their reluctance. The hero leaves the comfort zone of the ordinary world and ventures forth, crossing a threshold into an unfamiliar world. The hero is tested, confronts danger or their greatest fear, and wins by meeting tests of character. The hero is transformed by the experience, and returns to the ordinary world with knowledge or other gifts that are a benefit to their world (Duarte 2010, 32).

You can tell an effective story about an ordinary hero and their quest. Tell a personal story and then hook it to something larger. You want people not just to be moved by a story, but to feel that they are part of it, that this is their story (Lewis 2014).

Some Examples

You can find examples of storytelling techniques applied in all kinds of settings. Effective trial lawyers present their cases to juries in the form of stories (Ritter 2004, 6). When they are preparing a trial strategy, they try to uncover images, metaphors, and stories that are universally understood by jurors in their community. Then they find ways to explain details of the case using these familiar images. They appeal to shared values such as love, survival, family. Litigators select a single, coherent story line to present rather than being pulled off by a series of alternative arguments. The story has a theme, a strong beginning and ending, and is brought to life by verbal pictures, analogies, adages, and graphics. Without this organizing structure, all the evidence and testimony in a trial could appear to be just a series of random facts. So in the opening statement, the attorney essentially tells a story to the jury, giving them a framework within which to make sense of the information they will see and hear presented to them during the trial.

Theater is an art form that brings stories to life by presenting real people and their actions within a designed environment. During a performance, the theater is dark and the stage, with its carefully composed settings, is lit with lighting sequences designed by a lighting designer. The audience suspends disbelief and enters into the world on stage, where we join the actors in wrestling with ethics and ideas and where we can perhaps experience a healthier future. Theater is a realm where storytelling helps us clarify and embrace values. With certain plays, we can see ourselves in the goodness on stage, and perhaps feel impelled to live up to that (Carey 2016). Some modern theater directors, producers, and designers intentionally promote the greening of the theater, green dramaturgy, and sustainability in the arts, with such groups as EcoArts and Sustainability and the Arts showcasing ways to visualize sustainability and climate change topics, communicating through art and performance that change is possible. People who work in theater can feel disconnected and alone, a reason that many of us despair so easily, and a reason that connecting to like-minded others in the theater is important (ibid.) They remind us that no single play, no single performance needs to do it all; the world of theater and art is like an ecosystem where each species has a niche and no one organism does it all (ibid.) Drama can present multiple viewpoints in all their subtlety and can illustrate people acting collectively. In a vivid and immediate way, it can reach interested people who might not read written materials. The challenge, as with all communication, is to avoid the danger of falling into being didactic. Performances must be well done, and must avoid preaching to the audience (ISO 2006, 16).

Here is an example of storytelling technique used to engage readers in a sustainability issue. In a chapter of the book *The Sustainability Transformation,* author Alan AtKisson (2011) is talking about global warming and the collapse of marine fisheries. Instead of plodding through the details, he opens the chapter with a vivid story about a giant squid who attacked a racing trimaran in 2003. He then muses about how formerly elusive giant squid are washing up on beaches regularly these days, and he asks: What is going on? Now that the reader has experienced a concrete reality, is curious about what is going on, and has focused their attention on the situation, he can begin an explanation about cars burning fossil fuels, carbon dioxide in the atmosphere, and warming of the oceans, compounded by overharvesting of marine fisheries, a problem he then tells us can be summed up in one word: economics.

Like in the examples throughout this chapter, you can use the power of stories to communicate your message. Include human characters. Describe what they discovered or what challenges they overcame, and how things changed as a result. Structure your story with a beginning that introduces the characters and their challenge, a middle section where complications arise, and an ending where the conflict is resolved. Include something that is surprising or that makes your audience think about the theme that underpins your story.

6

INTERPRETIVE EXHIBITS AND SIGNS

Interpretation

People who work in sustainability often communicate by developing exhibits or creating explanatory signage. This is a field of practice known as interpretation, in which we communicate with non-captive audiences in a leisure or free-choice setting (Ham 2002, 162). Although we mostly associate it with museums, in fact the principles of interpretation lie at the heart of communicating sustainability to all kinds of people in all kinds of settings.

In a formal classroom setting, students are involved in a prescribed, sequential learning process. In an interpretive setting, however, participation is voluntary and the experience is usually a short-term episode (Knapp 2007, 54). People are present for a few minutes, and then they are gone. Our goal is to create positive impact and lasting memories from the short interludes with audiences, who are free to walk away at any moment. There are no external incentives like grades or examinations, so interpretation needs to be understandable, easy to process, and engaging. Audiences include both first-time and repeat visitors and come from a wide range of knowledge, ages, abilities, and cultures, so they need a varied menu of guided and self-guided activities and opportunities that allow for diverse learning styles and preferences.

Your goals in this free-choice setting include encouraging curiosity and exploration, challenging attitudes and assumptions, encouraging people to think about ethical issues, helping people to learn, and provoking people to find their own meanings (Moscardo et al. 2007, 69). People who do interpretation see their role not as teachers or givers of facts, but as facilitators of something more important: the making of meaning (Ham 2013, 7).

An interpreter is someone who translates meanings from one language into another. We do something similar when we help audiences understand the sustainability ideas we interpret. John Muir is credited with first using the word "interpretation" in this way (Mayo and Larsen 2009, 5). In his Yosemite note-book, he wrote, "I'll interpret the rocks, learn the language of flood, storm and the avalanche. I'll acquaint myself with the glaciers and wild gardens, and get as near the heart of the world as I can" (Muir 1896, 271).

Freeman Tilden first defined the practice of interpretation in 1957. Tilden was a journalist. At age 58, a friend invited him to work with the National Park Service, and as he traveled to various parks, he studied their interpretive interactions and communication. The basic principles he outlined in his seminal book, *Interpreting Our Heritage*, have been considered the standard ever since (Jacobson 2009, 304). The modern pillar of interpretation is Sam Ham, who developed principles of thematic interpretation based on his research in communication psychology. His theme-based communication principles have become central to the work of environmental and heritage interpretation (Mayo and Larsen 2009, 6).

Traditional interpretation happens at all kinds of sites, including museums, zoos, aquaria, historic sites, interpretive centers, nature centers, parks, and botanical gardens. It also happens at schools, colleges and universities, city sustainability programs, and community sustainability events.

There are two general categories of interpretation: personal and nonpersonal. Personal interpretation is face to face and gives visitors an opportunity to interact with an interpreter in person, which could involve a guided tour, a talk, a demonstration, a performance, or an informal conversation. These are good ways to showcase sustainability projects including solar panels, rainwater harvesting, composting, community gardens, and bioswales. With all but informal contacts, the interpreter generally determines the sequence. Personal interpretation reaches fewer people but is often more immersive and allows for two-way communication, resulting in greater impact for visitors.

Nonpersonal interpretation involves communicating a message without personal interaction. Examples include exhibits, information kiosks, signage, posters, brochures, maps, audio tours, websites, and smartphone apps. This kind of communication is nonsequential, and audiences determine to what information to pay attention, and in what order (Ham 2013, 174). Nonpersonal interpretation can reach broad audiences by using multiple formats and in multiple languages. Media products are more enduring and can be returned to multiple times.

Interpretation: Making Meaning, Provoking Connections

Interpretation is more than simply communicating factual information. According to the National Association for Interpretation (NAI), "Interpretation is a mission-based communication process that forges emotional and intellectual connections between the interests of the audience and meanings inherent in the resource" (Ham 2013, 7). Ham defines it as "a mission-based approach to communication aimed at provoking in audiences the discovery of personal meaning and the forging of personal connections with things, places, people, and concepts" (ibid., 252). Tilden argued that the goal of interpretation is not to teach anyone in the traditional sense, but rather to provoke them to do their own thinking and to make their own meanings (Knapp 2007, x). Interpretation creates opportunities for audiences to form their own intellectual and emotional connections. It goes beyond making connections to the next logical step of making a difference (Brochu 2003, 3), echoing the title of Ham's 2013 classic handbook, *Interpretation: Making a Difference on Purpose.*

Tilden asserted, and those who came after him have confirmed, that interpretation is not instruction but provocation. It is not what the interpreter does (communicate information) but what the audience does (think) that shows us whether interpretation has been successful (Ham 2013, xvii). In reality, the only meanings a visitor can attach to a subject are those that they make themselves, in their own minds (ibid., 7).

The primary goal of interpretation is to provoke audiences to think their own thoughts, and in so doing, to find their own meanings and connections (Ham 2013, 57). Research has shown repeatedly that increased knowledge does not impact visitors' attitudes (ibid., 84). Rather, it is their own thinking about a subject which produces meanings about the subject that then impacts their point of view about the subject. If something is meaningful to them, it is because they have thought about it and interacted with it and formed multiple connections related to it.

In order to have an impact on an audience's attitude toward a thing, you must provoke them to think about it themselves. And this has several requirements: First, they must see the interpretive material as easy to process, and for that to happen, it must be clearly organized. Then, in order to be motivated to process the information, they must see it as relevant. But because these are non-captive audiences, they are free to ignore the information if they choose; that means that processing it must be enjoyable (ibid., 86). Your goal is not to teach an audience your idea; it is to provoke them to think their own thoughts about the idea.

Gianna Moscardo (1999) first developed formal principles for making interpretation thought-provoking, built on psychological research into what makes us mindful, that is, what causes us to pay attention to the world around us (Moscardo 1999, 21). When we are mindful, we can process new information and are able to form new ways of seeing the world. Research reveals several factors which block mindful information processing: relying on familiar or repetitive routines, accepting a given description or stereotype and allowing it to guide our behavior, and deciding that the available information is not important or relevant. Thus, audiences are more likely to be mindful when they are in new or unfamiliar situations and when they perceive information as important or personally relevant (ibid., 22). When situations are dynamic and changing, we don't have a routine we can borrow from somewhere else. Dynamic circumstances require us to make decisions, which means we must process information mindfully. Giving people control in a situation means two things: that they must make their own decisions and that the outcome will be more important to them.

Principles for Interpretation

Tilden's principles are still considered fundamental to interpretation. They include the following principles: Interpretation is an educational process that relates "what is being displayed or described to something within the personality or experience of the visitor." While interpretation does include information, "information, as such, is not interpretation." Interpretation is an art which can be learned. It should strive "to present a whole, rather than a part." And the most essential of Tilden's principles is that "the chief aim of interpretation is not instruction, but provocation" (Tilden 1957, 15).

Interpretation builds on communication theories, cognitive psychology, and theories about how people learn (Mayo and Larsen 2009, 17). Ham's interpretive approach to communication came from a large body of research about how humans respond to communication done well. His principles said that effective interpretation has a theme, is organized, is relevant, and is enjoyable, which he captured with the acronym TORE (Ham 2013, 14).

Theme

The theme is the simple, big idea you want your audience to think about. Its purpose is to provide a focus for the personal connections audiences will make for themselves (Larsen 2001, 1). The theme answers the question, "so what?" A theme attracts attention, stimulates curiosity, and provokes the audience to think (Ham 2013, 122). It is not about memorizing facts. Your exhibit or sign does convey an idea, but the audience will make their own connections and take away their own meanings. Your theme can result in any number of different themes arising in the audience's mind. A solid theme will probably provoke connections you did not anticipate and may never be aware of (Mayo and Larsen 2009, 38).

A theme is different from a topic, which is simply the subject matter. For example, you may want to prepare an exhibit or create a sign about water pollution. "Water pollution" is a topic, but it is not a theme. Now consider this title as a theme: "We're Polluting the Water that Dinosaurs Drank" (Ham 2013, 212). Or you may want to prepare an exhibit or create a sign about fire. "Fire in nature" is a topic, but it is not a theme. Your theme might be, "Fire is a natural process that creates life out of death" (Mayo and Larsen 2009, 39). Notice how the themes made you think.

A theme must be simple. You are interpreting ideas for non-captive audiences in a free-choice setting, who will not invest a lot of effort into trying to understand something that is difficult to follow. A theme should be expressed in everyday, conversational language that an audience would typically use to describe the same idea. Think of people who have successfully interpreted science for lay audiences: Carl Sagan, David Attenborough, Neil deGrasse Tyson. They all explain complicated topics using plain, everyday language.

The theme should tie something tangible to something intangible, a universal concept. A tangible thing is concrete; it has qualities that can be perceived with the senses. Examples include an ecosystem, a tree, water, a neighborhood, or an event. Often one tangible thing is selected as an icon to represent the larger ideas of the theme. Intangibles are abstract and include relationships, feelings, ideas, and values. Links between tangibles, intangibles, and universal concepts are the basic building blocks for interpretation, giving audiences opportunities to make connections that are meaningful for themselves. A US National Park Service guide says that "all successful interpretation can be described as linking a tangible resource to its intangible meanings. Effective interpretation is about connecting one to the other" (Larsen 2003, 92).

A universal concept is an intangible meaning to which everyone can relate, even though no two people will see it just the same way (Mayo and Larsen 2009, 9). Universal concepts are ideas, values, and emotions that speak fundamentally to the human condition. They include experiences such as life, work, love, change, death, survival, and family; emotions such as love, fear, elation, and sorrow; biological imperatives such as birth, death, and hunger; and "human fascination with uncertainty, the cosmos, mystery, and suspense" (Ham 2013, 33). Almost every good story revolves around one or more universal concepts.

Connecting tangible things to universal concepts makes them relevant and valuable to the broadest audience. These connections can be intellectual, made through insight or better understanding, or they can be emotional, provoking feelings such as empathy, wonder, or concern. It is making these connections that helps audiences care about the subjects of your theme. People who come to see a thing or a place as socially significant, personally relevant, and meaningful are more likely to care for it so that it can continue into the long-term future.

Note that just proclaiming an abstract idea does not provoke the making of personal meaning. A universal concept must be linked to something tangible in order for audiences to make their own meaningful connections.

Organization

Exhibits and other interpretive materials should be organized, with content that is clear and easy to follow. As with all communication, having a clear structure minimizes the amount of effort required from the audience. People unconsciously weigh tradeoffs between rewards or potential benefits and the amount of effort required to attain them (Ham 2013, 26). Audiences are non-captive, and they will stop paying attention if they have to work too hard to follow an idea.

Relevance

Remember the definition of interpretation from the National Association for Interpretation (NAI): "Interpretation is a mission-based communication process that forges emotional and intellectual connections between the interests of the audience and meanings inherent in the resource" (Ham 2013, 7). The most important element of this form of communication is the making of connections.

That means a theme must be relevant. That is, it needs to be something that relates to the audience's experience and connects to their interests. It is only when the link between tangibles and intangibles is personally relevant that individuals connect to a subject. Interpretation should link to something people not only know about but also something they care about. Relevance motivates the audience to think about the words and ideas they see.

Research by Tulving (1983, 9) and others indicates that three important factors aid in increasing the ability to remember experiences and facts: One is repeated exposure to the concept. The second is the concept's relevance to individual person. Audiences have better recall when they are exposed to information that is practical in nature, based on experiences from real life, and seen as related to their own everyday lives. Third is having active, hands-on experiences (Knapp 2007, 11).

Enjoyability

Ham's evidence-based TORE principles say that to be effective, interpretation must have a theme, be organized, be relevant, and be enjoyable (Ham 2013, 14). Research repeatedly shows that learning and recall are much greater if audiences are engaged and enjoying themselves (Moscardo et al. 2007, 8). Interpretation that is enjoyable and entertaining is informal. It uses active verbs, shows relationships between cause and effect, has features that are unusual or surprising such as exaggerated scale, includes stories about people, and gives audiences opportunities to touch and manipulate things.

Research in cognitive psychology shows that content in our long-term memory consists of at least two main types: semantic and episodic memory (Tulving 1972, 381). Semantic memory is the conceptual knowledge of facts. When you are in a classroom, teachers often focus on semantic memory. But retaining facts in short-term memory has been shown to be a poor predictor of long-term learning (Knapp 2007, x).

Episodic memory is autobiographical; it is a memory of experiences, events in which we ourselves have participated. Memories are retrieved from long-term memory by means of cues which were stored along with the memory of the experience, including images, feelings, and other specific details related to the past event (Knapp 2007, 10). If you aim to provoke audiences to make their own meanings, then helping them to make episodic memories should be your goal (Ham 2013, 82), and that comes from providing experiences that are vivid and enjoyable.

Engaging Audiences

Multiple studies on what factors help create lasting impacts have shown that those which generate the richest and longest-lasting memories happen in novel settings, with hands-on opportunities, with personal interactions, and with links between tangible and intangible elements (Knapp 2007, 117). Things that are known to be of high interest to most people include other humans, movement, things that are dangerous, and things that are unusual or surprising (Ham 2013, 130).

An interpretive setting is different from a classroom. There are no exams or grades, and so people are free to ignore information without punishment or loss of reward. The reward for a non-captive audience is their own satisfaction or pleasure. If they receive information that is more engaging than other things around them, their brains will reward them by releasing the neurotransmitter dopamine and hormonal endorphins, and they will continue to pay attention (Ham 2013, 12). Information that is boring or difficult to process will cause them to look for pleasure elsewhere. Until you have captured your audience's attention, any other efforts will be wasted.

Variety

Cognitive psychology research tells us something about what will capture an audience's attention. The human neurological system has an old brain, concerned with survival; a mid-brain, which processes emotions; and the logical, reasoning new brain. The old brain developed first and its job is to scan the environment constantly for three critical things: food, mates, and danger. That is why anything new or novel will capture our attention (Weinschenk 2011, 110).

We instinctively pay attention to differences and changes in our environment. After we see a signal or pattern repeated several times, our old brain begins to ignore it. That is why research shows that visitors to an exhibit will have an initial burst of interest, then move through with less and less attention as if they were browsing (Moscardo et al. 2007, 8). Providing variety can help to restore interest: variety in setting, differences in style, and changes in pace, using multiple frames and from a variety of perspectives. Not only does this increase the chance of being novel enough to capture attention and encourage mindfulness (Moscardo 1999, 75), it also makes connections possible for more kinds of audiences, with people from varied cultural backgrounds. Variety also makes it more likely that visitors will visit a setting or exhibit more than once, because they anticipate new experiences (Moscardo 1999, 81).

We are drawn to things that stand out from the ordinary: something that is unusual or unexpected, something that is bigger than or contrasts with its surroundings. This is related to the reason we use contrast in graphic design and the reason that landmarks are useful in wayfinding. We are drawn to mystery: something with uncertainty or intrigue. In an unfamiliar situation, we cannot borrow a routine from somewhere else and our old brain will compel us to keep paying attention (Moscardo 1999, 22).

Scale

Shifts in scale, where we see things at either a larger or a smaller scale than we are accustomed, captures our attention and provokes us to see reality in new ways.

The American Museum of Natural History in New York City does a lot with scale in their special exhibitions, often beginning with a special entry, a threshold which visitors experience as a portal to another world (Meister 2015). At the Field Museum in Chicago, the *Underground Adventure* exhibit uses transition rooms to "shrink" visitors to 1/100th of their actual size and, using giant "soil" particles and animatronics, gives visitors a vivid, bug's-eye view of life in the soil, including how various invertebrate parents care for their young and how roots and fungal hyphae find nourishment in the soil (Chicone and Kissel 2013, 83).

Exaggerated timescales are effective, too. Some natural history museums use exhibits that let audiences experience time going by at a magnified rate. For example, they might use animation to show time speeded up so that 1000 years goes by every second, allowing the visitor to watch continental drift occur as if it were in real time. As a planner, you need to consider that things you find fascinating may or may not be interesting to your visitors. Make sure that your use of exaggerated scales is based on what you know about your audience (Ham 2013, 146).

Familiarity and Personal Connection

Associations play a fundamental role in our thinking and learning (Chen 2002, 69). For a new idea to be meaningful, it must relate to something that is already encoded in our brains (Jacobson 2009, 349). People learn by making connections between pieces of information and by fitting new information into their existing framework (Moscardo et al. 2007, 70).

Thus, interpretation needs to relate new information to something the visitor already knows. A well-crafted theme for an exhibit or sign helps audiences to make connections between new information and things they already know. The relationships may be obvious to you, but may not be obvious to audiences who do not have your knowledge or experience with the topic. Using a theme to present an interpretive story can link the pieces together for them (Moscardo et al. 2007, 74).

We help audiences make connections by working from the familiar to the unfamiliar, from the known to the unknown. One way to do this is by using examples, analogies, and metaphors (Ham 2013, 31). For example, if you were talking about transportation, you could say, "In 1889, horses were as common as automobiles are today" (Lake Champlain Basin Program 2004, 5).

We are drawn to situations that involve other living things, especially humans. Facts can be more relevant to audiences when they are framed in a human context. At the Field Museum in Chicago, the *Evolving Planet* exhibit explains that some sauropods had up to 80 individual vertebrae in their tails. This may not have meant much to visitors, until they read the next sentence: "You have 33 in your entire backbone." Comparing a dinosaur's tail to the visitor's own familiar body gives meaning to the impressive number of tail vertebrae (Chicone and Kissel 2013, 97).

Tilden gave an example of a label in a museum in Texas, which said, "Prehistoric mammoths were here in Texas just a few thousand years ago. They roamed the plains in great herds... The chances are that they browsed right where you are standing now" (Tilden 1977, 13). The mammoths thus were not far away, but were right beneath the visitor's own feet. The information related what was being described to "something within the experience of the visitor," as Tilden recommended in his first principle (ibid., 9).

If you are creating an exhibit on climate change, you could talk about how weather is short-term variations and climate is long-term trends. But that idea will be more understandable if you explain that when we say, "It's hot today," we are talking about weather, and when we say, "the cherry trees are blooming three weeks earlier than they did when I was a child," we are talking about climate. Or if you say, "weather tells you how to dress in the morning; climate tells you what to have in your closet" (Chicone and Kissel 2013, 98), you are relating these concepts to the audience's everyday lives.

Audiences will shift their attention to any information that is highly personal, information that reminds them of themselves, their families, their well-being, or their values (Ham 2013, 33). You can help people to connect new information to something with which they are familiar by saying, "Think about the last time you..." or "At one time or another, you have probably..." Research shows that simply asking an audience to use themselves and their experiences to judge the relevance of new information greatly improves learning and recall (Ham 2002, 163). The interests of your audience are usually different from your own interests. You need to find ways to make connections between what you talk about and what your audience cares about most.

As you are developing a theme, try inserting the personal pronoun "you" into the theme. It brings the audience into the story and in essence starts a conversation with them (Ham 2013, 126). Encourage audiences to interact with the theme actively. You can help them become involved by saying, "Look for the..." or "See if you can find the..." (Lake Champlain Basin Program 2004, 4).

Autonomy

The goal of the ancient part of your brain is to keep you out of danger and let you survive. It likes to feel that it is in control, because if it is, there is less likelihood you will be in danger (Weinschenk 2011, 142). This means that people are motivated by autonomy. They like to do things themselves, and they want to have choices. To engage audiences, give them opportunities to participate and interact, and to make choices about what and how much they do. Allow them to take control of their learning (Moscardo et al. 2007, 11). Allow them to touch and handle things (Moscardo 1999, 63).

Tilden saw that "the chief aim of interpretation is not instruction, but provocation" (Tilden 1957, 15). Decades of research have confirmed that the only meanings a visitor can attach to a subject are those that they make in their own mind. When audiences have control, they can use this control to find information that is personally relevant to them (Moscardo 1999, 67). The more they are provoked to do their own thinking and to make their own connections, the more enduring their understanding of the subject will be (Ham 2013, 8).

Circumstances that are unfamiliar, in which we do not have an existing routine we can follow, not only capture our attention, they require us to make decisions. And this decision making requires us to be mindful and results in feelings of autonomy (Moscardo 1999, 23). Wayfinding research shows that when people visit a new place, if they must explore by themselves rather than being guided by another person, on subsequent visits they will find their way better than if they had been shown around. Similarly, a person who is a passenger in a car will have more difficulty finding their way around than the person who is the driver of a car (Passini 1984, 80).

A walking tour is an effective strategy for enabling visitors to choose what to see and for how long. For example, you can map out a walking tour of green-building features in an urban neighborhood or Leadership in Energy and Environmental Design (LEED)-certified buildings on a college campus, with items on the map keyed to explanatory descriptions (Raphael 2013, 21). You can print a walking-tour map on a flyer or brochure and hand out copies at an event, and then make the map available on a website where it can remain in use for years. If you have the resources, consider adding signs and interpretive information that are also keyed to the map.

Stories

Visitor research shows that audiences prefer information presented as stories, and they prefer stories that relate to their immediate surroundings. They prefer cause-and-effect relationships over isolated facts or simple identification of objects. They want relationships between pieces of information to be clear, and they want to be able to make connections between that information and a larger context (Moscardo 1999, 84). Stories help them do this.

Stories are important interpretive techniques. They get audiences emotionally engaged and promote personal insights into subjects. They allow audiences not only to observe an event or idea, but to experience it. Effective interpretive stories convey emotions and share experiences of central characters (Moscardo et al. 2007, 65). For example, you might describe the thoughts, speech, and action of citizens of New Orleans in the days before or the years after Hurricane Katrina hit, or the citizens of Puerto Rico before and after Hurricane Maria hit. Stories are vivid because they necessarily include concrete details and specific examples. Often stories use a conversational tone and include informal language, anecdotes, and dialog.

Cognitive psychology research shows that when people are presented with different versions of the same story with identical content but differing organization, the comprehensibility and audience recall are determined by how much plot structure a story contains (Ham 2002, 166). Every interpretive presentation should have a beginning, middle, end, and a theme or big idea. A theme serves as plot structure and major organizer, giving continuity to the whole interpretive experience. The story should revolve around one or more universal concepts (Ham 2013, 33).

Within the narrative of an exhibit, you can illuminate details and make them relevant and engaging with smaller stories that present particular problems, place obstacles in the way, and finally reach a conclusion. These smaller stories should also have beginnings, middles, and ends, and should involve humans to whom visitors can relate (McKenna-Cress and Kamien 2010, 110). Include males and females, people of different ages, and people from different cultures or social groups. Audiences can choose to follow a character in whom they are most interested or who they think is most like themselves (Moscardo 1999, 69).

You can use an existing story or make up a story; locate it in the past, present, or future; and set up a hypothetical what-if scenario. Focus on an individual entity, who could be fictional, and provide details about what they experience. For example, you could tell a story about people in an indigenous family, or describe the last days of the final member of an extinct species, or follow a single water molecule through a full water cycle or through cycles across millions of years (Ham 2013, 48). In an exhibit about climate cycles and the most recent ice age, you could tell the story of how the Ice Age Floods carved out the Columbia River Gorge in Washington and Oregon. Instead of recounting simple facts about melting glaciers, basalt, and erosion, you could tell the dramatic story of geologist J. Harlan Bretz who first suspected that something enormous had happened, was mocked and ostracized for years by fellow scientists, but in the end was able to put the final pieces of evidence into place, upending beliefs worldwide about how geological processes worked. Let stories speak for themselves and let audiences find their own meanings; avoid summarizing a story or pointing out what you think is the moral (Mayo and Larsen 2009, 30).

Redundancy

Telling a story from more than one direction gives audiences greater opportunities to understand its meanings. When audiences have more perspectives from which to choose, they are more likely to form connections that are meaningful and relevant for them (Mayo and Larsen 2009, 17). Try to interpret a theme using multiple media and methods. Research on memory by Tulving and others has shown that exposure to a concept by different media and in different contexts strengthens both episodic memory, the memory of the experience, and semantic memory, the actual knowledge of the subject (Knapp 2007, 11). That redundancy makes the story available to everyone and means no one is left out. Research in sustainable tourism has shown that the more types of media and methods used to communicate, the greater the impacts for audiences in terms of what they know, what they feel, and how their behavior changes (Weiler and Smith 2009, 103).

Exhibit Design

An exhibit is "an organized arrangement of text, graphics, and objects that communicate a message or theme" (NAI 2007, 4). It can be a single, small element, or it can consist of multiple components. Effectively engaging audiences with exhibit content depends on attractiveness, brevity, clarity, and dynamism: exhibits must be attractive, brief, clear, and dynamic, sometimes referred to as the ABCDs of exhibit design (Jacobson 2009, 318).

An exhibit needs a distinct visual style in order to attract attention and communicate the theme and key messages from a distance. The text, images, and objects plus colors, materials, finishes, and sometimes lighting come together to create a complete physical experience (Chicone and Kissel 2013, 109).

Organization

In a larger, more structured installation, you can think of an exhibit as having a narrative that leads you on a journey, with an introduction, a body, and a conclusion (Meister 2015). If there is more than one panel, start with an introductory panel to tell audiences what the exhibit is about. The introduction needs to attract attention and create curiosity. It sets the stage for the conclusion. It tells the audience what to look for, gives them a mental road map of where the exhibit is going, and helps them make connections between pieces of information (Moscardo 1999, 89).

Then interpret, or develop the ideas, in the body of the exhibit. Panels in the body of the exhibit can follow a logical order to guide visitors through the exhibit, which can be cause and effect, timeline, problem and solution, progressing from parts to a whole (induction), or reasoning from general to specific (deduction) (Jacobson 2009, 322). However, remember that visitors are non-captive audiences and can choose to view panels in any order that interests them, so each panel must be able to communicate a complete concept on its own.

Add detail to bring the theme to life: stories, metaphors, examples, and facts that provoke thinking. Remember to make the content organized, relevant, and enjoyable as you support the theme (Ham 2013, 175). As visitors progress, give them sections that engage them more deeply including, perhaps, opportunities to participate or to take action.

Provide a final section that reinforces the theme and advances their understanding. Have a strong theme and present it once in the introduction and again in the conclusion. Provoke audiences to think their own theme-related thoughts. The conclusion can summarize main points and suggest larger meanings. Or it can plant a seed that answers the question, "Now what?" and give them positive, proactive takeaways (Second Story Interactive Studios 2012).

Provide visual and verbal cues that reinforce the central theme in a variety of ways throughout the phases of the exhibit. Provide a complete experience that touches both the intellect and the emotions. Bringing together thinking and feeling allows audiences to internalize the theme and to take away a message that helps them commit to positive behavioral change in some way.

Present four main ideas or fewer since, as we've seen earlier, working memory is capable of handling only three to five items at one time. Use organization, size, and color to make it easy for audiences to distinguish between the main ideas and subordinate ideas.

It makes organizational sense to have a series of signs, objects, and experiences that reinforce the story line. Visitors decide in what order they want to access the information and may not follow the sequence you have laid out, or they may not interact with each element, so there may be gaps in the story for some people. In a sequential exhibit the designer or interpreter controls the order, and the structure has an introduction, a body, and a conclusion. Sequential arrangements work well if a story is linear, such as a geologic timeline or the evolution of a forest system. In a nonsequential exhibit each person decides where to pay attention and in what order. You cannot predict what order they will follow or how much time they will spend engaging with each element.

Designing Exhibits to Engage Visitors

Interpretation research has identified three general categories of audiences for exhibits and signs, sometimes called studiers, strollers, and streakers (Ham 2013, 207). Studiers view exhibits in depth, try everything, and read almost all of the text (Moscardo et al. 2007, 9); not many visitors fall into this group. Strollers browse through signs or exhibits. Multiple studies on museum visitors indicate that people spend an average of only a few seconds reading any particular label. Many visitors spend from one to eighteen seconds reading; the greatest number pass by an exhibit and read nothing (Falk and Dierking 2016, 73).

Most of an audience consists of streakers who spend one to six seconds, just long enough to read a title, glance at a primary design element, and perhaps form a broad impression (Ham 2013, 208). This underscores how essential it is to develop a provocative theme and then provide a title and design that work together to convey the essence of that theme to the greatest number of people, even those who pass by quickly. Your goal should be to provoke thinking in every person in an audience, regardless of how much time they spend processing the theme. People who spend more time, the strollers and studiers, will be rewarded with a richer development of the theme.

Audiences know a title will tell them what an exhibit is about, and will use the title to help them decide whether to spend more time on it. While they are reading the title, they will notice at least one other design element which will catch their attention, at least briefly. Seeing a title and visual element together will cause a visitor to look for an association between them, and once they make an association, some kind of impression or thought will follow. In this moment, even a very brief audience can be provoked to think one or more theme-related thoughts (Ham 2013, 210). This combination of title and visual element, perceived as a unit, is the best strategy for developing a theme whether visitors experience an exhibit sequentially or nonsequentially.

Visitors prefer to spend most of their time looking, listening, and touching rather than reading (Falk and Dierking 2016, 78). If people can touch, feel, lift, or operate something, their experience becomes tangible. Their visit changes from a focus on just one sense, sight, to an experience that enables them to use several senses. Visual information alone can be emotionally detached, but touch connects directly to a person's body. Allowing audiences to touch and handle things pulls in multiple senses and gives them choice and control, and in so doing encourages mindfulness (Moscardo 1999, 64). When visitors in research studies describe memories of interpretive experiences, the richest descriptions are consistently related to active involvement: touching and active, hands-on experiences (Knapp 2007, 36).

Research tells us that people are able to retain information better when it is practical in nature, based on real-life experiences, and seen to be connected to their own everyday lives (Knapp 2007, 11). Visitor memories of interpretive content are richest when they have been actively involved. We want interpretation that provokes audiences to think their own thoughts and make their own connections; through association, they construct new ideas based on their own past or present knowledge. You can help people make personal connections through the use of metaphors, analogies, stories, especially those with relatable characters, and opportunities to interact and to make their own choices about what to do and how to participate (Moscardo et al. 2007, 6).

Hands-On Connections that Engage Visitors

Being involved in hands-on activity leads to stronger episodic memory, or the memory of experiences, for people of all ages. The strongest memories and the richest descriptions of memories connect to active involvement (Knapp 2007, 36). Research confirms that people of all ages remember actions they performed themselves better than actions they simply observed (Falk et al. 2007, 49).

Involve visitors in an active way as much as possible. For example, in a talk about the Lewis and Clark expedition, an interpreter provided a cloth tape measure cut to the length of the circumference of a tree Lewis and Clark recorded in their journals. Visitors stood in a group and held the cloth tape to encircle the group, forming themselves into a circle that represented the size of the ancient tree's diameter (Scherbaum 2006, 4). Allowing visitors to touch and handle things gives them control, provides variety, gives them ways to make personal connections, and encourages mindfulness (Moscardo 1999, 32). You can also involve visitors in an active way by asking questions such as, "How can you help?" that suggest actions they can take after leaving the site.

Designers of interactive exhibits can turn to principles of user-centered design, which is design with the needs of the user in mind. This approach to design thinking came into the mainstream through the work of cognitive scientist

Donald Norman (2013). The goal is to design objects and exhibits that are intuitive, that people can understand and use almost immediately without conscious effort. In such cases, users will know what to do just by looking, with no explanation or label required. For example, people know that knobs are for turning, and based on cultural standards, they know that turning a knob clockwise increases the amount of something (Falk et al. 2007, 45). Since working memory is capable of handling only three to five items at one time, limit the number of available controls or interactive features on an exhibit element to one small group at a time. Good design requires good communication about how to use the design: its features communicate what a thing is for, how it is structured, and how it is operated (Norman 2013, 19).

Accessibility

Use a mix of media, including signage, sound, and tactile features, so that communication is available to everyone and no one has to miss out. Be sure that similar experiences are available to all visitors. Consider having your design proposals tested or evaluated by people with a variety of physical abilities to ensure you have considered accessibility appropriately.

Do not underestimate the importance of adequate seating. Studies show that visitors who use available seating spend more time engaged with exhibits (Chicone and Kissel 2013, 121). All people enjoy experiences more when they are comfortable and if they can choose when to rest. Physical limitations or health make it necessary for some visitors in particular to rest often, so seating can determine whether they can form their own connections and meanings, or not.

Green Exhibits

When you plan, design, and fabricate exhibits you have choices to make about materials. Five green-exhibit strategies can help you create exhibits that are healthy for people and that reduce the environmental impacts of producing them (Willcox 2009, 14). (1) Reduce new material consumption. Design with an eye to using fewer materials, reuse material from previous exhibits or former buildings, use materials with recycled content, and use rapidly renewable materials such as bamboo and hemp; if you use wood or paper products, choose those that are FSC certified (Forest Stewardship Council). (2) Use local resources. Specify raw materials and manufactured products from within 500 miles of your site, hire local contractors for labor, and combine orders into batches to reduce packaging. (3) Reduce waste. Design components that can be re-purposed, use construction methods that allow components to be disassembled, use materials that can be recycled, eliminate the use of consumables that would be sent to a landfill, and design for durability. (4) Reduce energy consumption. Use fewer energy-consuming components and interfaces, choose energy-efficient components, use automatic shutoffs, and use alternative energy sources where possible.

(5) Reduce products with toxic emissions. Avoid wood products and textiles that contain formaldehyde or other volatile organic compounds (VOCs), use low-VOC finishes, use non-toxic cleaning products, and avoid PVC (Newman and Urizar 2013, 4).

Personal Interpretation

If you are leading a tour, giving a presentation, talking about a physical exhibit, or having conversations with visitors, then you are a personal interpreter. Personal interpretation occurs when visitors interact directly with an interpreter, and it has a big effect. Years of research have shown that personal contacts result in stronger memories and greater impact than impersonal interpretation alone (Knapp 2007, 116). Visitors see the individual interpreter as one of the most important and memorable parts of their visit. And the more the information communicated is relevant to the visitors' lives, the greater the impact.

Many exhibits include an introduction, a body, and a conclusion. You can provide the same structure when you are doing personal interpretation by speaking and interacting with audiences. Plan an introduction, a brochure, or an introductory area that establishes the theme and orients the visitor. Helping them understand the organization of the content will make learning easier. As architect Richard Wurman, co-founder of the TED Conference, said, "Knowing how to look for information gives you the freedom to find it" (Wurman 1989, 52).

Your goal is to promote connections with visitors and enhance the personal meanings they acquire from their visit. As with all forms of interpretation, this means provoking them to think their own thoughts and make their own meanings, rather than simply providing a one-way delivery of facts. When you talk with people informally, ask them questions like, "If you had my job what would you tell people?" Or, "What did you hope you would find here?" (Larsen 2003, 22).

Roving interpretation is personalized, one-on-one communication. Although it appears spontaneous to visitors, roving interpretation is organized and planned by interpreters (Knapp 2007, 74). It requires interpreters who want to talk to people and are willing to seek them out. Roving takes advantage of teachable moments. Find locations to walk around where people are most likely to end their visit and more likely to have questions, and be ready to stop and chat whenever someone seems interested. Consider having a prop or things that visitors can touch or handle to attract their interest. When you interact with people, be sensitive to signals that they have had enough conversation. You want memories from these close encounters to be only positive.

Personal Interpretation that Engages Visitors

Use open-ended questions to foster the thinking process. For example, you can encourage mental activity by saying, "You just left the rainforest. Now you are entering the mangrove forest. How are they different?" This process takes time, so allow time for an answer, the five to fifteen seconds that interpreters call "wait-time" (Mayo and Larsen 2009, 28). Allowing longer time usually results in better answers. If no one offers a response leave the question open, to be answered later, or try rephrasing; never answer your own questions (Regnier, Gross, and Zimmerman 1994, 30). Acknowledge visitors' willingness to think and participate, even if the answers are wrong, and avoid judging the value or correctness of the answer (Mayo and Larsen 2009, 28).

You can also use an invitation to engage visitors. For example, "Watch for monarch butterflies quietly landing on the milkweed." Or suggest that they take a walk along a creek on the site and invite them to notice how the understory plants begin to change as they near the creek. Or invite them to transport themselves into another time: "Imagine what it was like 15,000 years ago when the place where you are standing now was a lake, with mastodons and camels grazing nearby."

Ask people to compare similarities and differences. Ham gives an example of comparing two pine trees, both of which carry needles in bundles of three and grow in similar places; invite visitors to smell the bark and notice that one smells like vanilla while the other smells like turpentine (Ham 2013, 32). Encourage audiences to focus on multiple senses and promote mindfulness with suggestions or questions. For example, you can suggest people stop, close their eyes, and listen for particular sounds. Or suggest they close their eyes and use touch to compare differences between the bark of two trees (Scherbaum 2006, 35). Consider using these approaches in brochures for self-guided walks as well as on guided walks.

Use thought-provoking questions to engage visitors. Avoid asking questions such as, "Did you know...?" or, "Can anyone tell me...?" Such questions reinforce your possession of exclusive knowledge and their lack of knowledge. Avoid asking questions that assume prior knowledge or require guesswork, both potentially frustrating. Instead, ask provocative questions that encourage visitors to think about possible answers. Encourage them to look at the rest of an exhibit, site, or sign to discover the answer, giving them an intrinsic reward for their effort (Moscardo et al. 2007, 53). Those questions can be posed in writing or in person.

Interpretive Signage

Signs in interpretive settings are of three general types: orientation/information, warning, and interpretive signs or labels (Moscardo et al. 2007, 2). Orientation signs help visitors find their way, and include things like maps, floor plans, and words with direction arrows. Information signs give basic facts about such things as hours, admission cost, and activities. Warning and safety signs alert visitors to potential dangers and often include messages about how to minimize risk or increase safety.

Interpretive signs translate facts, figures, and information into a format that engages the audience and provokes in them theme-related thoughts. Text tells audiences what the exhibit is about. Most audiences read only a fraction of the text, so the titles, subtitles, and images must attract attention and communicate the theme quickly.

Present the messages in your sign in a hierarchy. Tell the same story with different levels of detail to accommodate different people. Some interpretive signage designers call this the 3–30–3 rule: Most visitors will look at a sign for at least 3 seconds, enough time to perceive an intriguing, theme-related title and large, focal graphic. Some visitors will continue looking at a sign for an additional 30 seconds. This is enough time to read the main message, which should be presented in large text and one to two paragraphs long. A few visitors will be interested enough in the topic to look at a sign for up to 3 minutes. Provide smaller, secondary graphics and text with more detailed information for this group of studiers (Gross, Zimmerman, and Buchholz 2006, 53). Visitors should be able to get your main message easily by reading only the top level of the sign.

Visitors will first notice the title and at least one other visually dominant design element, usually a graphic image that creates a focal point. Then they will look at subtitles, if there are any, or the main body of text. Finally, some will read any area of smaller sub-text. Some signs also go into greater detail for those who are interested using smaller, secondary graphics and text boxes with differently colored background fill. Distinguish each level in some way, such as size of text, use of subheadings, and grouping information into blocks.

Text on Signs

The title should relate to the theme, rather than just identifying a topic. Visitors will spend only a few seconds reading the title, and will use it to help them decide whether to spend any more time with the exhibit. On indoor signs, title typeface should be at least ¾ to 1 inch tall; outdoors, it should be 4 to 6 inches tall. Subtitles should be at least ½ to ¾ inch indoors or 3 to 5 inches tall outdoors (Jacobson 2009, 324).

Once a thematic title has attracted audiences, it is the subtitles and body text that have potential to hold them. Text and graphics should convey the story line of the exhibit. Remember that audiences are non-captive; they will only look at signs they want to look at, so designs must be engaging and clear. A visitor quickly assesses whether there is likely to be a reward for the effort of reading. If they conclude that there will be too much work for little reward, they will ignore the sign. Use a simple, memorable title to capture people's attention; use a subtitle to give them a little detail and tell them what to expect (Meister 2015).

Three factors determine how readable a piece of text is: its physical features, including typeface, line length, and size; the interestingness and relevance of its topic to the reader; and its use of plain language that is comprehensible to most readers (Moscardo et al. 2007, 56).

Body text for general audiences should be written at a 12- to 15-year-old, or sixth- to eighth-grade, reading level. You can check the reading level using a test such as the Flesch readability scale or the Fry test, both of which count the number of words per sentence and number of syllables per word. According to the Fry test, for example, at the 12- to 15-year-old age level there should be 10 to 20 words per sentence, with 5 to 10 sentences totaling 120 to 150 syllables in every 100 words (Jacobson 2009, 323).

Lines of text will be hard to read if they are either too short or too long. It is generally agreed that lines should be 40 to 65 characters in length, including spaces, or about 10 words per line (Moscardo et al. 2007, 41). Text is easiest to read when it has a flush left margin and ragged right margin, which allows standard word spacing.

Use plain language and familiar terms, and avoid jargon. Use concrete nouns and active verbs to create imagery. Write for reading aloud (Chicone and Kissel 2013, 95). Try reading your sign out loud, testing to see whether words have a comfortable rhythm and are easy to say. Notice that when people converse with each other aloud, they tend to use active, rather than passive, sentence structure (Moscardo et al. 2007, 62). Keep ideas focused and pare down wordiness by limiting the use of adjectives and adverbs. Illustrate ideas using metaphors, analogies, and real examples. Present the content so that it relates to something within the visitor's experience. Write like you are having a conversation with the visitor; use personal pronouns and personal language (Gross et al. 2006, 56). Words can have cultural connotations, so it is a good idea to have your proposed signage reviewed by people from a variety of backgrounds.

People are more likely to read signs that they believe to be short. Using only two or three pieces of information per sign and breaking up text using headings, short paragraphs, and graphics are effective ways to make signs appear short and accessible (Moscardo et al. 2007, 43). The average visitor will spend only a few seconds in front of each sign, so limit text to no more than 150 to 200 words per sign or panel, and try to break blocks of text into paragraphs of no more than 50 words each (Caputo et al. 2008, 15). People are more likely to read three short paragraphs than one long paragraph. If a concept requires a lengthier, more detailed explanation, consider creating a handout sheet or booklet that can be taken by people who are interested in learning more.

Research shows that people understand and remember text more easily when it is accompanied by graphics (Moscardo et al. 2007, 76). Remember that white space is a design element, along with text and images.

Graphics on Signs

Images have more impact than words on interpretive signage. Besides focusing attention and leading the reader through a message, images convey detailed information in concise and dramatic ways and are easier to understand than text descriptions (Gross et al. 2006, 36). For example, an interpretive sign in Badlands National Park in South Dakota stands in front of a moon-like landscape with layers of sediment visible in the hills of a dry, nearly bare terrain.

The attention-grabbing title of the sign, however, says, "Jungle on a Seabed." The subtitle says, "A jungle grew here. Before that, a shallow sea covered the land. Both are gone now, but both left evidence of their passing." Along the side of the panel, filling most of the sign, is the focal graphic, a diagram of geological layers with three simple photographs of undersea creatures who once lived there and whose fossils can now be found in the rocks. For visitors who want to learn more, three paragraphs of smaller text give details about what happened geologically and when.

Graphic images should generally do more than duplicate what is already visible; they should reveal hidden ideas and meanings. An exception occurs when there is a feature in the landscape that you would like to label and explain. For example, signs throughout Arches National Park in Utah feature color photographs identical to the landscapes beyond them, together with labels, explanatory text and, often, suggestions about how visitors can help protect this fragile place.

What grabs audiences' attention? Color, contrast, variety, movement, extremes, other people. Color inherently attracts attention. Warm colors appear closer and larger than cool colors and appear to be advancing toward the reader. Contrasts in color attract attention, especially bright color and strong contrast. Dark-colored text on a light background is particularly legible (Moscardo et al. 2007, 51). Contrasts in size stand out, such as large text for titles.

If you use multiple signs, you need to find a balance between contrast and harmony. Signs need to have enough elements in common that they are seen as parts of a whole. Separate signs can be linked by common style elements while also offering variety. Avoid monotonous repetition, and use variety to attract and hold attention. Variety can include font size, typeface, sentence length, paragraph length, amount of text, use of humor, and ranges of suggested activities. For variety, you can even use an occasional word that is more complex or colorful than most of the language in your text; if most language and syntax are accessible, readers can still derive meaning from reading the sign as a whole.

It is highly recommended that you use a copyeditor to review text and a professional designer for graphics and layout.

Signage Installation

Position signs within visitors' line of vision so that important information is easy to see (Moscardo et al. 2007, 75). People typically stand 18 to 36 inches from vertical sign panels. Keep text within a comfortable range to be seen, at a height of 36 to 72 inches above the ground (Brochu 2003, 116). Do not assume that every visitor's eye level is like your own; some people are very tall, some very short, some are children, and some use wheelchairs. A visual center between 50 and 60 inches from the ground will accommodate the greatest number of viewers.

Consider sign locations and think about where visitors may actually walk or stop. Locate signs at entrances and major decision points as well as key interpretive points and natural stopping areas such as viewpoints. Placing signs near a bench, an overlook, or on a path between a parking lot and restroom increases their chances of being seen. People are physically and mentally fresh when they enter an interpretive area, so are more willing to read signs near the beginning of a visit. Themes and primary ideas are best located near an entrance or beginning of an interpretive area, and perpendicular to the line of approach. For exhibits in multistory buildings, signs on the first floor are more likely to be read than signs on higher floors. The farther a sign is from the entrance, the less likely people are to read it. Signs near exits or near the end tend to be read the least (Moscardo et al. 2007, 27).

Lighting must allow visitors to read signs comfortably. For indoor signs, check for shadows caused by lighting placement that could affect readability. For outdoor signs in bright sunlight, the most readable have light-colored type on dark backgrounds. Outdoor signs in shaded areas are most readable with dark type on light backgrounds (Moscardo et al. 2007, 51). If people will be moving from outdoors to indoors, or from brightly lit to dimly lit conditions, their eyes will need to adapt to differences in light levels. A series of areas with progressively lower light levels will help eyes to adapt and prevent signs from appearing too dark. For signage written in Braille, remember that if they are made of metal and placed in full sun, the signs may get dangerously hot; consider a different material or a cooler location.

Signs can be fabricated using a range of materials, including wood, plastic laminates, cast bronze, and steel, and in a variety of technologies, including sandblasting, paint, porcelainized enamel, and color embedded in resin. Plan for vandalism; some materials deter or recover better than others. If you can, look at examples of signs that are several years old in other sites with conditions similar to yours. Consult signage professionals and handbooks on signage so you can make an informed decision.

Plan for periodic maintenance if your exhibit is to be somewhat permanent. Maintenance affects how visitors perceive and remember your message. Well-maintained exhibits or signs communicate to visitors that you value your message and their experience (Moscardo et al. 2007, 21).

Art

Art is another medium used for interpretation. The ISO environmental management standard for environmental communication, ISO 14063, specifically lists "Art Exhibitions," that is, using "display of artworks organized around environmental themes," as an environmental communication technique (ISO 2006, 17). A strength of this medium is that it encourages engagement by people who might not be attracted by more conventional approaches.

Boulder, Colorado, is home to the University of Colorado and the National Center for Atmospheric Research (NCAR). It is also the headquarters of EcoArts, an interdisciplinary organization that promotes collaborations between artists and scientists. In 2007 they organized "Weather Report: Art and Climate Change," a show curated by art critic Lucy Lippard which paired dozens of artists including Mary Miss with scientists to create both indoor and outdoor pieces to communicate ideas about climate change (Dederer 2007). In 2008 the "Weather Report" exhibit included visual art, dance, film, and lectures at venues across three cities. Being built on a scientific foundation allowed the art to express reality accurately, and art allowed people to grasp scientific information in a meaningful way by connecting through passion and emotion.

In 2010, the Museum of Modern Art (MoMA) in New York City featured an exhibit in collaboration with the P.S. 1 Contemporary Art Center titled "Rising Currents," which presented architectural proposals for adapting to sea level rise around New York Harbor. In the proposal stage before the exhibit opened, the artists' brief from the curator told architects, "Your mission is to come up with images that are so compelling they can't be forgotten and so realistic that they can't be dismissed" (Braasch 2013, 39).

Maya Lin first caught the world's attention in 1981 with her minimalist design for the Vietnam Veterans Memorial in Washington, DC, a design that is intimate in scale and still one of the world's most moving monuments. A prolific artist, in 2012 she began work on what she calls her "last memorial," a multimedia project titled "What Is Missing?" (Toomey 2012). Global in scale, richly layered, and centered around an interactive website including digital maps, videos, animations, images, and sound recordings, "What Is Missing?" marries art and science to draw attention to the increasingly rapid loss of biodiversity. In this subtle but profoundly moving opus, Lin uses the power of art to shift perceptions, offering different ways of seeing data points and awakening viewers to dramatic changes which had been invisible to most of us (Lin 2012). It is both an elegy and a call to action, with reports of positive changes happening now, hopeful scenarios for the future, and descriptions of simple actions each of us can take in our everyday lives that make a difference (Toomey 2012).

Planning for Interpretation

Like any activity, interpretation begins with planning. Exhibits, signage, printed and online materials, and the overall interpretive program all require a plan. Successful exhibit development depends on an organized process and teamwork. The planning process happens first and is followed by design, production, implementation, and evaluation. A plan not only increases the chances of a successful program, it enables you to attract the support you need, whether from grant funding, money from donors, volunteer effort, administrative work, or political support.

Form a project team and identify a leader. As with any organized planning effort, you need a team of motivated, engaged people representing everyone who will be affected by the implementation of the plan, together with a project manager to keep the process organized and moving forward (Robertson 2017, 298). Identify who will work on the project and determine each person's role

(Lake Champlain Basin Program 2004, 2). Maintain communication within the team through regular meetings, online collaboration tools, and regular status reports (Chicone and Kissel 2013, 46).

After you identify your goal, then determine strategies, which are the projects you will do that will get you to your goal. Then identify objectives, which are specific, relevant, measurable, and attainable. Finally, determine the tactics, or actions and sub-actions, which make up your to-do list. You may start by thinking there are only eight or ten, but in fact there are probably hundreds (Hayward 2015). Depending on who can be involved, help your team figure out your goal, strategy, objectives, and tactics, or figure them out yourself and then assign tasks to volunteers.

Develop a timeline with milestones. You can use a scheduling tool like a Gantt chart, or you can set this up with a simple spreadsheet. Start with where you want to be, then work backwards to milestones with dates. Many planners estimate the time required for each action item. Whatever time you estimate, you should probably allow several times that much. On your schedule, list tasks, who is responsible, priority, status, and date completed. Set up a regular tracking system and check on the list every day (ibid.). Monitor people who agreed to do a particular task. Have other team members review the timeline document on a regular basis (Brochu 2003, 57).

The plan needs a budget, which can include design fees, fabrication costs, marketing, operations, and other staff costs, depending on the size of your project. Begin developing the budget by attaching a cost to each action item in your timeline (Brochu 2003, 57). The budget should also include a contingency for changes or unexpected expenses (Chicone and Kissel 2013, 128). The plan should identify resources that will be needed. Resources include finances, staff, and facilities. Staffing needs can include things like design, operations, and maintenance.

The process used by the US National Park Service follows these steps: Select a tangible thing, place, or event you want visitors to care about. Identify intangible meanings. Identify universal concepts. Identify the potential audience. Develop a theme and include a universal concept. Use interpretive methods to link tangible things to their intangible meanings and to provide opportunities for visitors to make connections to meanings (Mayo and Larsen 2009, 35–40).

Begin by identifying your goal. Goals are generally not measurable. They can involve qualities like enhancing understanding, increasing awareness, or fostering participation. Depending upon the project, you may find it helpful to begin first by stating your organization's mission; this is a clear statement of your purpose, your reason for existence; it answers the question, "Why are we here?"

Develop the theme early in your planning process. The theme is a single whole idea that expresses meaning, captured in a phrase or sentence, sometimes two. You might or might not tell the audience what your theme is. It does not necessarily appear anywhere in your exhibit, although it can. This big idea is your guide as you develop a story line, research what to include, create and build the final product. The theme allows you to see how to organize your facts and details; it does for interpretation what plot does for a movie. Every element you include in an exhibit or sign should lead the audience to think ideas that hover somewhere around the theme (Ham 2013, 24). Be aware that crafting the theme statement is one of the most challenging steps in developing an interpretive exhibit or sign, requiring discipline and the patience to struggle through multiple iterations.

In the early stages of planning, allow for periods of brainstorming and creative chaos within the group process (Parman and Flowers 2008, 9). Team participation is crucial, but recognize that it may be difficult actually to craft a theme statement as a group. A more efficient approach is to collect words and ideas together, allow one planner to draft a theme statement, then to review and approve it as a group (Brochu 2003, 100). Wordsmithing a theme statement is typically not a good use of time, since it may not appear anywhere but in the planning document.

Select the best interpretive medium and techniques that communicate your theme and that link the tangible resources with the intangible meanings they represent (Mayo and Larsen 2009, 34).

Depending upon the topic, you may choose to develop subthemes, which allow a logical progression into story lines. If you use subthemes, avoid a fragmented plan by limiting them to no more than three to five subthemes (Brochu 2003, 103).

Organize the interpretive materials around a story line. Develop opportunities for visitors to make connections to meanings. Verify that the intangible meanings include universal concepts that are relevant for most people (Mayo and Larsen 2009, 34). Identify what is special about this topic or place; evaluate your topic or site to identify hooks, the particular tangible or intangible features that help create lasting impacts with visitors (Knapp 2007, 117). Some sites or topics may have a tangible feature that can serve as an icon for the focus of interpretive efforts (Mayo and Larsen 2009, 34). For example, if you are interpreting a wetland, you may decide that a great blue heron can serve as its icon.

Conduct front-end evaluation, which we will discuss in the final section of this chapter. Identify potential audiences for whom your message is intended. Conduct visitor research to determine who you expect will see your exhibit and signs.

Conduct research on information and images to be included. Write, review, and revise the text. Arrange for text to be translated by a qualified translator, if your interpretive exhibit or signage are to be presented in more than one language.

Select a graphic designer. Lay out the design, with information and images presented in hierarchical layers. Review and revise the design.

Consider allowing time in your project plan for making prototypes to test ideas and see how they work. Prototypes can be as simple as cardboard, markers, and duct tape. In fact, if prototypes are clearly rudimentary, people will recognize them as opportunities to contribute to the design process. Test multiple iterations with a variety of people. Try not to explain your prototypes; just watch and listen to how potential visitors interact with them (Chicone and Kissel 2013, 78).

Once the design is finalized, your team can move on to coordinate the printing, fabrication, construction, and installation.

Sign Plans and Other Plans

If your project includes signage, you should consider creating a separate sign plan. This type of plan includes an inventory of all the signs needed, broken down by category: orientation, information, safety, and interpretive signs; a map that shows the location of every sign; design guidelines to ensure consistency; and a maintenance schedule (Brochu 2003, 9). Depending upon size and location, determine whether sign permits are needed.

Interpretive signs are expensive and are designed to remain in place for long periods of time, so they should be planned with care. They can be a cost-effective way to reach large numbers of people. However, once constructed they have limited flexibility and cannot be changed easily. Before leaping ahead to the design phase, think about whether signs are the best option for your particular purpose (Moscardo et al. 2007, 21). Often they are, but it is a question worth considering.

If your project includes anything beyond a simple publication, consider creating a communication plan (Caputo et al. 2008, 66). Determine what kinds of publications, multimedia, and online resources exist or need to be created, and how they, your exhibit, and your signage relate to form a unified program (Lake Champlain Basin Program 2004, 2).

Evaluation

Every planning or design process needs a feedback step so that planners can know whether the plan's objectives have been achieved. Feedback also helps planners understand what can be done to make either this plan or future plans better. With evaluation, you collect and analyze information about interpretive materials or their impacts on visitors with the goal of improving your ability to serve audiences in the ways you intended (Moscardo 1999, 101).

Evaluation is an important element of all planning. It is the careful study of something, either to determine its feasibility or to determine its effectiveness at meeting goals and objectives (NAI 2007, 4). It is done at the beginning of a planning process to shape the development of themes and interpretive media and at the end of the planning process to foster learning and impact future products in a cycle of continuous improvement.

Front-end evaluation is conducted during the planning phase to provide background information prior to design in order to explore the interests, learning styles, general knowledge, experiences, and expectations of potential visitors

(NAI 2007, 4). It is about knowing who your visitors are and what they expect (Moscardo 1999, 102). You want to ensure that the needs of visitors drive development of themes and design of exhibits and signage. In this stage, you identify who the potential visitors are, their interests, their level of interest and how much time they are likely to spend, whether they are likely to visit more than once, their level of knowledge, and whether there are misconceptions that should be addressed. Interviews with focus groups are a good way to conduct front-end evaluation (Moscardo et al. 2007, 116).

Formative evaluation is done during the design process. It evaluates the potential for proposed signs and exhibits to communicate, while they are still under development, and provides information about how they can be improved (NAI 2007, 4). Mock-ups and prototypes are a good way to check assumptions and test tentative design solutions with potential visitors (Moscardo et al. 2007, 116). In this stage, you should determine whether exhibits or signs make sense to visitors and try to find out what visitors think are the main messages or themes being communicated. Notice which aspects attract the most attention and whether any are being ignored. Observe potential visitors, if possible, and notice whether they appear to be focused and absorbed in the material and whether they appear comfortable in the setting. Formative evaluation is an iterative process in which you use inexpensive mock-ups, prototypes, and temporary printed signs to test, then revise, then test again. It allows testing of design and material choices before committing to costly design and fabrication expenses.

Summative evaluation, the most common form of evaluation, is conducted after a project is completed to assess the quality and impact of a project that is already in place (Moscardo 1999, 102). It involves real visitors engaging with real exhibits and signs. What is assessed should be tied to the goals and objectives you developed early in your planning process (NAI 2007, 4). In this stage you evaluate whether your project is meeting its stated goals and objectives, that is, whether visitors are getting the messages you hoped to send. One method is to conduct exit interviews or surveys. Focus groups are also a good way to conduct this step of evaluation. Open-ended questions are effective. For example, ask participants to complete a sentence such as, "I did not know that..." or "this made me realize that..." (Moscardo et al. 2007, 118) or "the main thing I take from this image is..." (Ham 2013, 214).

A survey or interview is not intended to test how much knowledge visitors acquired. Rather, it tests the exhibit's or sign's impact using visitors' self-reported understanding. Look for clues that it provoked visitors to think their own thoughts, or to feel emotions such as caring more about something, or to modify their behavior in some way (Weiler and Smith 2009, 96).

In a method called thought listing, you simply ask people to tell you, either orally or in writing, what they are thinking about the topics in an exhibit or sign. This can tell you about the extent to which your interpretive material has provoked them to think, what they are thinking about, and whether their thoughts are within your zone of tolerance (Ham 2013, 167). With this information, what you can do to improve becomes more clear. Ham suggests that as an alternative to formal research methodology, you can also be guided by your own reactions: if you find yourself smiling as you read or listen to their reactions, then what they are saying can be considered to fall within your zone of tolerance. If a thought they express does not cause you to smile, you can count it as lying outside your zone of tolerance (ibid.)

You can do formal or informal observations, using counters to gage level of use and noting how much time visitors spend in front of a particular exhibit or sign, whether any are being ignored, and whether any seem to encourage conversations among visitors. Formal observations use methods from the field of environment–behavior. These methods include observing physical traces, such as litter or paths worn across a lawn; observing behavior to see how people use physical settings and recording those observations in checklists, written notes, on maps, and with photographs or video; focused interviews; structured questionnaires; and archival records such as information about questions received by staff (Zeisel 2006). Observations give us a lot of information but they do not tell us why visitors behave in particular ways, which is why surveys, interviews, and focus groups are important (Moscardo 1999, 104).

Summative evaluation is a helpful learning tool that allows you to make minor adjustments to existing media or to refine your plans for the future. Be prepared to make changes to an existing exhibit if your evaluation results show that changes are needed.

Planning is an iterative process that does not stop with completion of a plan. Plans do not remain fixed in time, and every plan should be considered a work in progress. Conditions change, visitors change, and current knowledge changes. Each plan should be submitted to periodic review, and modifications or even new plans will be required to meet changing conditions. Experience should be fed back into the process at every level of planning and design. Many interpretive planners explicitly build into their plans a method for reviewing and revising, with a suggested timeline and titles of the people who will be responsible for this evaluation (Brochu 2003, 78).

7

WAYFINDING

Wayfinding means, literally, finding one's way. It also refers to the information systems such as signs and maps that guide people through places. Why include a chapter on wayfinding in a book about communication? Because the process of finding your way in physical space has much in common with using communication materials, and the principles involved in wayfinding are directly applicable to principles for communication.

The study of wayfinding integrates cognitive science with design and planning (Berger 2009). Environmental graphic design (EGD) applies this knowledge in the design of information systems to guide people through physical environments, to help them form mental maps of a place, and to help them understand and experience the space. EGD is concerned with visual aspects of wayfinding and communicating information and can include signage, maps, symbols, colors, architecture, landscape, sculptural objects, and digital displays.

Wayfinding and the Ancient Human Brain

Wayfinding originated deep in our evolutionary past. Thigmotaxis, or wall-hugging, is a primal, subconscious wayfinding strategy. It is believed that navigation and spatial traits such as thigmotaxis are governed by the hippocampus in the limbic system in the more ancient part of our brains (Sussman and Hollander 2015, 20). Thigmotaxis can be any movement in response to the touch of a solid object, and is a behavior that evolves when responding to physical objects would result in greater safety or other survival benefits (Pelletier 2010). In many animals, including humans, thigmotaxis is wall-hugging behavior. In prey animals such as mice, wall-hugging is a way to avoid open spaces where they are in danger from predators. Humans, too, instinctively avoid the centers of large open spaces. Thigmotaxis helps us sense the borders of a space and its escape routes. This helps us feel more safe and protected when navigating through a new space and it helps us construct a mental map of the space (Sussman and Hollander 2015, 25).

People want to understand what is going on and do not like being disoriented or confused (UNEP 2005, 15). Being able to make sense of the world, including the physical environment we are in, is critical to feeling competent, safe, and secure (Kaplan et al. 1998, 147). A model known as Maslow's hierarchy of needs describes how feeling safe and competent is a prerequisite to learning. Psychologist Abraham Maslow (1943) developed the theory of human motivation known as the hierarchy of needs. He identified five sets of basic needs common to all humans which he labeled physiological, safety, love/belonging, esteem, and self-actualization. These are typically drawn as a pyramid, with physiological needs forming the broad base and self-actualization the peak. Physiological needs include those basic to survival: breathing, food, water, sex, and sleep. Until they are satisfied, all other needs are pushed into the background or become non-existent (Maslow 1970, 11). Once these needs are satisfied, higher needs emerge. At this point the lower needs are no longer active motivators, and the higher needs organize our behavior (ibid.)

The next level above physiological in the hierarchy is safety, and it is satisfied when we are oriented, know where we are, and know how to get where we are going. When the lower needs are satisfied, new and higher needs emerge, including the motivation to discover, explore, and learn new things; these are aspects of self-actualization.

The Wayfinding Process

As with understanding information generally, people navigate from general to more specific destinations in a series of steps (Calori 2007, 86). For example, if you are traveling to visit a friend in the hospital, you do not need to see the room number on the highway exit sign. From the highway, a sign directs you to the hospital complex in general. When you arrive at the main entrance, signs then direct you to various buildings. Once you enter the appropriate building, information about zones within that building appears, and a directory and map give you department and elevator locations. Once you reach the elevator you need, you find information about room locations. When you reach a specific area, signs along a hallway direct you to room numbers, and you find the one you need. In this kind of wayfinding system, signs or maps are located at decision points, destination names are added to signs when more detail is needed and are deleted from signs once they have been reached.

The physical structure and hierarchy of the circulation system or patterns of paths affect how easy it is to form mental maps and to make choices at decision points (Arthur and Passini 1992). In an ideal design we might not need maps or signs at all. Once we arrived at a new destination it would be obvious from the structure and architecture where the next directions should go, and finding our way would require little effort (Calori 2007, viii).

When we are finding our way to a place, whether we are using maps or navigating on our own, we form knowledge about the place in stages. First, we learn information about key landmarks. Then, we develop knowledge about routes that connect one location to another. Finally, we form a mental map of the spatial complex (Ware 2013, 359).

The consensus is that we humans have two general strategies for finding our way, sometimes called route and survey (Thompson and Travlou 2007, 112). In one strategy people learn routes and make a sequential series of turns at particular locations from an imagined viewpoint within the space. In the other strategy, survey knowledge, people form an overall view constructed from an understanding of the structure of the space, with mental maps assembled from landmarks and their relationships to each other, a hierarchical network connecting them, and an imagined viewpoint above the space (Raphael 2013, 3). Survey knowledge is more flexible than route knowledge, and it allows people to develop their own routes and shortcuts. Some people start with landmarks and use them as anchor points and then connect them with paths; others assume that routes are the main structuring element. In an unfamiliar space, we may start with one strategy and then switch to the other as the place becomes more familiar.

The most efficient wayfinding strategy is based on using landmarks as anchor points. But what constitutes a landmark is different for different people. So as in other areas of communication, redundancy, with clear structure and offering multiple anchor points, makes it more likely that people will feel comfortable and find their way easily (Arthur and Passini 1992).

Cognitive Maps

Cognitive maps are mental representations of physical places. They are mental constructs of places which cannot be seen from a single vantage point and so must be constructed into a whole from a series of individual views that have been seen in parts (Arthur and Passini 1992, 19). Animals, including humans, use them to remember important features of a place and to find their way. During our evolution, cognitive maps helped us efficiently find food, shelter, and other members of our social group.

When we are new to a place, most of us build cognitive maps by first remembering landmarks and then by learning routes that connect a sequence of landmarks. Landmarks can be used as anchors for new information because they are easy to remember and easy to identify. Landmarks located at decision points are particularly useful in constructing cognitive maps (Moscardo 1999, 49). The main disorienting quality of a labyrinth or maze is that, lacking a clear overall spatial structure, it cannot be represented in a cognitive map (Arthur and Passini 1992, 19).

In an influential work on the perception of urban environments, the planner Kevin Lynch studied what makes cities legible. Legibility of a place, according to Lynch, means "the ease with which its parts can be recognized and can be organized into a coherent pattern" (Lynch 1964, 2). He asked residents of three US cities to draw quick maps with the main features of their city from memory, to give directions for their daily trip from home to work, and to participate in several additional exercises. As a result of this research, he identified five elements of legibility, five elements that make a place easy to understand: paths, edges, districts, nodes, and landmarks.[1] A landmark is a distinct physical object, a visual anchor. A node is a distinct hub of activity (Chen 2002, 70). A district is a recognizable region with an identifying character, where it is clear to an observer whether they are inside or outside. An edge is a boundary, a linear element that is not a path. A path is a linear element along which people can move that connects landmarks, nodes, or districts (Lynch 1964, 47). Lynch compared the legibility of a printed page, which "can be visually grasped as a related pattern of recognizable symbols" (ibid., 2), with the legibility of a city, where districts, landmarks, and pathways are easily identifiable and can be grouped into an overall pattern.

Lynch showed that cognitive science was a field which could be applied to design and planning work (Berger 2009). Research in neuroscience has shown parallels between the wayfinding structures Lynch discovered and processes operating in the hippocampus, a region of the mid-brain known to be important in our understanding of space. The hippocampus contains three types of neurons related to spatial navigation: Border cells signal impenetrable edges, place cells signal specific locations, and grid cells maintain an updated cognitive map of where we are (Ware 2013, 361).

Lynch's conclusions reinforced the principles of Maslow's hierarchy of needs. He pointed out that if a place is legible, it feels safe and offers security. He then pointed out that if a place is legible and thus safe, it "heightens potential depth and intensity of human experience" (Lynch 1964, 5); that is, it allows the user to move to the higher self-actualization level in the hierarchy of needs. Note the parallel between legible places and the legibility of signage and clarity of communication in written text: If communication is legible and structured, the audience feels competent, do not need to struggle to understand its content, and can move on to thinking their own thoughts and making their own connections.

Landmarks and Background

Wayfinding, whether in printed material, signage, or physical places, depends upon two contrasting features: landmarks and background. A successful landmark is visually distinct from every other element, easy to identify, separate from the background and, as much as possible, recognizable at all scales (Ware 2013, 361). Its essential characteristic is its contrast with the background (Lynch 1964, 100). The more distinctive and startling an object, the more effective it is as a landmark (Arthur and Passini 1992, 198). In physical space, landmarks are significant elements that make up a wayfinding system before signage is considered; landmarks can be districts, major buildings, and distinctive objects. In a theme park like Disneyland, for example, landmarks and icons are highly visible from a distance and from multiple viewing directions; they help visitors stay oriented (Meister 2015). The Eiffel Tower does this for visitors in Paris. On a college campus or a city street, landmarks stand out from the background and are easy to recognize.

For some buildings to function as landmarks, most buildings must be background and there must be only a few that stand out. In order to be prominent, a thing must be set against a background of something that is not prominent. Things that are important, whether objects, images, or text, may only exist for us when there is a contrast with things that are less important (Hall 2007, 106). As Tufte explained about the need for visual hierarchy, "When everything is emphasized, nothing is emphasized" (Tufte 1997, 73).

Humans are able to perceive things as foreground and background (Hall 2007, 84). In the perceptual tendency of figure/ground, identified as one of the principles of Gestalt psychology, our brains separate visual patterns into figure and background. Figures are the focus of our attention; the background is everything else, and it appears to lie behind the figure. Early research indicated that we need a continuous background surface in order to understand space and distance (Gibson 1950, 20). This concept is confirmed by classrooms, where children are able to focus their attention more easily in a calm, understated background with a few landmarks or focal points. Research shows that young children in highly decorated classrooms are easily distracted and struggle to stay on task, but are able to focus and make greater learning gains when irrelevant decorations are removed (Fisher, Godwin, and Seltman 2014, 1362).

Navigation and wayfinding, like other communication endeavors, exemplify cognitive psychology concepts such as association, discussed in Chapter 2. You might have noticed that when you are traveling, you notice more detail and remember the place more clearly if you feel oriented and know where you are, but if you do not know where you are, your memory of the place tends to be partial and vague. We take in new information by connecting it to what we already know (Moscardo 1999, 33). Our brains use association to relate the things we see around us to information that has already been encoded in our brains (Jacobson 2009, 349).

Cognitive psychology also tells us that we acquire and remember more information if we consolidate the diverse pieces into cognitive chunks (Ham 2002, 166). Our pattern-seeking brains are able to distill the mass of visual input around us into just a few chunks of information using landmarks and routes. From these chunks we unconsciously build cognitive frameworks onto which we can hang pieces of new information as a range of associations is automatically activated in our brains (Ware 2013, 323).

Environmental psychology research shows that humans have two basic needs when navigating an environment: understanding and exploration, to understand their surroundings and to have opportunities for exploration. Legibility allows understanding; mystery promotes exploration.

Coherent and legible places enable us to understand and make sense of our surroundings; they give us a feeling of security (Kaplan et al. 1998, 10). Places that are well organized, with clear hierarchies of paths and spaces, are easier to understand. Chaotic settings, such as commercial strips along roads with jumbles of signs and no underlying plan, overwhelm us with masses of information and few cues to help us determine which information is relevant (ibid., 8). Coherence comes from clear structure, discernible regions or districts, a distinctive landmark, and repeating themes, with spatial information laid out so that we can perceive it as a small number of chunks. Landmarks and coherent regions make places easy to understand as long as they are distinctive, memorable, visible from some distance, and few in number (ibid., 53). They function as organizing elements, similar to headings and subheadings on a brochure or interpretive sign. Understanding and making sense of your environment leads you to feel less overwhelmed and more competent (ibid., 150).

Exploration

Once the need for safety is taken care of, we feel motivated to expand our horizons, find new information, and seek new challenges. The tendency to explore and to seek out optimal conditions is found in most animals. Exploration is the activity which leads animals to discover places with conditions that afford survival, as well as to identify places which are dangerous that should be avoided and to identify paths for escape (Appleton 1975, 48). Seeking behavior kept ancient humans moving through the world and helped them survive. We are an exploring animal, driven to find out where things are and what they mean for us. At a physiological level, we and other animals are impelled to explore by neurotransmitters, which are communication chemicals such as dopamine. Dopamine is a neurochemical associated with pleasure and reward that motivates us to take action to move toward rewards (Weinschenk 2011, 121). It operates in the brains of all vertebrates, from lizards to humans, but human brains have evolved to use a great deal of it (Deans 2011). Humans are motivated on multiple levels—food, safety, aesthetics, ideas—to seek out, search, and learn, and research indicates that ideas are more fascinating to us if we must do some work to understand them (Hall 2007, 33).

Complexity and mystery suggest the potential for exploration, in both communication media and places. In the context of wayfinding, complexity does not mean confusion; it means there are multiple, interrelated layers of meaning. A place can be both complex and highly coherent (Kaplan et al. 1998, 13). In both physical places and communication media, providing bits of information in increments together with providing a way for people to get more information results in more exploratory, information-seeking behavior (Weinschenk 2011, 124).

In physical spaces, mystery leads to fascination and encourages exploration. Mystery results from such features as a winding path, an opening with filtered light, a narrow screen, or vegetation that partially blocks a view, all of which hint at what might lie ahead. A sense of depth pulls us onward, an experience that is enhanced by multiple layers and landmarks (Kaplan et al. 1998, 13).

A place which is coherent but which offers some layers of complexity affords some mystery and impels us to go find out. Landmarks allow us to remain oriented. Without landmarks, the appearance of sameness or large expanses of undifferentiated space suggest the risk of becoming lost (Kaplan et al. 1998, 11). A space with large, monochrome, unarticulated surfaces is like a white poster with a few plain words and no pictures: there is not enough information to hold our interest.

Wayfinding Planning and Design

A wayfinding system consists of two aspects: spatial planning and environmental communication (Arthur and Passini 1992, 42). Spatial planning provides sight lines, landmarks, entrances, and other built-in features of the environment (Calori 2007, 83). Environmental communication consists of signs, maps, directories, color coding, and other active elements of wayfinding design.

Spatial information is fundamental. Even the best graphic information usually cannot replace missing or misplaced spatial information (Arthur and Passini 1992, 45). Wayfinders need memorable, imageable spaces. In an ideal environment, people understand places intuitively and these spaces communicate so clearly that few signs are needed. This design approach is important in the field of therapeutic garden design and especially valuable in outdoor spaces for Alzheimer's patients, where residents can understand a garden's organization from anywhere in the setting without needing to rely on signs, maps, or memory (Thompson and Travlou 2007, 143).

Integrated spatial wayfinding elements include landmarks that can be used as anchor points as people move through the space; identifiable decision points; clear sight lines to decision points; gateways and entrances that look like entrances, clearly marked by materials, scale, and lighting; outdoor paths or indoor hallways that are differentiated from each other by size, texture, color, and artwork; and a minimal number of turns in routes from one destination to another (Calori 2007, 83). Borders or edges and a small number of coherent areas distinguishable from other areas make a space easier to understand. Gateways and entrances serve as landmarks and signal a transition from one identifiable area to another, and often provide a view into the next area (Kaplan et al. 1998, 150). Each of these elements must be distinct from the others. Distinctiveness allows people to make decisions readily, while uniformity leads to confusion and indecision.

As with other forms of communication, redundancy is important in wayfinding communication. People's brains process information in a variety of ways, and different people have different sensory abilities. Using multiple ways to communicate the same information is the best way to ensure that messages are received (Arthur and Passini 1992, 45).

Our brains can consciously process only a limited amount of information at one time. A wayfinding system provides only the information a visitor needs at that moment, progressively disclosing other information as it is needed (Weinschenk 2011, 62). If people are presented with too much information at once, they can feel overwhelmed with the result that they simply ignore the information altogether. A better approach is not to do everything at once, but to introduce information a step at a time (Arthur and Passini 1992, 45). Good wayfinding design allows people to form cognitive maps, then gives them finer-grained information as needed at decision points.

Signs and maps orient people to a place and help them navigate it (Calori 2007, 4).

The environmental graphic designer breaks down each complex wayfinding problem into smaller problems that need no more than three or four decisions to solve. The visitor can think about a particular aspect of the wayfinding problem and still keep in mind the problem as a whole (Arthur and Passini 1992, 30). The designer starts with a general plan to move from one location to a final destination; this translates into a series of tasks and sub-tasks which become more detailed as one gets closer to the destination (Thompson and Travlou 2007, 113). If the words used on signs remain consistent throughout a wayfinding system, the signs maintain what is referred to as a bread-crumb trail of information that helps people find their way through the space (Calori 2007, 83).

Signage

A signage program consists of three systems: the information content; the graphics, or the signs themselves; and the hardware. The information is planned first. Then the graphics and the hardware can be designed. All the various types of signs in a sign program share common visual features so that wayfinders can recognize them as related to each other (Calori 2007, 160).

The designer prepares a sign plan, which consists of sign location plans and an inventory of signs to be fabricated and installed, entered into a spreadsheet. Maintenance and replacement information is also included in the plan. Each sign is given a sign number and the signs are categorized by type, with a schedule of the message vocabulary, typeface and fonts, symbols, images, color, materials, finishes, elevations, and sizes. The designer produces a drawing package which includes sign location plans; top, front, and side views of each sign type; hardware drawings; graphic layout drawings; and written specifications. The sign fabricator produces the final digital artwork from which they will print each sign (Calori 2007, 41).

A wayfinding signage program contains several types of directional and identifying signs. There will be a hierarchy of standard sign types, including trailblazers, directional signs, and identifiers.

A trailblazer is a directional sign, located at each decision point. Trailblazers with primary information directing visitors to major destination zones are given

more visual importance than signs which lead to sub-zones or individual destinations (Arthur and Passini 1992, 51).

Each trailblazer should contain no more than five or six pieces of information,
including the sign itself, and no more than three pieces of written information
(Arthur and Passini 1992, 50–51). If more than three items must be included,
information should be chunked, grouped together into no more than three packages. If more information must be provided, then additional signs are needed.

For directional signs that include arrows, there are three options for grouping
destinations: Destinations reached in the same direction can be grouped together
on the sign, rather than separated, with destinations to the left first, then straight
ahead, then destinations to the right, which is the grouping preferred by many
wayfinding experts. They can be listed in the order in which wayfinders will
encounter them. Or they can be listed in alphabetical order. However they are
grouped, the arrows should be placed on the side of the message to which the
visitor is being directed. Left-pointing arrows should be placed on the left side of
the sign; right-pointing arrows should be placed on the right (Raphael 2013, 12).

An identifier is used to confirm the wayfinder's location, and identifies each
space or building.

Designers begin by studying decision points and circulation routes and then
indicating on a map where signs will be needed and what type they should be
(Calori 2007, 76). They visit each proposed sign location and evaluate viewing
distances, viewing angles, sight lines, obstructions, lighting conditions, and any
other conditions that could affect signage design and use (ibid., 80).

If you are involved in this process, plan to locate directional signs at every
decision point and locate identification signs at every destination to which people
have been directed. On long paths, provide additional signs at regular intervals
to reinforce the route and to assure people that they are still headed in the right
direction. Once a destination is listed on a directional sign, it must be included
on every subsequent directional sign until the wayfinder reaches the destination
(Arthur and Passini 1992, 200).

People need three things when they are in a new setting: information to make
decisions, information to execute decisions, and information to conclude the
process. The information that enables them to make decisions includes general
orientation with an overview of shapes, routes, and where their destination is
located so that they can form a cognitive map. Maps, floor plans, and models give
them this understanding. The information to execute decisions is what directs
them to their destination. Directional signs with arrows, simple descriptions that
include landmarks, directories near elevators, and color coding allow them to
execute the decisions they have made. Finally, identifying information that confirms when they have arrived at a destination comes from identifying signs, with
names, numbers, or icons (Arthur and Passini 1992, 143).

Symbols or icons provide a space-efficient graphic shortcut. Although the
terms "symbol" and "icon" are often used interchangeably, technically an icon
is representative and a symbol is abstract (Lannon and Gurak 2017, 265). An icon

resembles the thing it represents, such as an icon of a file folder on a computer or a simplified graphic of a person in a wheelchair to represent an accessible route. A symbol can be more abstract, such as a question mark to represent a place to get help, or the international symbol for a radioactive biohazard.

When symbols and icons convey information that would have needed many words to communicate, they allow faster recognition time for readers (Raphael 2013, 13). They are a universal form of communication which can be understood by people who speak other languages, children or people who do not read, and people with some forms of cognitive disability (Finke 1994, 108). Consider cultural context and use symbols and icons with care. For example, the use of a pointing index finger can signify rudeness in some cultures including Venezuela and Sri Lanka (Bosley 1996, 5).

Color is an additional way to encode information on signs. Both color and shape can be recognized from a greater distance than words or symbols (Raphael 2013, 14). Bright, saturated colors stand out from their surroundings and neutral, more subtle colors recede into their surroundings. When you use color, remember that some readers have varying degrees of colorblindness.

In complex environments, color coding links a particular message with a particular color, differentiating it from other messages. Using the same color code on signs and on architectural elements reinforces the message. For example, signs in an airport might code elevators, escalators, stairs, and ramps with yellow and then paint those same physical elements bright yellow within the building (Arthur and Passini 1992, 51). Hospitals often use systems of color coding to identify zones, repeating the same colors on directional and identifier signs, on walls, and in path-like stripes on floors. Color is often used to link maps and actual places in zoos and theme parks; if an area is given a color on a map, then that color is also used in signs, paths, and structures in that physical area (Moscardo 1999, 55).

To be visible by people with low vision, the Americans with Disabilities Act (ADA) recommends a minimum of 70 percent contrast between figure and background (Calori 2007, 128). Research shows that light-colored letters on dark backgrounds provide better contrast than do dark letters on light backgrounds, particularly in outdoor light (Raphael 2013, 15). Highway signs are an example of this. In shaded or indoor areas, dark letters on light backgrounds are more readable (Moscardo et al. 2007, 51).

The Society for Experiential Graphic Design (SEGD) recommends that non-rounded capital letters such as E, H, or I on signs be a minimum of one inch in height for every 25 feet of viewing distance, with a minimum of three inches of capital height. That means that for a sign that must be read from 150 feet away, a desirable height for capital letters would be six inches (Raphael 2013, 14). SEGD is the organization for environmental graphic designers, professionals concerned with the work of placemaking, interpretation, and wayfinding.

Environmental graphic designers lay out signs using elements of typeface, graphics, color, shape, and composition. Before spending the majority of money from a sign budget, designers make prototypes to try out size, typeface, color, and hardware (Calori 2007, 35). Then final drawings are made and detailed specifications are written. Once approved, finished designs are submitted to sign fabricators for formal bidding.

Maps

A map can convey more information, and more complex information, than directional signs alone because it shows spatial relationships (Raphael 2013, 16). When people read a map, they use it first to form a mental image of the spatial framework. In a subsequent step they add landmarks into their cognitive map, forming a single, integrated image (Chen 2002, 6). Using a map involves mentally comparing images on a flat surface with objects in the physical world (Ware 2013, 365).

Some people struggle to understand maps. Maps are small, often vertical, two-dimensional, and abstract. They are at different scales than the places we actually see. They are abstractions of places and do not look like the places they represent. Maps mounted on signs hold reality up vertically, when the physical world is approximately flat (Arthur and Passini 1992, 146). However, maps have the ability to reduce complicated surroundings to a simple representation, and a cognitive map of a place can be formed much more readily by reading an actual map than by moving through the physical place (Ware 2013, 360).

Maps can be portable. They can be printed on paper that visitors can take with them, or can be included in websites along with other directional information. When maps are mounted permanently on signs or kiosks, it is helpful and reassuring to place them at each decision point.

To be useful, a map should show only as much information as is needed to make decisions. If it shows too much detail, some readers feel overwhelmed and simply give up. Research shows that when people form cognitive maps, angles and directions are not as important as sequences, so maps are still useful even when simplified and stylized (Moscardo 1999, 51). The best maps are selective in their use of color, text, and symbols.

On an effective map, representing the visually strongest aspects of a place provides an overview, showing the main features and the path structure that connects them. Three kinds of information on maps help visitors get oriented: distinctive landmarks, large, relatively uniform areas such as woods or fields, and decision points where choices must be made (Kaplan et al. 1998, 58).

Every map should include a prominent "you-are-here" label to orient the reader. Some maps give these indicators as triangles pointing in the direction the viewer is facing. Walking circles, which are concentric circles that represent walking times in five-minute intervals, can be used in urban environments. Centered on the you-are-here indicator, they communicate a sense of scale while they promote walking instead of driving (Raphael 2013, 18).

As with other forms of graphic communication, maps are more helpful when labels are placed right on the map features. Using a menu of symbols with a legend is less useful because it forces people to hold pieces of information in memory while looking back and forth between a map and a legend which explains it.

Map Orientation

Two options for orienting maps are possible. One is to orient the map with north at the top, which is probably the most common. Experienced navigators often prefer this orientation because it provides a consistent frame of reference for geographic information (Ware 2013, 365). However, some people become confused when the orientation of the map they are reading does not match the orientation on the ground. Some readers find it too difficult to make mental rotations, and simply give up.

The other choice orients the top of the map in the direction the reader is facing, known as heads-up orientation (Calori 2007, 123). In this forward-up orientation, a line between two points on the ground is parallel to a line connecting those two points on the map (Chen 2002, 72). It can cause confusion for people accustomed to looking for north at the top, so clear labeling is essential. But it is easier to use for many people because what they are facing in physical reality is also directly ahead of them on the map, features which are physically on their left are on the left side of the map, and so forth. This orientation is sometimes known as track-up orientation, so called because if you were in a vehicle, the direction your vehicle was heading would be in the vertical direction on the map (Ware 2013, 364). A disadvantage of this orientation is that you need different rotations of maps, including rotations of legends, labels, and symbols, for different locations on the ground. Including a concise map of the area being shown, oriented to the correct compass direction, will help readers understand where they and the map are in space (Finke 1994, 108).

Plan View and Bird's-Eye View

Most maps are shown in plan view, that is, as if seen from an airplane looking straight down. Plan view is useful for understanding the structure of paths or roads (Kaplan et al. 1998, 60). It is also the best choice for interior settings. It is less useful for three-dimensional landmarks, which can be hard to recognize in plan view. An oblique or bird's-eye view makes landmarks easier to understand. An especially useful solution combines plan view for paths with an oblique perspective for buildings and other landmarks. This approach is often seen in university campus maps.

Another approach takes realism further by replacing a map with an illustration of the real scene the viewer is actually looking at. The scene can be a photograph, a hand drawing, or a rendering generated by computer graphics, with labels added to identify elements (Arthur and Passini 1992, 145). In some parks, outline drawings are applied to shatterproof glass and placed in front of the scene, perfectly aligned to the setting itself. The setting is viewed through the glass, with labels superimposed on landmarks or buildings (ibid., 189).

A photograph taken either from directly overhead or from an oblique angle of around 60 degrees can be used as a base for a map, with words added to label features. The realism of renderings and photographs overcomes the difficulty some people have with abstract, stylized maps. This is seen often in software such as Google Maps.

The best tool for many people is a three-dimensional, physical model of a site, displayed horizontally like the real world and oriented in the same direction as the reality it represents. Although models do abstract details and reduce the complexities of the real site, they are easy to understand. Not only do they represent reality and facilitate the formation of cognitive maps, the shift in scale holds fascination for many people. If done carefully, a model can also be used by people with visual impairment to understand a space.

Note

1 Lynch limited the scope of his research to the effects of physical objects. He did not try to deal with social and cultural influences, which he acknowledged were also significant to the image and meaning of a place.

8

VISIBLE PROCESSES

When you want to help people understand how living systems and sustainable human systems work, one approach is to describe and illustrate them with brochures, websites, presentations, exhibits, and interpretive signage. Another, more direct, way is to let these processes speak for themselves.

Models

When you offer a model of a system at smaller than full scale, you accomplish two things: First, you enable visitors to visualize things they could not otherwise see, to get an overview of the system that would not be possible at full size (Ritter 2004, 232). And second, you engage them. People are fascinated by things that are presented at unexpected scales. The *Underground Adventure* exhibit at the Field Museum in Chicago, which lets visitors imagine being 1/100th of their actual size as they roam through giant "soil" particles and come face to face with giant animatronic inhabitants of the soil, has drawn visitors into its world for years. The hallways of the Thorne Miniature Rooms at the Art Institute of Chicago are filled with 68 rooms meticulously built at a scale of one inch to one foot. Visitors become fascinated by historical periods from the thirteenth century to the 1940s and notice all kinds of details of architecture and everyday life, even though those same visitors might feel completely bored by a full-scale period room in a museum.

Harvard University manages 4000 acres of woodlands in western Massachusetts. Within this forest, the Fisher Museum displays seven miniature dioramas that illustrate how a single area of the forest has changed over a period of 300 years. The dioramas begin in 1700 with the forest mosaics which formed after early European explorers brought diseases that wiped out resident populations of Native Americans who had managed the land. Subsequent dioramas progress to clearing of the land by colonists to make farmland, to farms and orchards, to abandonment of farms and colonization by white pine forests, to the gradual succession of mixed hardwood forests in the twentieth century. These finely detailed miniatures compress both time and space, allowing visitors to think about human and natural processes and change over time.

Scale models of watersheds, with landscapes shaped from concrete and paint, are popular at zoos, aquaria, and interpretive centers. They allow people to try things out, to pour water and watch how it moves through the topography. Some watershed play tables include sand so that people can experience how streams form meanders and how they perform the work of erosion. People, especially children, are drawn to water and to an opportunity to touch it, becoming fascinated by the land-shaping processes of water. Research tells us that being able to touch things with our hands provokes us to make connections and to remember ideas in ways that renderings on a screen or pictures on a page do not (Knapp 2007, 117).

You can find representational models of water systems in parks and playgrounds all over the world. One example is the interactive Ballona Discovery Park in Playa Vista, near Los Angeles, positioned near an elementary school at the Ballona Wetlands trailhead. A representational model of the watershed allows humans to walk like giants alongside water as it moves from mountains, through an urbanized city, through a marsh and to the ocean. A stylized downtown has blocky buildings just the right size to sit or climb on. Visitors can watch a sprinkler soak a patch of conventional lawn, then see the water run down stylized streets and accumulate on impermeable paving where it builds up instead of soaking in, while in an adjacent vegetated strip water from the streets soaks in and disappears.

Concrete Representation

Models are typically smaller-scale replicas, miniature versions of things you cannot otherwise see. Another useful strategy is a representational model, which is like a concrete analogy (Ritter 2004, 232).

Concrete objects, or the terms that describe them, are stored in long-term memory more easily than abstract terms (Weinschenk 2011, 54). Ideas are easier to grasp mentally if you can hold them in your hand physically (Hamre 2017). Research in cognitive psychology reveals there are neurological reasons that concrete representations make concepts more vivid and memorable. Concrete information and abstract information are processed differently in the brain. Multiple methods of sensory input reinforce mental connections and make them much stronger (Mayer 2009, 129). Concrete stimuli become associated with both visual and verbal connection points, so that later they are remembered better (Kahle and Gurel-Atay 2013, 133). Or as another author put it, the sensory nature of concrete ideas helps to bind them to memory (Heath and Heath 2007, 5).

A famous story describes the concrete testimony of physicist Richard Feynman at the meeting of a presidential commission investigating the fatal 1986 explosion of the Space Shuttle Challenger. Testimony had gone on for days, with masses of inscrutable technical jargon by engineers and officials which did nothing to clarify the issues. Feynman realized the problem was that rubber O-rings had never been tested at temperatures below freezing. So he brought a C-clamp and an O-ring with him and let them rest in a glass of ice water he had ordered from the waiter. When it was time for him to testify, he lifted the rubber ring from the ice water, loosened the clamp and said simply, "I discovered that when you undo the clamp, the rubber doesn't spring back. In other words... there is no resilience in this particular material when it is at a temperature of 32 degrees. I believe that has some significance for our problem" (Tufte 1997, 50). Feynman's testimony was shown repeatedly on television news, and the public was able to see how clear thinking, simple language, and concrete examples can make engineering concepts comprehensible.

Visualizing Climate Change

You may be involved in developing a climate action plan or reporting on a greenhouse gas inventory, and you will report how many tons of carbon dioxide equivalent are in your organization's emissions. What does a ton of carbon dioxide look like? Concrete analogies are useful to help us make sense of invisible greenhouse gas emissions. A comparison such as "that is the same amount of carbon dioxide that 1000 cars would emit in a year" gives your audience context. In 2008, the US Environmental Protection Agency (EPA) developed a Greenhouse Gas Equivalencies Calculator that you can use to convert emission reductions into everyday terms. The EPA calculator converts passenger-vehicle miles driven, gallons of gasoline, or kilowatt-hours of electricity consumed into acres of tree seedlings, acres of pine or fir forests, tanker trucks of gasoline, railcars of coal, and other equivalents. For example, one ton of carbon dioxide equals 114 gallons of gasoline consumed, or 2.3 barrels of oil, or 0.01 acres of forest preserved from deforestation (US EPA 2017).

The 2006 documentary *An Inconvenient Truth* was created from former vice president Al Gore's slideshow about climate change. The producers filmed in front of a live audience on a soundstage in Hollywood. Gore showed a graph of carbon dioxide concentrations over time, gesturing toward data points on a screen that was 90 feet wide. The dramatic reveal happened when he showed audiences that the carbon dioxide levels continue to rise, and at the current end of the timeline the audience gasped as Gore's hand followed the hockey stick-shaped graph while a scissor lift raised him 50 feet up in the air (Galloway 2016).

Energy

Vivid images make concepts real. An energy technician from a utility may tell a resident that heat can escape under their doors, and that news might not have impact. But when they explain that the cracks would add up to a hole the size of a football in a living room wall, residents are more likely to understand why weatherstripping is important (James 2010, 4). When some citizens in an Iowa town were reluctant to spend money on insulation, the local utility posted in the town hall an aerial photograph taken using infrared that showed heat leaking through every roof. The residents realized how heat was escaping, and learned to insulate their houses (Lovins 2011, 113).

Comparisons of Size and Volume

To give people a feel for size, think of a local landmark or something else with which they are already familiar and use it for comparison. Sustainability consultants working with a large law firm wanted to help them understand how much paper they consumed in a year. Rather than reporting the firm's consumption in dollars or cases of paper, they visualized reams of paper in a stack and reported how many times the height of the firm's skyscraper that much paper represented. They also reported how many stories high each individual attorney's stack of paper usage would be (Hitchcock and Willard 2008, 68).

To give people a feel for weight, think of something familiar, look up its weight, and then use that for a metric. For example, what is its weight in elephants? An average African elephant weights about 7 tons, or 14,000 pounds. What is its weight in cars? Or hippopotamuses? An average midsize car weighs 3500 pounds, and an average male hippopotamus weighs 6600 to 9900 pounds. Research partners at several universities calculated how much plastic has been produced and discarded (Geyer, Jambeck, and Law 2017). To give readers a feel for what the numbers meant, a designer at the University of Georgia created an infographic with simple pictures illustrating that since 1950, plastic equivalent to the weight of 822,000 Eiffel Towers, or 80 million blue whales, or one billion elephants has been manufactured, most of which is now buried in landfills (Beckley 2017).

If you want to communicate the volume of water used, you could measure it in numbers of swimming pools. An Olympic-size swimming pool contains a little more than 660,000 gallons of water. To find the number of swimming pools, divide your quantity in gallons by 660,000.

How about area? The ecological footprint is an indicator of human impact that uses area. It is a measure of the demand humans place on nature expressed as land area in global hectares, or converted to acres in the US. For people who don't know what an acre is, you can tell them that an acre is about the size of an American football field without the end zones[1] (Moscardo 1999, 69). A soccer field is slightly larger. If you want to help people grasp the size of an acre, instead of just looking at a field, take them to a football field and have them walk the perimeter. They will get a little exercise and fresh air while physically feeling the concept of an area measurement.

Do you know any math students who would be interested in a challenge? Ask them to calculate the volume in their school's football stadium. Then find out how much trash their school, or perhaps their city, sent to the landfill in the previous year, or even better, how much was diverted from the landfill by recycling. You could use a photograph of the stadium to make a poster to communicate the comparison. For example, your poster might explain that "the amount of waste our city diverted from the landfill last year by recycling would fill the high school's football stadium to the top bleachers."

A professor at the California Polytechnic State University wanted to express a quantity of waste in a way that was vivid and concrete. Instead of just reporting that Californians generated 1300 pounds of waste per person each year, she described it as "enough to fill a two-lane highway, 10 feet deep from Oregon to the Mexican border" (McKenzie-Mohr and Smith 1999, 85). A microbiologist who wanted to describe paper consumption calculated that the paper produced in the US in one year would be enough to build a wall from the east to the west coast 11 to 12 feet high (Maczulak 2010, 28).

Visualizing Waste

A waste audit is a physical analysis of an organization's waste stream which provides a snapshot of the contents of the waste stream, identifying the types of trash generated and in what quantities. A waste audit is also a graphic and effective way to make often-abstract waste and recycling concepts visible. For many people, recycling is their first connection to sustainability efforts, and a waste audit gives them real-world feedback. Waste is collected into trash bags and labeled by date and location. Each bag is weighed, and the total weight and volume from each location is calculated and recorded on worksheets. Volunteers then carefully lift out waste by hand and deposit it into appropriate sorting bins. One university placed a symbolic display of one day's garbage for the campus into a pile in the main quad. Another displayed food waste in a livestock trough equal to the amount from one day in the dining hall (Barlett and Chase 2004, 30).

To illustrate plastic waste a London artist, Tatiana Woolrych, created an infographic titled "Plastic Is Not Fantastic." A photograph showed a square stack about five feet high made from one month's use of plastic in a typical London household of five, with layers that include produce trays, clamshell containers, plastic milk cartons, water and juice bottles, spray bottles, plastic packaging, and foam packing peanuts. Beneath the photo was information about each of the seven recyclable plastics with their uses, the time needed to biodegrade, and information that four of the seven are typically not recycled at all because of the mixture of compounds they are made from (Ehmann et al. 2012, 53).

Life Magazine wanted to illustrate what a consumptive lifestyle means. So they placed all the possessions of one American family on the front lawn of their house and photographed it. Then they photographed all the possessions of a family from a Third World country in front of their house. When they ran the two photographs side by side in a magazine spread, the extreme contrast in environmental impact was vivid (McKenzie-Mohr and Smith 1999, 87).

Photographer Chris Jordan communicates statistics with images, using photographs to depict the magnitude of consumption and waste. Each of his images portrays a specific quantity of something. To depict the number of disposable paper cups people use for coffee and tea in one day of cup consumption, Jordan stacked digital images of 40 million white cups in rows that filled a large projection screen. He told audiences that these stacks are the height of a 42-story building, and for scale he added people, barely visible in the lower corner of the image, and then the Statue of Liberty, dwarfed by the stacks of white cups (Gallo 2014, 220). In another image, a large-format photograph of a young woman is a mosaic of 78,000 plastic water bottles; a caption explains that the number of bottles in the image equals $1/10,000^{th}$ of the number of people worldwide who lack access to safe drinking water, that showing the entire statistic would require 10,000 copies of the 60 x 70-inch image, and that when lined up side by side the images would stretch ten miles (Jordan 2015).

Visualizing Water Levels

How much was the older New York Harbor filled to create what is now Manhattan? In 1980 artist Eric Arctander painted two parallel lines 7000 feet long marking the original shoreline of the southern end of the island, often hundreds of yards from the modern shoreline, in a full-scale map titled "Nieuw Amsterdam." The blue and green stripes, accompanied by signs, cut across streets, through buildings, and through Battery Park, dramatizing in a concrete way the filling of the harbor (Helphand 1995, 14).

Designers who want to communicate with citizens about the history of floods in their cities sometimes install flood markers to mark past water levels. They show past events compared to existing sites. For example, sculptural flood markers along the sidewalks in Boulder, Colorado's Central Park mark the levels of 50-year, 100-year, and larger floods that have actually occurred along Boulder Creek. The markers, with water lines many feet above pedestrians' heads, interpretive signage, and historic photographs, all placed in front of the creek where floods rose, make the events real for visitors. The existing site provides a reference point for the experience.

Visualizing What's in Our Food

You may have seen displays about nutritional content of foods at science fairs or community events. When a nutritionist wants to teach people about the sugar content of processed foods, they could simply place a label in front of each item reporting a quantity, but a more attention-grabbing approach is to add a small glass dish containing a pile of sugar in a measured amount of the actual sugar content. Or to show the fat content in each food, in addition to a label they can place a plate containing a measured amount of white shortening that corresponds to the fat content of the item. Many people are shocked when they see the sizes of the blobs of fat. Because these displays are both concrete and surprising, they capture audience attention and the information is remembered long after the event.

Michael Pollan is known for his bestselling books and documentaries about food. In one talk, he wanted to demonstrate the environmental impact of a meat diet by showing how much petroleum is required to produce one hamburger. After pulling a burger from a fast-food chain's paper bag, he produced a container of dark brown crude oil and began to pour the oil into 8 ounce glasses as he spoke. It turned out that it took 26 ounces of petroleum to produce that one burger, so by the time he finished speaking the audience was looking at 3¼ glasses filled with crude oil alongside that burger (Duarte 2010, 151). The image was vivid, concrete, and memorable.

Frames

We can help to focus attention through framing devices. In written communication, framing is the act of helping audiences understand complex topics by selecting and organizing ideas (Corbett 2006, 236). In outdoor physical spaces, framing begins with choosing where paths are located and which views are framed.[2] A Boy Scout troupe cleaning up trash in the New York City area made viewing tubes of PVC pipe. Some framed landmark skyscrapers in Manhattan, but adjacent pipes pointed at nature in the city, framing remnants of a New Jersey volcanic rock formation known as Snake Hill (Griswold 1993, 81). University of Oregon students installed a temporary series of frames along the Old Columbia River Highway; some focused the visitor's attention on spectacular views of the gorge, while others focused on close-up elements such as the bark of an old tree (Helphand 1995, 15).

Signs and billboards are not just for advertising. They can be used as comparative graphic devices by placing an illustration of a place as it used to be at a time in the past alongside the place itself. The illustration reproduces the same perspective and viewpoint from which an observer is likely to be viewing the physical place. For example, the Bay Boards project in California chronicled the evolution of the local landscape. It placed signs and billboards near office buildings, warehouses, and rail yards of San Francisco and Oakland, where viewers could compare the places where they now stood with illustrations of the blue waters, beaches, marshes, and hills that had been there 150 years earlier (Biggar 2004).

Infrastructure

Infrastructure refers to the basic facilities and services needed for the functioning of a community. *Infra* and *sub* are both Latin words meaning "below," and so the words *infrastructure* and *substructure* contain the same meaning: "the structure below." But while *substructure* points to physical objects, *infrastructure* is about relationships and functions. It is the systems used to transport people, goods, water, waste disposal, energy, and information. Contemporary infrastructure is the complex of technological support systems—including water supply, wastewater treatment, power, gas, communications, roads, harbors, and bridges—that underlie and make possible human culture, and it is a physical manifestation of the social life we hold in common. Nearly all infrastructure is made of flows.

Often infrastructure is invisible. Water distribution systems are placed underground to avoid freezing or prevent crushing of pipes. Sometimes, however, we hide infrastructure just because we see it as unattractive; we prefer to enjoy its benefits but avoid its costs. But in hiding these systems, we lose our connection with the earth and its processes (Thayer 1985).

Even visible infrastructure often goes unnoticed. To test this, try to take a photograph of a visually attractive urban space; do you need to struggle to dodge "non-scenic" elements in order to get a good composition? Or, print a photograph of an attractive urban street, and then using orange or another bright paint color, paint all the utilities in the picture. How much of your scene is now filled with orange paint?

When we look at countrysides and cities, we see the patterns that we expect to see: landscapes, urban forms, buildings, and open spaces. We experience confirmation bias and tend not to notice elements which do not fit our internal image, particularly if they are not scenic. This is not just abstract. A habit of selective non-seeing makes it even more difficult to see the world clearly. We may not realize that we are not seeing, and we become perceptually numb. Rene Dubos reminded us decades ago, "The worst thing we can do to our children is to convince them that ugliness is normal" (quoted in Orr 1998, 229).

Systems of water and energy can be built in ways that reveal the hidden processes that make communities work. Some of the most moving landscapes in pre-industrial cities were nothing more than the irrigation, water supply, sanitary sewer, and flood control systems of the time (Strang 1996, 8).

Green Infrastructure

Water that falls as rain is called stormwater. In the conventional approach to managing stormwater, sometimes known as "gray infrastructure," surface streets and buried pipes bypass natural processes and take the place of streambeds; water disappears into hidden pipes made of concrete and steel which send the water to detention ponds or straight to streams. "Green infrastructure" replaces those concrete pipes and channels with rain gardens and vegetated swales to cleanse the water with plants and microorganisms and then let it infiltrate the soil.

When stormwater processes are visible and celebrated, they communicate messages. They say, "this is how we view the natural world and our place in it" and "this is something we value." Then they communicate the next message: "this is how this system works." When we make environmental systems visible, people see more easily where resources come from and where wastes go.

In a tightly packed downtown area of Berlin, Potsdamer Platz is a three-acre recreational plaza which captures, treats, and stores rainwater. In this dense urban setting, visitors see water being cleansed as it flows through wetland plants in visible, textured channels. Using water as a sculptural medium, the plaza makes the concepts of rainfall volume and water quality perceptible as a pleasant byproduct of providing artful urban spaces for walking, resting, and socializing (Dreiseitl, Grau, and Ludwig 2001, 44).

In Portland, Oregon, the city's Water Pollution Control Laboratory is surrounded by parklike ponds and a dramatic stone water flume that curls in a spiral. Runoff from 50 acres of nearby streets and parking lots flows down the flume and into the water gardens around the building, which break down and remove toxins and cleanse the water before it flows into the adjacent river. The rising curve of the stone water flume makes the uphill sources of the water visible.

The Rain Garden at the Oregon Convention Center, also in Portland, is a lush, beautifully designed landscape that receives stormwater as it runs off the convention center's 5.5-acre roof. During rainstorms, visitors watch as large volumes of water rush through steel scuppers, flow down four stone spillways, over the tops of stone weirs made of local basalt, and through plants and cobbles in a series of seven terraced basins. What begins as untreated runoff is filtered and clean by the time it reaches the end of the last basin, where the clean water flows into the Willamette River. The entire system, from roof scupper to spillway to basin to river on the other side of an industrial-area freeway are visible and comprehensible to the visitor.

Buildings and Sites

We practice environmental communication with actions as well as with words and graphics. How we build, what we plant, what food we eat, how we travel, how we consume resources, how we handle rainfall, whether we let our streams flow or send them into storm drains, all these convey ideas and illustrate our policies about the world (Corbett 2006, 6).

School grounds and campus landscapes are increasingly used as resources for learning and for environmental communication. Students at schools where schoolyards contain functioning ecosystems and healthy habitat learn that "the environment" is not just a place far away, in a tropical rainforest or on a mountain. They experience it as the biosphere that surrounds and supports us all, including in our own neighborhoods.

A range of strategies help students learn about nature's rhythms and timescales. One of the most direct activities is planting, growing, and harvesting food in a garden. Other activities can involve wildlife, their habitats, and local native plants which change with changing seasons. Growing native plants that produce food for wildlife allows students to be part of the life cycles of wild birds and other animals. Engaging in stream or ecosystem restoration projects allows students to watch, up close, the changes over time as a system comes back to life.

In buildings which are made of local materials, powered by renewable energy, with systems for capturing and reusing water, students have opportunities to learn about energy flows and interconnectedness. But even so-called green building features may not teach if students do not know that the features are there or why they were done that way. Schools can take advantage of these potential opportunities by studying building features as part of class learning activities, by posting signs identifying and explaining the features, and by providing real-time feedback, such as a gage showing the amount of stored rainwater in a cistern or an electronic dashboard illustrating the current rate of energy use.

In the Bertschi Center in Seattle, Washington, for example, because the Science Wing is certified as a Living Building (a step beyond LEED Platinum) it must maintain net-zero water and net-zero energy balances, and so numerous monitoring and control systems are located throughout the building. Fourth- and fifth-grade students monitor usage and production of water and energy using these instruments as part of their science curriculum.

A building which collects rainwater or reuses graywater can make the collection and filtration systems visible rather than hidden in a mechanical room. It can use an electronic dashboard to display quantities and flow rates and can provide attractive interpretive signs to make sense of the system. The hydrology laboratory in the Engineering Building at Portland State University in Oregon is an example of a building which does this.

Some schools install sundials to make visible how sun angles change with changing seasons. School buildings designed to use natural daylighting or passive solar heating also illustrate in an immediate way the changing angles of the sun.

Many buildings built with green-building principles include information dashboards, digital information screens that display overviews of data such as temperature, water use, and energy use. Dashboards allow people to monitor what is going on within a building in real time.

Artists find ways to communicate succinctly within buildings. For example, the design firm Hu2 Design in Paris developed decals to apply to light switches consisting of black silhouettes. One places a factory with a smoke cloud stamped "CO_2" above the switch plate, with a black cord connecting it to the switch plate. Another places an oil rig above the switch plate with flares coming out of its stacks, a pipe from the rig winding around the switch plate and plugging into it, and a large drop stamped "OIL" dripping from the bottom of the pipe run. A third is simply a hemisphere of the Earth with a polar bear floating on a tiny iceberg at the top and a banner stamped with the word "THINK" (Ehmann et al. 2012, 18).

Notes

1 An American football field including the end zones is about 1.32 acres or 0.53 hectares.
2 Chinese scholars' gardens, with their continually changing vistas composed and framed like paintings, are exemplars of this strategy.

PART III
Practical Details

9

GRAPHIC DESIGN 101

Graphic design is a creative process that combines text and images to communicate ideas or tell a story. Its primary function is to make information accessible. Using a combination of art and technology, graphic design synthesizes text and images to organize and convey information and solve problems (Caputo et al. 2008, 83). The designer brings together logical, analytical thinking, which takes place on the left side of the brain, with intuitive, subjective thinking, which takes place on the right side of the brain, allowing the audience to integrate the two hemispheres of the brain (ibid., 21). The combination of words and images creates a synergy in which the whole effect is greater than the sum of the individual parts (Barnes 2011, 90). Elements of design include shapes, color, typography, and images; composition arranges these elements together into a whole.

Shapes

Our brains respond to four types of forms: dots, lines, shapes, and volumes. Dots or points have visual energy that attract the eye (Barnes 2011, 22). Connecting two points creates a line. Straight lines are rare in nature but common in objects made by humans. In some preliterate cultures, such as the Nazca and Inca of Peru or the builders of Stonehenge in England, straight lines took on sacred significance (Aveni 2000, 171; Parker Pearson 2014, 245); that may be because they were so rarely seen in the natural world. Horizontal and vertical directions align with the human view of the horizon and the central axis of the body; horizontal and vertical lines create stability (Barnes 2011, 25). Diagonal lines appear unstable; they suggest movement and energy (Shepard 2002, 7). Lines can be used to create shapes, including triangles and rectangles. Circles are composed of curved lines. Curved shapes suggest natural features, liquid, warmth, and enclosure. Regular or symmetrical shapes are perceived to have more weight than irregular shapes (Barnes 2011, 25).

Color

Properties of Color

Color is a property of visible light waves. Electromagnetic waves travel through the universe across a spectrum of wavelengths. The longest electromagnetic waves include radio waves, microwaves, and infrared radiation. The shortest electromagnetic waves include ultraviolet rays, X-rays, and gamma rays. Visible light consists of electromagnetic waves at a range in between, in that part of the spectrum to which the human eye can respond. Light is visible at different wavelengths for different kinds of animals; for humans, light waves are visible from about 390 to about 700 nanometers (Nm) in length. A nanometer is a billionth of a meter. Blue has a wavelength around 400 Nm; red is around 700 Nm.

Research shows that primary terms for the colors red, green, yellow, and blue are used consistently across multiple cultures and languages (Ware 2013, 109). Particular hues can have very different meanings among different cultures, however. While color perception appears to be physiological, symbolic color associations are learned and are not consistent across cultures (Zettl 1998, 64).

Designers describe color using three attributes: hue, saturation, and brightness. Hue is the color itself, such as red or blue. Saturation, or chroma, is the intensity or purity of the color. Brightness, or value, is the degree of darkness or lightness, a measure of how much light the color reflects. A hue plus white gives a lighter color, or tint; a hue plus black gives a darker color, or shade. These three attributes, hue, saturation, and brightness, are mapped in three-dimensional color space whose shape resembles an American football with bulges. The vertical axis in the center, the value, is the grayscale, from white to black. Hues are arranged around the value axis like branches. The farther away from the axis a color lies, the more saturated it is (Zettl 1998, 48). A color at 100 percent saturation contains no white or black (Caputo et al. 2008, 28). The strongest colors occur midway in the value scale, which is why the color map is football-shaped, not cylindrical.

You can visualize this color space as a building with an elevator at its center. The elevator is gray inside. On the bottom floor the value is very black; on the top floor the value is very white. You ride the elevator to a floor and get off there. Corridors radiate from the elevator, each one a different hue. One corridor is red, for example. You look down the corridor and see that the red becomes more intense or saturated farther down the hall; the outside of the building is the strongest red. Turning, you see another corridor radiating away from the elevator; this corridor is blue, and the section of corridor at the outside of the building is the strongest blue.

When we mix colors with light, such as on a computer screen, we use the RGB system. RGB stands for red, green, and blue, the three primary colors of light. RGB is used with transmitted light. It is an additive color system: if you add the three colors of light together, you get white.

When we mix colors with pigment, such as in printed documents, we use the CMYK system. CMYK stands for cyan, magenta, yellow, and black. Blue (cyan), red (magenta), and yellow are the three primary colors of pigment. CMYK is used with reflected light. It is a subtractive color system, where white is the absence of color and black is all colors added together. In the printing process, each of the colors is printed separately.

Graphics software products, such as Photoshop, allow you to change from RGB to CMYK. Various software products also allow you to change from RGB, which offers millions of colors, to something called Index Color, which uses only 256 colors. Although Index Color has a limited palette of colors, it results in reduced file size and is still adequate for many applications.

A tool called the color wheel was developed in the seventeenth century by Sir Isaac Newton from his experiments with prisms. The color wheel is based on the three primary colors of pigment: red, blue, and yellow, arranged 120 degrees apart. Mixing two adjacent primary colors creates the secondary colors: purple, green, and orange. Mixing adjacent primary and secondary colors creates tertiary colors, such as red-purple, blue-purple, blue-green, yellow-green, yellow-orange, and red-orange. When a color wheel includes tertiary colors, it contains twelve colors.

The color wheel helps you to understand how colors work together and to select colors for color schemes. You can use the three primary colors to create a color scheme that feels basic and even childlike. For maximum contrast and a bold look you can use complementary colors, which are pairs of colors directly opposite each other on the color wheel, such as yellow and purple, blue and orange, or red and green. Complementary colors add emphasis and create energy. For a more subtle, calm look you can use analogous colors, which are any two or three adjacent colors on the color wheel, such as yellow, yellow-green, and green. Analogous colors create a unified feel. A monochromatic color scheme uses a single hue presented in different shades, by adding black, and tints, by adding white.

We perceive color differently under different conditions. The same physical color can look very different to us, depending on the size of the object, glossiness, variations in lighting, and surrounding background. We perceive color not as an absolute but as a difference between the surrounding color and the color we are focusing on (Few 2009, 48).

Early in our evolution our sensory systems needed to be able to find food and see danger in a variety of conditions, so we are wired to detect differences rather than absolute values. In the case of vision, when neurons transmit information from our eyes to our brain, they are signaling not the amount of light but the relative amount of light. They behave not like light meters but like change meters (Ware 2013, 69). This means that any one color can look quite different when placed on different-colored backgrounds (Knight and Glaser 2009, 4). A color in front of a dark background looks brighter than its real value; in front of a similar color, it can almost disappear. A color generally takes on a slight tint that is complementary, or opposite on the color wheel, to the background color (Zettl 1998, 56).

Metamerism is the phenomenon in which colors change under different light sources. Two colors may appear to match under one light, but appear to be different shades under another light. In daylight, the time of day, direction of sunlight, weather, and season can all affect color. Indoors, fluorescent light is notorious for causing this effect. Reflected light from walls or ceilings can also cause colors to change.

Color can be specified with precision using its three attributes of hue, value, and chroma. Design software allows you to specify colors in RGB, for websites and computer screens, and in CMYK, for printing. Other systems are available as well. The Natural Color System (NCS) is a color-naming system widely used in Europe. In the US, the Munsell system is used in manufacturing and the Pantone system is used in printing and design. Pantone is a color-matching system; users can specify a color by Pantone name or number.

Colors can be measured and verified with instruments. A device that measures color, that is, wavelengths of visible light, is called a spectrophotometer. To make consistent measurements, this instrument is usually mounted inside a booth with gray walls and a standard light source; hand-held versions are also available.

Communicating with Color

Choose colors thoughtfully. Have a reason for each color you select.

Warm colors, those with red in them, attract and hold attention. They appear larger and nearer than cool colors, and can give the impression that they are advancing toward the viewer. Warm colors feel more personal and intimate than cool colors (Caputo et al. 2008, 28). Cool colors, those with blue in them, are regarded as more relaxing than warm colors. These colors make objects look farther away (Zettl 1998, 57) and create a sense of emotional distance (Caputo et al. 2008, 28).

Colors can be used to indicate particular topics. Red can signify fire or sunlight, and can imply movement or energy. Blue can signify water, ice, moonlight, clouds, winter, or serenity (Moscardo et al. 2007, 50). Green can signify nature or spring. Shades of green found in nature are calming (Tufte 1990, 90); this is the reason for the traditional color of theater green rooms (Zettl 1998, 57). Be aware of cultural differences. For example, the color green is associated with safety in the US but carries strong political connotations in Northern Ireland (Lannon and Gurak 2017, 275).

The impact a color has on a viewer depends on hue, saturation, brightness, size, and the degree of contrast with background colors. Items with darker colors appear larger and closer and are perceived as more important than items of the same size in lighter colors ((Lannon and Gurak 2017, 272).

Clear, strong contrast helps highlight main points or key aspects of a sign, document, webpage, or illustration. Viewers are drawn to whatever looks different on a page (White 2002, 65). You will have greater impact if you use less color, rather than more. For legibility, make sure you highlight only a few elements; a colorful, chaotic mess is not legible.

Many people with color blindness cannot distinguish between red and green, between blue and purple, or between pairs of dark colors (Johnson 2014, 46). If you need to show gradations, such as in a graph or diagram, sequences along a scale of black to white or along a scale of blue to yellow will be distinguishable to people with color blindness (Ware 2013, 133). Make color a redundant attribute; differentiate features using attributes in addition to color that can be understood in black and white, such as shape, size, location, or font (Lannon and Gurak 2017, 272).

Our eyes are more sensitive to differences between large patches of color and our ability to distinguish colors decreases with size (Few 2012, 78). Especially if you are using low-saturation colors, differences in large patches are easier to detect, while differences in small patches are hard to detect (Ware 2013, 107).

Use less saturated colors for a background and more saturated symbols or shapes on the foreground. If you are using different colors as codes in a map or diagram, use more saturated colors for small areas so they will be recognizable, but use less saturated colors for large areas. To see why, study a high-quality map, with regions distinguished by less saturated colors, and compare that to a homemade map made with strongly colored regions, if you can find one; notice how the map with intense colors is hard to look at or understand. If you need to reduce the contrast between two adjacent color areas for some reason, one trick is to outline one of them with a thin white or black border (Ware 2013, 123).

Adjacent colors affect each other. Complementary colors that are highly saturated, such as red and green, can cause an impression that the colors are vibrating. Saturated colors are high energy. Designers typically place small areas of saturated or high-energy color against background areas of less saturated or lower-energy color (Zettl 1998, 65). Using a background of high energy, saturated color actually tends to reduce the energy of any foreground element (ibid., 66).

Communication has a better chance of reaching its viewer if information comes on more than one channel. So for example, if you want to distinguish between different items using color, use differences in saturation and brightness as well as hue, and use other cues such as symbols or contrasting shapes (Johnson 2014, 45).

Typography

Typography is the art of arranging letters and words. A typeface is a particular design for an alphabet created by a type designer. Helvetica is a typeface. A typeface is a family of fonts; a font is a subset of a typeface with a particular size and weight. Helvetica bold and Helvetica italic are fonts which are part of the Helvetica typeface.

We place typefaces in two broad categories: serif and sans serif. Serifs are the short horizontal strokes at the top and bottom of letters in typefaces such as Times New Roman and Garamond. They were invented by ancient Romans who carved letters into stone with broad chisels, finishing letter strokes with a perpendicular hit (Calori 2007, 105). *Sans* is the French word meaning "without," so sans serif typefaces are those without serifs, such as Arial and Helvetica.

Researchers still debate the question of whether we read by decoding letters, words, or overall shapes, and therefore whether serif typefaces are easier to read than sans serif, and whether upper- and lowercase text is easier to read than all capitals. Many designers believe that lowercase words are easier to scan and recognize, especially at a distance, because words set in lowercase have distinctive shapes formed by capitals, ascenders, and descenders, rather than the simple rectangles formed by words in all capitals which are always the same shape. You can find research that supports both sides of the issue. What we know is that our brains must be trained to recognize that certain shapes represent certain letters, and if a typeface is unfamiliar or its shapes are hard to distinguish, reading will be disrupted (Johnson 2014, 76).

If you must use all capitals, increase the spacing between letters to help readers recognize them more easily (Caputo et al. 2008, 31). If a person has trouble reading a typeface, that feeling of difficulty will transfer to the meaning itself, and the person might decide that the content of the text is hard to understand (Weinschenk 2011, 39).

Printers and word-processing software measure type size in points and picas. One point is 1/72 of an inch, so a 12-point typeface is 1/6 of an inch high. A pica is 12 points. The point size includes the height of the body of lowercase letters, known as x-height, plus ascenders which rise above the x-height and descenders which lie below the x-height. That is why different 12-point typefaces can appear to be different sizes.

Selecting Typefaces

Typeface design is a specialized, time-consuming process that requires specialized skills, and many existing typefaces are highly legible. Most designers use existing typefaces, rather than designing new ones. The most legible typefaces have large x-height, easily recognizable shapes, medium stroke widths that are not overly thick nor thin, and medium character widths that are not overly expanded nor condensed.

Many designers consider the horizontal strokes of serifs to be helpful for reading large blocks of small text. Serif typefaces also connote a traditional or refined theme. Because letters in serif typefaces contain both thick and thin stroke widths, they may be too delicate for large graphics on signs (Calori 2007, 108).

Sans serif typefaces have relatively uniform stroke widths and are more readable from a distance (Thomas et al. 2006, 16). They are useful for headings and large type of signs. They also connote a modern theme.

Your goal when selecting typefaces and fonts is to minimize the effort readers need to exert to understand your message. Time-tested typefaces like Times New Roman, Arial, and Helvetica are easy to read. By not drawing attention to themselves, they allow your message's content to come through. Using typefaces that are already in common use also minimizes problems when you share files with other people or send files to printers. Use standard-width fonts; sans serif styles are difficult to read when they are condensed, and serif fonts are difficult to read when they are stretched. Use italics for emphasis or subheadings only; don't use italics for the body of text, as they are difficult to read. Avoid gimmicky typefaces, drop shadows, and other special effects.

Limit your document, presentation, or signage to no more than two typeface families; you could use one serif and one sans serif typeface for contrast. Select one typeface as primary, and a very different typeface to provide contrast for devices like titles and headings (Caputo et al. 2008, 30). Typefaces are your visual voice. Using regular, bold, and italic fonts in each of two typefaces, for a total of six, is similar to having six voices speak, allowing you enough variation to convey any message (White 2002, 121).

Maintaining consistent typography throughout means viewers do not have to keep reorienting themselves and so helps them stay focused on the content of your message. Continue to maintain this consistency if you have multiple document and website types.

Type Size and Spacing

You want your text to be readable by everyone. What size to choose depends upon how far away you think your readers will be. In print documents, 9 to 12 points is typical for body text. You may want to use 14 points or more for posters. In interpretive exhibits, a good guide is to make body text, individual labels, and captions 18 to 24 points; focus labels and theme labels 24 to 40 points; subtitles or key points 100 to 120 points; and main titles two to three inches high (Chicone and Kissel 2013, 105). For signage under ideal conditions, a guideline is to allow one inch of letter height per 50 feet of viewing distance (Arthur and Passini 1992, 165). For outdoor signage used in wayfinding systems, allow one inch of letter height per 25 feet of viewing distance (Raphael 2013, 14).

Line spacing used to be called leading, left over from the days when typesetters used strips of lead as spacers between lines. Now we just call it line spacing. Spacing is measured from the base of one line to the top of a capital letter on a line below. For signs and posters, allow a minimum of half the capital letter's height, which works out to a spacing of one and a half capital heights, or 150 percent, from one baseline to the next baseline (Calori 2007, 139). For printed documents, 120 to 145 percent is typical (Goodman-Khasani 2014, 36). Looser line spacing is easier for viewers to read (Caputo et al. 2008, 32), up to a point; if there is too much white space between lines, readers will have difficulty locating the next line (Barnes 2011, 86).

Text Layout

Use contrast between text and background, both to attract attention and to make your text legible. On printed matter, dark-colored text on a light background is especially legible; on a projected slide or backlit sign, the reverse is true (Moscardo et al. 2007, 51). Avoid patterned backgrounds in general; they produce visual noise that makes characters and words hard to recognize. If you must use a patterned background, be sure that the color of text in front of it is a clear contrast.

Cluster words together to form chunks. Help your reader by breaking text into chunks and making paragraphs short. Where you can, provide visual landmarks such as headings, bullets, and images.

You can choose to set headings in all capital letters, if you wish. However, be aware that many designers feel that title case—lowercase letters with initial letters of each word capitalized—is easier to read because it results in distinctive word shapes. Also, all-capital words take up more space than title case (Calori 2007, 111).

Short- and medium-length lines are easiest to read. Various studies have shown the optimal number of characters including spaces and punctuation per line to be 39 to 52 (White 2002, 111), 45 to 72 (Weinschenk 2011, 43), 40 to 65 (Moscardo et al. 2007, 41), or 60 to 70 (Barnes 2011, 86), which works out to about 10 to 12 words per line. Watch out for very short lines. They break up the text too much and are also hard to read. Since the ideal width contains 40 to 72 characters, type size must be proportional to the length of line; the longer the line, the larger the type must be.

Justification means that a block of text is aligned with one or both side margins. The easiest to read is left justification, also known as flush left, ragged right, because it gives the reader a predictable beginning point with consistent word spacing. Justifying both left and right can result in awkwardly long spaces between words. Avoid using centered text or right-justified text in paragraphs; use them sparingly as needed in design situations.

Avoid what are known as widows and orphans in your text where possible. A widow is a single word or very short line at the end of a paragraph. An orphan is a single syllable of a hyphenated word on a line by itself at the end of a paragraph. Avoid placing the last line of a paragraph at the top of a column or page.

Composition and Design

Design principles in graphic design have much in common with principles of wayfinding. Some of the problems are similar: Faced with a mass of information and stimuli, how does the reader figure out where they are and where they are going? Use two general devices to guide readers: highlight and organize. Highlight the information using contrast, and organize it using visual hierarchies. Visual design leads the reader through the material in a sequence that tells your story.

When you bring together elements into a layout, your goal is to make it as easy as you can for a reader to see and understand ideas. The way you lay out a page or a poster helps your reader understand where to start, where to move next, and how all the elements relate. You do this with pattern, visual hierarchies, contrast, and balance. Well-designed layouts feature contrast, consistency, white space as a design element, and above all, structure and hierarchy.

Our brains are pattern-seeking devices. Use patterns in your layouts; people will be automatically looking for them. You can create pattern with grouping and white space. Use titles and headings to give your reader clues to help them find their way through the layout. Position related items close together. For consistency, repeat some design elements throughout, such as typeface, a shape, a graphic element, or a color theme. At the same time, avoid boredom by providing contrast and emphasis. You can think about different layout options using rough thumbnail sketches. These sketches do not have to be artistic; they are just tools to help you think.

Design every layout with the goal of making it as easy as possible for people to comprehend its content. The visual systems in our brains are set up to perceive structure in our environment. This is how we make sense of what is around us. The more you structure your layout, the more easily people will be able to scan and understand it. People quickly forget isolated fragments, but if those pieces fit into a previously established structure, they are much easier to remember.

Use some kind of visual hierarchy for organizing elements in a layout. Don't make every element equal in dominance; have a single, primary element or focal point to make it clear to readers where to start. Break material into sections, and break large sections into subsections. Label each section and subsection prominently, and make the higher-level headings more prominent than the lower-level subsection headings. Determine which elements are the most important, and render them with the greatest contrast to their surroundings.

Contrast attracts attention and is an important way to achieve hierarchy. The stronger the contrast, the higher the hierarchy level will be. Use size, boldness, shape, and color to create contrast. Our eyes are naturally drawn to strong color, so contrast in color is a way to enhance legibility. You can contrast strong spot colors with less saturated colors. You can also create contrast through size, shape, position, and texture differences. Render elements that are second in importance with somewhat less contrast. When you choose an element to create contrast, change only one element. Elements should be similar in every way except the one feature that is contrasted. The more you increase the number of things that are different, the less they stand out. Objects which contrast or differ from their surroundings will pop out and be detected even in peripheral vision (Johnson 2014, 63).

Use formatting, color, and white space to make your key message clearly visible at a glance. Consider a hierarchy of headings that are very clearly seen, with a title in large, bold font; section headings in large, bold font, perhaps centered over the section, and a different color, depending on the document; subheadings in smaller, bold font; bold, italicized subheadings as the first sentence of some paragraphs; bullet points to make key ideas visible; ample white space; narrow columns; and perhaps one summary or key block of text highlighted with a shaded background. Start directly with your main point, not background information and context.

Use about three levels of hierarchy: headings for the most important, subheadings for the less important, and all the remaining information of equivalent importance. More than three levels can be confusing, depending on the document (White 2002, 65). Provide a focal point. The primary level is the attention-grabber, with large, bold text or a compelling image. The element with the highest degree of contrast will be the primary level of hierarchy. Choose either text or an image to be the first element seen, and be sure they do not compete with each other for attention. Once readers have been drawn in by the primary level, they move on to the secondary and tertiary levels to learn more.

When a pattern is organized simply and is clearly different from its environment, it can be easily recognized (Arnheim 1997, 29). If you want to focus attention on a key element, you can consider leaving large areas of white space. Or move a key paragraph out of alignment with the rest of the text.

Use chunking to reduce the effort of reading as much as possible so that readers are unaware of the act of reading. Use white space, graphics, and hierarchies of headings to chunk information into no more than four items. Use empty space and structure to allow readers to scan a page and to grasp the main ideas with one scan. As designers say, this helps to conserve the most valuable resource you have: attention (Goodman-Khasani 2014, 13).

Two complementary qualities contribute to good design and clear communication: contrast and unity. Contrast attracts attention. Unity allows all the parts of a design to support each other so that they are part of a unified whole, with the whole more significant than any of the parts. Structuring the elements within a visual hierarchy is part of a unified whole. So is careful attention to similarity: of typeface, color scheme, shape, position and alignment, and texture, together with the internal organization of a grid system. Introduce enough variety to keep the reader interested. Instead of constant repetition, think of the design as a theme with variations.

Objects have visual weight. Position them so that there is an even balance. A symmetrical arrangement is more formal and suggests rest and connection. An asymmetrical arrangement is more informal, more dynamic and interesting, and suggests motion and opening. Symmetry achieves balance through similarity; asymmetry achieves balance through contrast.

Create a balance and provide a visual hierarchy that leads the reader through the message. Think about what you want your audience to see first, whether it is a word, a phrase, or an image, and make that element the most prominent.

White space is the term designers use to refer to space that does not contain text or graphics. It plays a significant role in graphic design. Treat it as a design element, just like text and graphics. Use it to provide a path for readers' eyes to follow or to make elements more recognizable by providing contrast.

In Western culture, people read from left to right and top to bottom, with a bias toward the horizontal (Barnes 2011, 30). Eye-tracking research shows that for people who read in a language that moves left to right, their eyes move in a Z pattern from top to bottom. The reader's eyes focus first on the center of the layout, then shift to the upper left and move across to the right, where they make a decision about whether to continue. If the reader decides to continue, their eyes drop down and to the left, moving across to the right again. If the reader decides not to continue, their eyes drop to the lower left corner, scanning in between as they go to be sure nothing is missed (Caputo et al. 2008, 77). Since people tend to begin at the top left corner of a page or layout, that is a good location for your primary message or title and any other information you want to be sure readers see.

In signs, posters, and book pages, images near the edge have greater visual weight that those in the center (Moscardo et al. 2007, 48). In printing and signage, extending an image or other design element all the way to an edge is called bleeding. Bleeds can be on one or more edges or on all four. Talk with your printer or sign fabricator if you need bleeding, since printed matter with bleeds tends to be more expensive to produce and may require bleeding elements to extend beyond the boundary of the layout medium.

Grids and Other Layouts

The rule of thirds is a simple approach to layout used by many designers. Simply divide the layout or page into thirds, both vertically and horizontally. Put important content at the intersection of those imaginary grid lines, or put content along one or more of the lines.

Most designers use a grid. Like the unseen skeleton inside an animal that gives it its shape or the unseen framing beneath the skin of a building that gives it shape, a design grid provides a structure over which visible elements of words and images are placed. A grid divides a page into modular units. Over that framework, a designer can vary the placement of elements for interest and contrast while maintaining unity. A number of grid structures are possible.

First, use vertical guidelines to create columns. Using an odd number of columns, such as three or five columns, is visually appealing and offers choices. A seven-column grid is often used in page design. Seven columns allow you to spread elements across two or three grid lines, and you can vary when that occurs.

Use horizontal guidelines to create a series of three or more evenly spaced horizontal axes. Hang the top of an element from the horizontal guide so that tops are aligned, rather than having bottoms aligned. Since people read from top to bottom, designers typically hang the most important elements from the top or primary horizontal axis, secondary information from the next axis, and tertiary information from the third axis.

Use the same grid on all pages of a document, or on all signs in an exhibit. Thus similar elements will appear in similar locations on each. Readers learn where to look for a particular kind of information, so information becomes easier to find.

The Golden Section

The golden section, or golden ratio, has been used by architects and designers since the ancient Greeks first recognized its role in nature and its proportions in the human body. It is the ratio between two sides of a rectangle, or two sections of a line, where the shorter is to the longer length as the longer length is to the sum of both lengths.

To say this mathematically, if the two lengths are labeled a and b, then $a/b = b/(a+b)$. The ratios are approximately 1 to 1.618, which is also .618 to 1, a proportion designated by the Greek letter Φ (phi). In a rectangle with these proportions, each time a square is constructed on the smaller side and subtracted from the original rectangle, the smaller rectangle which remains has the same proportions.

The golden section is intimately related to growth, and this proportion turns up constantly in growing forms. The golden spiral forms within a golden rectangle. The growth of spirals in seashells, such as the chambered nautilus, are based on this ratio. A series of ratios called the Fibonacci numbers is related to the golden section, and is seen in the ratios of plant leaves as they emerge from stems, sunflower seed heads, and pine cone scales.

Research on vision indicates that a horizontal golden rectangle is an efficient shape for humans to see. Human have binocular vision, and the fields of vision from our two eyes overlap. We evolved for fast horizontal scanning, since danger more often appeared from the sides, not from above or below. The rectangle formed by our field of vision has a ratio of 1 to 1.47, which approximates the golden rectangle of 1 to 1.618. We can scan an area of this proportion easily, without much effort. Looking up requires more effort, for tilting the head, and looking at the periphery requires more effort, for turning the head. Neurons in our visual cortex are specialized, with some activated when we read horizontal lines, others activated for vertical lines, and others for slanted lines (Sussman and Hollander 2015, 96). Research shows that we are able to scan a rectangle and process its contents the most efficiently when its proportions are about 3 to 2, or approximating the golden ratio (Bejan 2009, 97).

Shapes with this ratio are inherently attractive. You can see these proportions used in Greek temples such as the Parthenon in Athens and in Renaissance architecture such as Notre Dame cathedral in Paris (Sussman and Hollander 2015, 93). Graphic designers often use this ratio in layouts and cropping of images. The golden ratio, 1 to 1.618, is not far from a ratio of 2 to 3. So the rule of thirds is a simple guide to layout that will result in proportions inherently attractive to humans.

Doing Design

Desktop publishing software makes it possible for anyone to lay out pages, brochures, posters, or signs. But owning the software does not automatically turn us into designers. What can you do?

First, look at what others have done. Collect examples of color themes and layouts. Find examples which you think represent good design that communicates well. You will not copy other people's work directly, but having examples to look at will give you ideas about how to put elements together.

Second, use templates. Many software companies hire professional designers to create samples that are included with the software and are free to use.

Third, learn design rules and base your decisions on them. You can break a rule if you have a good reason to do so, once you know the rules and you believe you can communicate more clearly by breaking one.

Fourth, make a goal-based plan. Behind every decision to leave something out or add something in lies a clearly defined set of goals. Make conscious decisions. Know and be able to explain what you are doing and why you are doing it.

10

IMAGES

Images—photographs and drawings—promote deeper understanding of a concept when chosen carefully. They can lead to new understanding or deepen emotional connection. The best illustrations describe a process or tell a story. Images help us visualize things we could not otherwise see, such as symbiotic fungi living around the roots of a tree or what it is like inside a beaver's den. They help us understand abstract ideas, illustrating things like food webs, ecosystems, and the hydrologic cycle.

Images Have Impact

Photography has had a profound impact on the ways in which we view the world, allowing us to see things we would not otherwise have access to. As we saw in Chapter 3, the 1968 photograph of Earth from the Apollo 8 moon mission known as "Earthrise" was a powerful reminder that the world on which we live is finite and the only home we have. It was followed in 1972 by the photograph of Earth floating in space known as the "Blue Marble." These two images, "Earthrise" and "Blue Marble," allowed people to conceive of their world on a global scale in a way they had not been able to before.

Photographs often have an emotional impact that words do not. They let us see animals as fellow beings with feelings of their own, and they let us see landscapes as places with intrinsic value. Images can connect us with fellow creatures on a personal level. For example, we may see pictures of cave paintings of now-extinct woolly mammoths, and the paintings allow us to imagine them as denizens of some other world, not ours. But when we see actual photographs documenting now-extinct animals who were alive but are no longer with us, we may be better able to see them as fellow beings and to recognize the impact of their loss.

Memes

A meme is a self-replicating unit of cultural information, usually an image, that spreads rapidly, allowing an idea to replicate (Blackmore 2000, 53). The term was coined by biologist Richard Dawkins as analogous to "gene," using a shortened form of a Greek word meaning to imitate. Memes have power to spread "contagious" ideas (Broda-Bahm 2012b). What this phenomenon illustrates about communication is that a simple, single image or small bit of text containing a single idea is effective. A meme is simple, it contains a single, complete thought, and it is often visual.

Images and Climate Change

Before-and-after photographs or artwork are compelling because they convey evidence without words or logical argument. Repeat photography is a technique in which two photographs from different time periods, both taken from the same location and having the same field of view, are compared and contrasted. The Repeat Photography Project by the US Geological Survey is a tool for communicating the effects of climate change. Scientists document landscape change in Glacier Bay National Park and Preserve, Alaska, and in Glacier National Park, Montana, by placing historic photos of glaciers, some from the nineteenth century and some from the 1930s, alongside contemporary photos in places where formerly massive glaciers have retreated dramatically or disappeared altogether. The striking images created by these pairs of photos make the subject of climate change relevant and visible.

Research on communicating about climate change indicates there are two broad categories of images. Some images capture attention and reinforce the sense that climate change is significant. Others promote a feeling of efficacy, a sense of being able to take action. Few images fall into both categories (O'Neill et al. 2013, 413).

These disparate categories illustrate why it is important to determine first what your goals are, and then to select images in line with those goals. Dramatic images of climate impacts showing such things as melting glaciers, floods, and polar bears act as persuasive evidence that climate change is real and important. On the other hand, these things are distant from viewers, may not seem relevant to individual lives, and may even cause people to feel helpless and to disengage from the subject.

Images that depict distant damage caused by climate change do not resonate with many people. Effective images show the effects of climate change in local places and then show how people to whom we can relate are adapting to change. It is interesting to note that climate skepticism communication typically does not use images (Braasch 2013, 37).

Images of wind farms, solar panels, and electric cars promote positive engagement with the subject; they illustrate choices that individuals can make and help people feel empowered to take specific actions. Images that show alternate energy futures, or using less energy in a home, or changing one's travel behavior, or reducing red meat consumption increase people's feelings that there are things they can do to make a difference (O'Neill et al. 2013, 419). These images enable people to build a connection with climate change in a positive way and to create possibilities for engagement and action (Braasch 2013, 38).

Images and Urban Planning

Many people, including some trained urban planners, have difficulty estimating density in suburban developments and cities. When we see monotonous, inhuman developments we tend to overestimate their density, and when we see examples of smart growth and well-designed, walkable neighborhoods we tend to underestimate their density. The Lincoln Institute of Land Policy published a collection of photographs with a broad sample of densities at various levels in order to help readers get a feel for what each looks like. At the same time, these photographs make clear that it is design, rather than density, that shapes the character of a place (Campoli and MacLean 2007, 21).

Comparing Photographs and Drawings

Photographs and drawings are two ways to communicate with images. Because we believe they represent reality, photos can provide a powerful visual punch. We tend to think of photos as reality without filters (Ritter 2004, 295). Once a frame and point of view are selected, a photo shows every detail within the frame, so that it is a challenge to suppress irrelevant details and emphasize important details (Mijksenaar 1997, 50).

Because a drawing is able to filter out some elements and to focus on others, some people think a drawing is "visual opinion" (Hogben 2009, 5), while they think a photograph is factual. However, photographs are not neutral. How a photographer selects a camera angle, how they choose what to include in a frame and choose what to exclude influences how viewers interpret the image. And a drawing or diagram still has the potential to be perceived as reliable fact.

Simple drawings have a powerful communicative function, in some cases communicating better than photographs. Surprisingly, research on perception has shown that people can identify a human hand more quickly when they see it as a simplified line drawing than when they see a photograph of a hand (Ware 2013, 302). Silhouettes are especially important in perceiving the structure of objects. Many objects have what are known as canonical silhouettes, shapes that are particularly recognizable from a certain point of view, which is often perpendicular to a major axis of symmetry. The outline of a person is an example. There are limits to how far we can change the viewing direction before a drawing becomes hard to recognize. Babies early in life can identify faces when they are upright, but not when they are inverted (Sussman and Hollander 2015, 61).

Try looking at an outline of North America turned upside down and notice how unrecognizable its shape is. What this tells us is that if we use a drawing to stand for a category of things, we should use a canonical shape in its normal orientation.

Choosing Images

How do you go about choosing images? By planning first. Determine the goals of your message, develop a theme, then develop text. Once you have completed these steps, then choose illustrations to support your theme and message. Try not to use generic photos of nature just for the sake of having an illustration.

Look for hard-working images that support the goal of your message. Find images that add information to the message you are communicating, allow the viewer to make a positive connection with the subject, and help the viewer understand it. Research shows that images with negative messages can induce feelings of helplessness and then apathy (Braasch 2013, 38). Even benign photos like wind turbine farms, which do show positive solutions, still can be distant, at an inhuman scale, and impersonal, and are so familiar they can become clichés.

Images that allow the viewer to connect in a specific and positive manner are more likely to make a person feel there are possibilities for engagement and action. For example, positive images that are especially effective show the effects of climate change in a local place and convey a story about how people there are adapting to climate change.

Clip art is generic, cartoonish artwork that comes free with software. Do not use it. Use photographs or high-quality illustrations that add meaning to information you are communicating.

Use stock photos with care. If a photo is too perfect and too beautiful, the viewer will recognize that it is staged and inauthentic, and will feel disconnected. This is especially true of stock photos of people: never use them.

People respond to images that tell a story. A photo of a static object does not tell a story. If nothing is happening in a photo, then there is no story. A story takes shape when something happens. A single photo often tells a story. Study images on the front pages of major newspapers, and you will see a story line in what is depicted. Usually such a photo shows action at a moment frozen in time; the viewer can imagine what might have come before and what might come after.

You can also consider organizing multiple photos in a sequence to show change over time or cause and effect, or to allow a viewer to zoom in at progressively closer and more intimate scales. Revealing information gradually adds fascination and engages viewers in the story.

People respond to images that contain other people. We do not respond to all visual inputs equally; faces are special objects in human perception and our brains prioritize them. The visual cortex takes up a sizable portion of the brain's resources, but there is an area outside the visual cortex called the fusiform gyrus dedicated solely to recognizing faces. When we look at a face, the visual signal bypasses the brain's usual channels and we process the face more quickly than we would any other object (Weinschenk 2011, 9).

Humans even tend to see faces in inanimate objects when faces are not actually there. This was important for survival in our evolutionary past, when it was important to recognize threats quickly. If you mistook a blade of grass for a snake, there was little harm done; but failing to recognize a poisonous snake in the grass could prove fatal (Sussman and Hollander 2015, 69). It was also important to survival to identify human faces quickly, both friend and foe. Infants learn about faces faster than they do any other object. For ancient humans, infants who were able to recognize faces quickly smiled back more, were more likely to win the hearts of their parents, and so were more likely to prosper (Sagan 1995, 45). We are a social species, visually attuned to other people. The brain devotes more area to recognition of faces than to recognition of any other visual object (Kandel 2012, 333).

If you are communicating about the dangers of climate change, for example, use images that put people in the middle of the story about climate change. Dramatic photographs of hurricanes, floods, rising seas, and forest fires are compelling, but they have a more personal impact when they show vulnerable people caught in these disasters (Braasch 2013, 36). It is the human connection that makes these issues matter to most of us.

We have a tendency to prefer curves over straight or sharp lines, subconscious tendencies that are rooted again in our evolutionary past (Sussman and Hollander 2015, 150). For ancient humans, pointed shapes appeared in sharp teeth, big claws, quills, and thorns, and it was advantageous to be able to notice them and escape if needed.

Also rooted in our evolutionary past is our tendency to favor visual complexity. Biophilia, which literally means a love for nature, is the genetically encoded emotional need of human beings to affiliate with nature and with other living organisms, rooted in human biology and evolution (Wilson 2002, 134). Biophilia evolved as an adaptive mechanism to protect people from hazards and to help them access such resources as food, water, and shelter. Modern humans exhibit a strong preference for features that suggest those evolutionary roots. People are aesthetically drawn to features that have proven instrumental in human survival, including clean flowing water, rich vegetation, and bright flowering colors that frequently signify presence of food, all features with a degree of visual complexity.

Be aware that we don't all see the same image in the same way. Cultural studies tell us that differences in social and economic class within the same culture shape the ways we perceive imagery and symbols (Barnes 2011, 246). People from different cultures inhabit different sensory worlds, and people of each culture selectively filter sensory data so that they perceive some visual elements differently from people in another culture (Hall 1969, 2). Culture influences the ways we interpret visual messages. For example, cognitive research shows that when looking at images, people from East Asia pay more attention to figure–ground relationships and holistic context, while people from the US pay more attention to individual foreground objects (Weinschenk 2011, 93). Research in linguistics tells us that the language we speak shapes the ways we perceive reality, both socially and physically.

Composing Photographs

Several attributes can influence the way viewers interpret photographic images. One is the camera angle. Shooting from a different vantage point can result in a dramatic image.

Time of day affects lighting. For outdoor images, quality of light is best in the early morning or late afternoon, when the sun is low in the sky. At midday, light is harsh, shadows are scarce, and objects appear flatter.

Depth of field is the apparent distance from the nearest to the most distant objects that still appear relatively in-focus in an image. A greater depth of field and a distinct plane of focus make for a more compelling image. Look for images in which the subject is in sharp focus, while the background and foreground are less focused (Caputo et al. 2008, 42).

Use the rule of thirds to help you choose or compose photographs. Divide the image into thirds, both vertically and horizontally. Important elements, and the horizon, should align with those imaginary grid lines. For some images, dividing into fifths is also effective. The rule of thirds gives images dynamic balance. If a subject, or the horizon line, were centered in the picture, the image would be static and would not create any visual tension. You can use lines created by features like rivers, paths, or fences to draw the viewer's eye to the focal point of an image.

Images are more interesting when the eye is drawn from one edge to the other. Frame active elements to lead the viewer's eye into, rather than out of, the image. For example, if someone or something is moving from right to left, they should appear on the right side of the image so that they move into rather than out of the image. Or if someone is looking toward the left, they should be placed on the right side of the image (Caputo et al. 2008, 41).

Humans of all cultures appear to read diagonals from left to right, for reasons which are not known conclusively. We perceive a diagonal going from lower left to upper right as going up, and a diagonal going from upper left to lower right as going down. This is true regardless of the language in which we read, whether we are left- or right-handed, and whether we are left- or right-brained. You can use these tendencies to intensify the appearance of motion. So, for example, you can intensify the feeling that an object is rolling downhill by showing it descending on a diagonal from left to right (Zettl 1998, 97).

Look at each photo critically and think about whether the entire image contributes to your message. Crop images as needed to focus the viewer's attention on the essence of the image. Objects tend to have more graphic weight when they are framed so that they are shown close up (Zettl 1998, 81).

Digital Images: Rasters, Vectors, and Resolution

Computer graphics can be produced in either raster or vector format. Knowing about the advantages and disadvantages of each will help you to choose the format appropriate for your purpose.

Raster images are composed of pixels or tiny squares, each one coded with a particular color. The word "pixel" is a combination of the words "pictures" and "elements." Raster images are resolution-specific. When a raster image is scaled up too much, it becomes pixelated; that is, the individual squares are visible, making the image jagged and less crisp, and losing the subtlety of color gradations. Raster images have larger file sizes than vector images, and those with high resolution are significantly larger than those with low resolution. Raster images provide excellent color detail, but become blurry if enlarged too much.

Vector images are created by mathematical formulas that define geometric shapes. For example, a straight line is defined by the location of a point at each end, and a circle is defined by the path swept by a point as it rotates at a constant radius around a center point. Vector images are used for things like line art, logos, and symbols. They are also used to create accurate drawings of buildings, sites, and objects used for design and construction. Vector images are scalable and can be enlarged without losing quality, but their ability to manage complex and subtle color is limited. Vectors are not resolution-dependent; they allow you to print images at any size you want with no change in resolution. They result in smaller file size than raster images. In illustration software, type can be converted to vectors, eliminating concern over whether a printer has appropriate typefaces on their computers.

Resolution is measured in pixels per inch (ppi) for screen images and dots per inch (dpi) for printing. A pixel on a screen is square; a dot on a printed page is round. For printing, images are usually 300 ppi. That means that each one inch by one inch square will contain 300 pieces of information. The higher the resolution, the better an image's quality and the smoother its color gradations will be.

In years past, common wisdom said that images displayed on the web should be limited to 72 ppi, which was the standard screen resolution when Apple first began producing Macintosh computers. However, all screens now have resolutions much higher than 72 ppi, so that images display equally well online whether they are 72 or 300 or more ppi (Patterson 2017).

File types for raster images include TIFF (Targeted Image File Format), used for printing; JPEG or JPG (Joint Photographic Experts Group), used for screen images; BMP (bitmap), used mostly for black and white; PNG (Portable Network Graphics), used for screen images; and GIF (Graphic Interchange Format), used for screen images with index colors (not RGB or CMYK), especially those with sharp edges and no color blending. GIFs can be saved in an animated format. TIFF files have larger file size because they retain information about layers and colors; they are the best format for printing. The advantage of JPEG files is that they can be compressed; some quality is lost, but file sizes are smaller. PNG files can be compressed without loss of quality.

File types for vector images include EPS (Encapsulated Post Script), used for illustrations by software such as Adobe Illustrator; and DWG (drawing) for computer-aided design drawings. The most common software for creating raster images is Adobe Photoshop. Other software programs such as Adobe InDesign are used for assembling text, raster, and vector images into page layouts, which can be sent directly to a printer. Any file type can be converted to a PDF (Portable Document Format), a single file which allows the designer to share a file with someone else, whether or not they have specific typefaces or the same kind of software on which the file was created.

Finding and Using Images

How do you find images if you do not create your own? An online image search using carefully considered search terms will usually turn up a great number of choices. Remember, however, that art, including photographs, is intellectual property which often has copyright protection. When you find an image that suits your communication goal, the first thing to do is to find out whether this is a copyrighted or a copyright-free image. Do not assume that an image being used on a nonprofit organization's website belongs to that organization. Find out the source of that image and determine whether there is a copyright and what the image's owner requires in order to secure permission to use the image. Each organization is different, and some have specific ways they want an attribution written. Some images may be freely used for personal or educational purposes, but permission may be required for commercial uses.

An image is in the public domain if it is not under copyright protection. It may be in the public domain because its owner placed it in that category from the beginning, or it may be old enough that it is no longer under copyright protection. Works in the public domain may be used freely without the permission of the image's owner.

Images from any US government agency are in the public domain. There are two ways to search for US government images. One is to specify "site:.gov" as a limiting term when doing an online search. This will limit the number of images to those from government agencies, but you cannot necessarily use all of them. Only federal government images are certain to be copyright-free; those from state or county agencies may or may not be copyrighted, and you will need to check. Another way to search for US government images is to go to the extensive image galleries provided by each agency. Examples include the National Aeronautics and Space Administration (NASA), the National Oceanic and Atmospheric Administration (NOAA), the Department of Energy (DOE), the Environmental Protection Agency (EPA), the US Geological Survey (USGS), the National Park Service (NPS), the Library of Congress (LC), and so forth.

Creative Commons is an organization whose mission is to share knowledge and creativity. They offer several versions of licenses, from non-commercial to public domain. A number of nonprofit organizations and image-sharing sites provide collections of images in the public domain. Examples include Pexels, Freeimages (formerly known as Stock.Xchange), Morguefile, Image*After, PublicDomainPictures.net, and Dreamstime.

Good file management is essential. As you find images, save them in a way that will make it easy for you to find them again. Maintain a resource library of public domain images, sorted into folders by category. Be sure to keep track of the source for each image. Creating or finding effective images is time-consuming, and having your own resource library will save you time on future projects.

11

GRAPHS AND DIAGRAMS

Charts, consisting of tables, graphs, or diagrams, are tools in the field of information design. Information design is the practice of making complex information accessible and easily understood by users (SEGD 2014). These tools transfer complex data to two-dimensional representations, revealing information that was previously hidden or submerged (Schuller 2007). Information graphics, or infographics for short, is a term often used, especially informally, to describe graphic representations of data or information.

Information Graphics Help Us Understand Systems

The best information graphics tell an interesting story. The data you illustrate represent real life. There is meaning in those data, and a graphic helps you see what they have to say (Yau 2011, 2). Patterns and relationships help reveal the story. Good graphics tell a story by organizing collections of information and making patterns visible (Tufte 2001, 30).

Information design deals with making large sets of facts and their relationships comprehensible. Sustainability is about systems, which by their nature are complex. Graphics allow you to illustrate a view of a system which is simpler than the complex whole but still shows its important aspects (Stibbe 2009, 162). They allow readers to see relationships in complex data that would not have been visible otherwise. The value of a good graphic is that it lets viewers see patterns, and in so doing, it helps to create a shared view of a situation. By allowing you to see patterns, graphs and diagrams allow you to see emergent properties which you had not anticipated, which can lead you to new insight (Ware 2013, 2). Whenever we transform information from one form into another, we will learn something we did not know before (Few 2009, 1).

Not only do graphs and diagrams make patterns visible, they make quantities of data available to us that we could not have held all at once in our minds, and so they extend the capacity of our working memory (Few 2009, 6). Steve Duenes, graphics director of the *New York Times*, says, "If a reader can glance at a map or simple chart and quickly orient themselves or understand a statistic, and then continue reading the story without skipping a beat, it means we've edited and designed those graphics well" (Williams 2010, 40).

In other words, graphics provide external storage for our working memory. Research tells us that our working memory can handle only three to four chunks of information at a time. A table of numbers or a page of verbal explanation contains more than three or four, but when we put that information into a graphic image we are able to chunk that information together so that we can think about it simultaneously (Few 2009, 50). The number of facts we can hold and the insights that can emerge are multiplied.

Words are linear; graphics are presented all at once. If you tried to describe a complex system verbally, you might need many words, and viewers would need to read or hear them in sequential order. With a diagram, however, a viewer can see the larger scope in one view, can choose to look at the elements in any order they choose, and can loop back through detailed features as many times as needed (Lester 2011, 59).

Similar to the way a map helps us understand a landscape by selecting only some important features to highlight, a diagram helps us understand the key features of a system. And like a map, a diagram allows the viewer to study the system at various scales, looking at the whole, zooming in on particular details, then regarding the larger whole again. Graphics allow you to see both large- and small-scale features of information and data. When we focus on details, it is easy to lose a clear view of the larger context. When we regard the big picture, we lose track of details. A graphic allows us to keep both scales before us, to see both detail focus and whole context together (Few 2009, 113).

Diagrams and graphs are thinking tools, both for the viewer and for you. The process of creating a graphic forces you to step back and evaluate what it is you want people to understand, what is important, what your big ideas really are. It forces you to organize your ideas. While you are using a graphic to educate people, you, yourself, are learning more about your communication project. The process you go through as you are creating a graphic makes you better educated and a more effective advocate (Ritter 2004, 2). In the process of making decisions about how to illustrate your concepts you must clarify your thinking and your basic assumptions, and the result is often new insights (Frankel and DePace 2012, 3).

Information graphics come in various forms. Charts constitute a family of display methods which includes tables, graphs, and diagrams (Few 2012, 11).

Tables

Tables are collections of text and numbers arranged in rows and columns. While they may hide the main story, tables are useful for looking up individual facts and precise amounts. They feature precision of information and ease of reference. Cognitively, tables require us to process information sequentially and interact primarily with our verbal system, while graphs allow simultaneous processing of more information that involves visual perception (Few 2012, 11). Tables are a good choice for small sets of data of twenty or fewer numbers (Tufte 2001, 56).

Graphs

Graphs show patterns, trends, and quantitative relationships. They often include time. A graph is a visual display of quantitative information (Tufte 2001, 9), and by giving it shape a graph can show a large amount of data in a way that is readily understood. In a graph, you can see the image of thousands of values expressed as a single pattern. Trends show the overall nature of change during a period of time (Few 2012, 48) and so are a fundamental tool for evaluating progress.

Graphs let you see patterns that you would not have seen if you only looked at numbers in a table. Some of the most dramatic graphs make the fingerprints of climate change visible: the Keeling Curve, which shows the steady climb of carbon dioxide concentration levels in the atmosphere since 1958, and the graph of global average temperatures over the last millennium, sometimes called the "hockey stick" because of its dramatic sharp rise in the twentieth century. People who may think photographs are selective and non-representative of the climate-change phenomenon view graphs of rising temperatures as authoritative and scientific (Braasch 2013, 34).

A graph has two axes, each beginning at zero and moving away from the lower left corner. Each axis measures a variable, and the graph line shows a relationship between the variables. Often the horizontal axis represents time.

A line graph is good at showing trends. Some of the most powerful communication examples are simple line graphs showing human population, carbon dioxide concentration, or average global temperature over time. One way to compare multiple attributes is to show multiple graph lines on the same chart; if each graph line needs its own vertical axis, you can use one scale for the left vertical axis and a different scale for the right.

A bar graph, where each value is shown as a vertical column or horizontal bar, is good at showing differences in value. Because each bar is distinct, a bar graph is good at showing individual values.

Know your audience and use graphs with care. While many people find graphs quite useful, others in the general public have a negative reaction to what they think represents mathematics and may actually freeze up or stop thinking when presented with a graph (Ritter 2004, 288). You can avoid some of these reactions by choosing graphs that are simple and dramatic, with clear messages. Help your audience by describing the data in a graph, orally or with text, by saying, "What this tells you is…" (Baron 2010, 110).

Other Charts

Area Graphs

A pie chart shows each value as a wedge, expressed as part of a total. It shows general comparisons of size, but cannot show whether the pie is getting larger or smaller, or other trends, and its degree of visual accuracy is limited.

A bubble chart is a kind of scatter plot in which you use vertical and horizontal axes to locate two sets of values, and the area of each circle or bubble to represent a quantity.

Pie charts and bubble charts are area graphs; they display quantities in terms of the sizes of two-dimensional areas. The problem with area charts is that readers have a hard time interpreting quantities accurately. In a pie chart, our visual system cannot accurately determine quantities from two-dimensional areas. In a bubble chart, a large circle which appears to be twice the diameter of another circle actually contains four times the area of the smaller circle (Yau 2011, 18).

Triangular Graphs

A triangular coordinate graph is shaped like a triangle and has three axes, one on each side. Points within the triangle bring together values from each of the three categories. This kind of graph is used to illustrate subjects like soil texture.

Radar Graphs

A radar graph, also known as a star graph, spider graph, or amoeba graph, is a graph in a circular format that can show multiple metrics at the same time (Bell and Morse 2003, 45). It is laid out on a radial grid, like spokes on a wheel, with concentric circles representing quantities or percentages and multiple arms or axes with one characteristic displayed on each axis. Using a radar graph to display sustainability characteristics helps to illustrate strengths and gaps. Progress over time can be shown by representing past years with different line types.

A wind rose is a radar graph which summarizes how wind in a geographical region blows from different directions in each different season. A series of eight to sixteen equally spaced grid lines is drawn from the center, with one line for each compass direction. The length of bars or spokes drawn along those lines indicate what percentage of time the wind blows from each direction.

A radar graph was used to define planetary boundaries within which it is safe to operate for each of several interrelated systems, a "safe operating space" within which human society could continue to develop (Wijkman and Rockström 2012, 44). A group of scientists defined planetary boundaries for nine interdependent areas of the global commons: climate change, biodiversity loss, excess nitrogen and phosphorus production, stratospheric ozone depletion, ocean acidification, freshwater consumption, land-use change, air pollution, and chemical pollution. They mapped these onto a radial graph with one wedge for each area of concern and with boundaries denoted by concentric rings. The concept of planetary boundaries and their graphic illustration became a powerful way to communicate complex scientific issues to a broad lay audience (Folke 2013, 29).

Diagrams

Diagrams are graphics which show processes, conceptual frameworks, and relationships. They can be used to show nonquantitative relationships. Examples include cycle maps, such as those that illustrate the carbon cycle or the hydrologic cycle; organizational charts, which show formal reporting relationships; charts such as Gantt charts, used in project management to plan schedules graphically; process charts and other flowcharts, which show sequences of events and causal links.

A flowchart uses symbols to represent process steps: typically a rectangle indicates a step or activity; a tab with radiused ends indicates a start, stop, or pause; a diamond indicates a choice or decision; and arrows indicate relationships between steps (Harris 1996, 154). A Gantt chart shows the length of time each step takes, when it will start and end, and plots them against a time line; each step is shown on a separate line so that time dependencies and overlaps can be seen. A critical path method (CPM) chart, also known as a program evaluation review technique or PERT chart, represents the time required for each step by a line length drawn to scale; the path with the largest number of length units, the one that takes the longest, is the critical path, and it determines the minimum amount of time required to complete the whole process.

A diagram guides the viewer. Complex visualizations can be difficult to interpret, but a diagram simplifies the mass of facts and reduces the number of details so that the viewer can more easily think about the most important features (Barnes 2011, 62). Research shows that graphics and words together often communicate more effectively than either images or text alone (Ware 2013, 332).

A diagram groups together information that is used together to minimize searching and clarify thinking. These visual representations are typically in line with visual perception principles and easy for humans to understand (Card et al. 1999, 16). Diagrams are often intended to be studied with minimal additional explanation, at whatever level of detail the viewer chooses. Diagrams can tell stories, and they illustrate the classic rule of journalism, fiction writing, and movies: "show, don't tell."

Both diagrams and maps allow reading on both macro and micro levels. The viewer can first get an overall view of a concept, and then can look at a more specific level with the scale of detail they choose (Knight and Glaser 2009, 5). The viewer, not the designer, is in control of the information they collect. By providing high-density designs with multiple levels of detail at once, diagrams allow viewers to delve into the material without having to switch back and forth between various symbols or areas. This ability to provide information at micro and macro levels applies to many situations, from courtroom graphics to geographic maps to data displays.

Maps

Maps are representations of an area, usually on a flat surface, which show information about land or water geospatially. They show spatial and directional relationships between elements in physical space. Maps are created as the result of a selection process; they simplify reality by showing what people need to know in order to examine a place or find their way. The most simplified form of map is a schematic subway map. It is highly simplified because when people navigate a subway system, they only want to know which subway lines go to which stations; they do not need to know about landmarks or even distances (Johnson 2014, 177).

Indigenous cultures have developed ways to map their worlds using all sorts of materials. Polynesian sailors used navigation maps made of reeds tied in bundles (Turnbull 1994, 2000). In the Marshall Islands, navigators used stick charts that showed the relationships between wave masses and land masses, with grids made of palm ribs and shells or coral pieces representing islands (Raphael 2013, ii). Inuit navigators carve tactile maps from pieces of wood. They can hold the maps inside thick mittens and feel the abstracted contours of the coastline with their fingers, they can read them in the dark Arctic days, the wooden maps are waterproof, and they float if dropped in the water (Hall 2007, 14).

During presentations at the Roger Williams National Memorial, a park commemorating the founder of Rhode Island, National Park Service interpreters place a giant blue-and-green map of the area in the seventeenth century on the floor. As children reenact Williams' travels they place tangible objects on the map one at a time. By the end of the program, what was once a flat map has become a vivid world for them (Scherbaum 2006, 24).

The classic example of a map combined with a diagram to tell a story is the Minard map, the map showing the retreat of Napoleon's army from Russia in 1812 created in 1861 by French engineer Charles Joseph Minard as a visible way to protest the wastes of war (Ritter 2004, 119). A light-colored band traces the advance of troops on Moscow, a darker-colored band traces their retreat, and the width of each band reflects the number of troops, which dwindled from 422,000 to only 10,000 survivors at the end. Other bands show where auxiliary troops split off and their numbers. Rivers, city locations, and a graphic distance scale mark the geography. Changing widths each time a band intersects a river reflects the number of men who died there, either attempting to cross or in the battles that often occurred at these locations. A graph below the map shows the temperature at each point, which never rose above freezing and at one point fell to $-30°C$ or $-36°F$. Vertical lines show where the troops were and the numbers of deaths at each major drop in temperature. This is a remarkable graphic which plots at least seven variables.

Design

As with all visual communication, information in a chart should be presented hierarchically. Not everything is of equal value. Information which is more important should be more visually distinct than other information (Ware 2013, 14). Labels and other text help explain what the graphic shows; elements like color and line weight direct the viewer's eyes to what is important (Yau 2011, 4). These elements are like wayfinding for information graphics. Your graphic can make information available at several levels of detail, so that the viewer can choose a broad overview or finer detail.

We can learn fundamental principles of information design by studying the works of Edward Tufte, Stephen Few, and Colin Ware, well-known advocates of excellence in graphical information design. They tell us that information graphics consist of three visual layers: data, non-data elements, and background (Few 2012, 142). Of those elements, it is the data which should stand out. You want patterns to be easy to spot. Because our eyes are drawn to contrast, we should render important data elements using contrast: color, boldness, size, and form. Non-data elements should be just visible enough to do their jobs but should not draw attention to themselves, or as Tufte says, we should "concentrate the viewer's attention on data rather than data containers" (Tufte 1990, 64). You want the viewer to think about the content, not the technique. For example, you can render grid lines and axes with thin lines and light, neutral colors, and should make them as uniform as possible so that they do not stand out (Few 2012, 143). Consider eliminating grid lines altogether. The design should disappear enough so that it is the information that is the most visible.

For graphs, label each axis. Viewers may not have time to study your graph in detail; choose a title that tells the story clearly. Make the direction of graphs consistent. Design them so that one direction is always good, such as upward for increasing value, or downward for decreasing waste volumes.

With a graph, consider the scale so that you report information honestly. A graph of global average temperature that focuses on a short time period may make it appear that temperatures have decreased, while a graph that plots temperatures over a hundred or thousands of years will show a distinct rising trend over time, with decreases appearing realistically as minor variations. A quantitative graph should start at zero.

If you are designing a table, keep grid lines to a minimum. Grid lines, especially vertical lines, break the information into separate compartments and break up the flow of information. If you must use grid lines, thin lines are better than thick, and light gray are better than black lines. Consider using white space instead to guide readers' eyes, so that a simple absence of text replaces the grid. You can separate rows of data with a wider space, and if you need more visual guides, use halftone shading on alternate rows.

If you are designing a diagram, place text as close as possible to the parts of a diagram it explains, and link them graphically. The brain has a limited working memory capacity; placing text next to images reduces the need to hold information in memory while switching back and forth between locations (Ware 2013, 333). Labels on graphs are often small. Use a sans serif typeface to improve readability at small sizes (Thomas et al. 2006, 43).

You can use color to support naturally occurring information, for example using red colors to show increasing heat, or blue colors to show increasingly cooler temperatures. Colors found in nature, such as less saturated shades of gray, green, blue, and brown are easy to look at (Tufte 1990, 90). Strongly saturated colors are unpleasant to look at over large areas adjacent to each other, so use them sparingly to communicate a message. Saturated colors attract attention; use them as contrast to highlight particular information.

If you have charts or graphs you must print in black and white, use distinct shades of gray to distinguish categories or values. You can use value scales from light to dark to illustrate quantities. Avoid fill patterns in bar graphs; they are jarring and hard to distinguish.

Shapes, sizes, and colors must be distinctly different. Form and color are processed in different visual channels in the brain, and aspects of data should be displayed in different channels so that they are visually distinct (Ware 2013, 145). Make symbols distinct from each other and from the background. Strive to avoid visual clutter, which impedes understanding. You can use white space (which does not have to be literally white) to separate information.

Remember that people can hold only three or four chunks of information in their working memory at one time. If your graph has more than five colors or symbols with a legend for interpreting them, the viewer will be forced to look back and forth constantly to remember which one represents what. Instead, find a way to combine information into chunks that form large, coherent patterns so the chunks can be held in working memory.

Research shows that when reading a graph, we can distinguish preattentively up to eight different hues, four orientations, and four different sizes (Few 2012, 75). If your graph uses a greater number of characteristics, viewers can no longer distinguish them preattentively and must switch to attentive processing, which is slower. Avoid the temptation to combine attributes to create larger numbers of options; remember that preattentive processing can handle just one visual attribute at a time, such as color, shape, or size.

Just as you can collect a library of images, you can collect a style library. Once you develop some combinations of visual attributes that you think are successful, save them so you can use them again.

Information Visualization

Information visualization is a field of practice which uses visual representations of abstract data to amplify cognition (Card et al. 1999, 7). It is discussed briefly here in the interest of being thorough. This form of visualization is used as a tool for thinking in order to reveal invisible patterns from abstract data (Chen 2002, 101).

The process begins by mapping raw data into data tables; these data are then mapped into visual structures. It is powerful for knowledge visualization, where mapping of literatures and their multilevel citation links can reveal knowledge domains that turn out to be connected (ibid., 195). Scholars forage for information in citation indices, then use visualization software to reveal cluster structures.

Word clouds are a different kind of visualization tool, in which text data are analyzed based on word counts. A word or tag cloud is a collection of words in different type sizes, where larger size represents more frequent use of a particular word. When used with web-based searches, tag clouds can reveal opinion trends and areas of greater or lesser agreement (White 2013, 214). Various tag-cloud generator software products are available which produce word clouds. The use of word clouds is controversial, with some researchers viewing them as faddish and inaccurate.

12

REPORTING TOOLS

Indicators

It is common for people who work in sustainability to measure progress toward sustainability goals by developing and using indicator reports or similar tools for measuring. Data that describe current conditions and trends are called indicators. Like an indicator needle on a gage, data in an indicator report point to conditions, telling us something about the state of the system being measured. These measurements are similar to taking an inventory; they help a company, institution, or community understand where they are, identify gaps, and decide what needs to be done. Indicators can include waste and recycling quantities, percentage of waste stream recycled, water quality, water use, energy consumption, local employment, local poverty rates, and greenhouse gas emissions.

An indicator is a marker that helps gage progress toward a goal. One indicator gives a snapshot; measuring an indicator more than once over time reveals a pattern. Sustainability work is about recognizing and changing trajectories. When sustainability indicators are tracked over time, they help to measure progress toward sustainability goals.

In addition to gathering data, people working in sustainability need to make sense of the data and to present them so that other people can make sense of them, too. An indicator report can take several forms. Some people report quantities in a simple table. Many professionals use spreadsheets to track large quantities of data, then write a summary report to explain and interpret the data. A spreadsheet provides the ability to sort, to track changes over time, and to generate graphs and charts easily.

Types of Indicators

Indicators can be organized in various ways when deciding what to measure. One way is to organize by category. For example, a company or school might prepare an indicator report in each of several categories such as water use, energy use, waste and recycling rate, transportation, greenhouse gas emissions, pollution, economic development, and social impact. Reports organized by category tend to be easy for many people to understand.

Another approach is to organize measurement and reporting around a set of goals. Some communities work collaboratively to develop a set of sustainability goals, then organize their indicators to measure the extent to which each goal was addressed. At a national and global scale the United Nations established the Sustainable Development Goals, organized around a set of 17 goals subdivided into 169 quantifiable targets and indicators (UN 2012, 46).

Yet another way is to organize indicators around driving forces and responses, a method sometimes used by government agencies and other policymakers (Hart 2006b, 10). Driving forces can include factors such as drought, rate of pesticide use, land conversion, or political instability. This was the method used by the United Nations Commission on Sustainable Development (CSD) in the past; more recent CSD reports are organized around themes, such as poverty or climate change (ibid.).

Businesses typically report measurements using performance indicators. A company with an environmental management system establishes goals, then uses indicators to measure their progress toward meeting those goals. Each measurable goal includes a benchmark or reference point. For example, a company goal might be to reduce volume of water used per year by 10 percent relative to the 2005 water consumption rate. Or a goal might be to reduce energy use compared to the regional average by 10 percent per year.

Indicators can be a tool for community sustainability planning. For example, in 1990 business leaders, labor, educators, students, government representatives, and citizens of Seattle, Washington, came together to form a project known as Sustainable Seattle (Bell and Morse 2003, 52). They worked together to agree upon goals, then selected regional sustainability indicators to measure progress toward those goals. Indicators are measured and reevaluated regularly. Their Regional Sustainability Indicators are organized around four environments: the natural, built, social, and personal environments, with 20 sustainability goals, measured with a set of 36 indicators.

Selecting Indicators

As with any planning or management task, the first step in preparing indicator reports is to clarify goals. Goals provide a framework, pointing toward indicators that can be used to measure progress toward those goals. You should be clear about the purpose of collecting indicator data and about who makes up the intended audience. Spend time considering and developing a broad range of goals and be clear about ultimate goals before identifying indicators to make it more likely that the right things get measured (Bell and Morse 2003, 49).

Ensure a balanced picture by providing diversity in the types of indicators. You may want to consider a mix of lagging and leading indicators (Hitchcock and Willard 2008, 67). Lagging indicators measure past results, such as quantity of kilowatt-hours used in a month. Leading indicators help predict future trends; they are statistics that change before their results change, such as investment in energy conservation measures.

Decide whether to measure absolute numbers, such as total tons of carbon dioxide equivalent (CO_2e) emitted, or whether to measure ratios, such as tons of carbon dioxide equivalent per item produced. Data expressed as a ratio are known as normalized data and often provide a more clear understanding of progress. However, normalized data sometimes appear to show progress when in fact the impact continues to worsen. For example, a computer manufacturer's indicator report may show that the amount of greenhouse gas emissions per unit produced is lower than the previous year, which is positive. However, if the manufacturer is producing more computers than in the previous year, the impact on Earth's climate is still increasing. The best solution is to track and report both absolute and normalized data (ibid., 74).

People sometimes get focused on what they want to measure rather than on their goals. There is a risk of tracking only indicators for which data are readily available and avoiding indicators for which data do not appear to exist. The advantage is that, if others are tracking similar indicators, it is possible to make comparisons and even to share knowledge. But choosing indicators because they are easy to track means issues that should be analyzed can get overlooked. Set your priorities by developing sustainability goals first, and only selecting indicators once goals are established.

Sustainability indicators should be measurable; that usually means that they are quantitative rather than qualitative. Indicators should be relevant; that is, they should relate to the goals being assessed. They should be practical and easy to understand, including by people who are not experts. They should be based on data that are available and accessible, and data should be cost-effective to collect. Indicators should be reliable; they should dependably reflect conditions being measured, and their numbers should change as conditions change. Indicators need not be precise; given the complexity of sustainability issues precision is often not possible, and too much precision can imply reliability that is not realistic.

People can feel overwhelmed when dealing with numbers, so try to limit the quantity of indicators. Twenty to 30 indicators are generally considered adequate for community sustainability indicators; for businesses, fewer indicators may be appropriate (Bell and Morse 2008, 177). One strategy for streamlining the amount of data people must deal with is to cycle through indicators over time. You can focus on three or four indicators in one year and a different three or four indicators the next year. Some indicators should be tracked on an ongoing basis; others may only be needed to assess the effectiveness of a single project.

Another strategy for streamlining the management of data is for different people to track different indicators, with each person tracking the indicators that are most relevant to them. People then come together periodically to discuss how indicators might be interacting and to reassess goals.

Indicators are not ends in themselves; they are tools to foster learning and adaptation. Because they communicate the extent to which actions result in the achievement of performance goals, they can be used to guide policy change to make management decisions.

Indicators are communication tools as well as learning tools. When indicator data are communicated in written reports, make the names of categories unambiguous and descriptive. Use language that is objective and descriptive. Avoid judgment, unnecessary adjectives, and words such as "should" or "ought." Let the data speak for themselves.

Frameworks

As teams develop strategies and tactics for measuring progress, a framework can help to provide a common language and a common conceptual understanding. It can include standards and principles to help guide decision making and can suggest ways to conduct assessment and measurement. Commonly used frameworks include the triple bottom line, the Global Reporting Initiative (GRI), and The Natural Step. Some organizations develop their own hybrid sustainability framework.

The triple bottom line encompasses environmental, economic, and social dimensions of sustainability. As a reporting framework, the triple bottom line can be used to guide the measurement of sustainability performance in a business or region. Sustainable Seattle is an example of an initiative that uses a triple bottom line reporting framework.

The Global Reporting Initiative is the most widely used sustainability reporting framework worldwide. It provides detailed guidelines for measuring and reporting on environmental, economic, and social dimensions of an organization's activities. While it is a complex and comprehensive framework, particularly appropriate for large organizations and those with international audiences, its framework of sustainability indicators is useful in organizations of any size. The Sustainability Tracking, Assessment and Rating System (STARS) is a similar reporting framework used in institutions of higher education.

The Natural Step is a scientifically based framework designed to help organizations measure and implement sustainable practices. It includes a set of system conditions or principles and a planning method which together are known as The Natural Step Framework (Edwards 2005, 59–62). The four system conditions translate the laws of nature into understandable principles. Condition 1 relates to fossil fuels and minerals, Condition 2 relates to toxins, Condition 3 relates to resource extraction, and Condition 4 relates to equity and economics (Nattrass and Altomare 1999).

The Natural Step uses graphics and metaphors to make the planning process practical and accessible. The planning process, illustrated by simple drawings, is referred to as the ABCD approach, an acronym for the four steps: Awareness and Visioning, Baseline Mapping, Creative Solutions, and Decide on Priorities.

The Natural Step offers handbooks and training programs. Its framework is used by many cities, universities, design firms, and corporations (Nattrass and Altomare 2002).

Footprints

Ecological Footprint

The ecological footprint is a measure of the demand humans place on nature expressed as land area. It quantifies the amount of productive land and water area required to produce the resources we consume and to absorb the waste we generate. Calculating footprints allows us to compare human demand to the biosphere's carrying capacity. Ecological footprints can be calculated at any scale, from an individual person to an entire nation. They are understandable tools for communicating impact, and they monitor the combined impact of a variety of indicators. Footprint calculators are available through the Global Footprint Network website and from several other organizations' websites.

Water Footprint

Water footprint is also known as virtual water content. A water footprint represents the volume of freshwater required per unit of product or per unit of time. Water footprint is an indicator of water use related to consumption, and includes direct use, indirect use, and volume of water polluted. Water footprint calculators are available at several organizations' websites including the Water Footprint Network.

Carbon Footprint

A carbon footprint, when calculated as part of an ecological footprint, expresses greenhouse gas emissions in terms of area of land needed for carbon dioxide sequestration (Ewing et al. 2010, 101). A number of carbon calculators are available online. Many of them calculate the amount of carbon in tons or carbon dioxide equivalent in tons, rather than the amount of land needed to sequester carbon dioxide emissions. Many people use the term carbon footprint to mean the quantity of greenhouse gas emissions, rather than meaning footprint expressed as area.

Labels

A label is a concise and sometimes creative way to communicate information. A notable example was the Pharos Project, a system of colorful labels for green building materials launched in 2006 by architects from the USGBC and the Healthy Building Network and now discontinued. The Pharos framework organized a large amount of environmental and social information into a single graphic format. The organizational device was a radar graph called the lens, drawn from the metaphor of a navigational lighthouse. Pharos was the great lighthouse of ancient Alexandria. The circular lens presented 3 major sectors divided into 16 wedges, one for each social or environmental concern. Concentric circles measured the relative value of each issue for a given material, both numerically and with a color code. The colorful geometric layout in the form of a radar graph allowed users to grasp that a product may perform well in some categories and poorly in others and showed what was known and not known about a material in all of the categories. The lens was one element on a larger label, which included life-cycle data about content, embodied energy, biodegradability, recyclability, and whether the material was tested on animals. The label and lens were designed to allow users to make decisions about materials relatively quickly.

Eco-Labels

An eco-label is any label on a product that tells consumers that the product provides environmental or social benefit. The best labels and the systems they represent are third-party verified, with meaningful standards for environmental protection or social justice developed through a process that is open, public, and transparent, with broad stakeholder involvement.

ISO is the short name of the International Organization for Standardization, the developer and publisher of international standards. ISO is a consensus-based network of national standards institutes from 163 countries. ISO 14020, Environmental Labels, recognizes three types of environmental labels. Type I labels indicate that products are independently verified by a third party based on specific criteria; these are referred to by ISO as eco-labels. Like a seal of approval, an eco-label is applied when the product meets a certifying standard. "USDA Organic" and "FSC" are examples of this type. Type II labels are self-declarations about a product. They are claims that may or may not be verifiable. A Type II label makes claims using descriptive terms, such as "biodegradable." Type III labels are also eco-labels that indicate independent third-party verification. In addition, award of a Type III label is based on a full life-cycle assessment of the product.

In contrast to genuine eco-labels, the ubiquitous recycling symbol is more sly. The recycling logo was developed by the packaging industry. A few months after the first Earth Day the Container Corporation of America commissioned the recycling symbol, a triangle made of chasing arrows, leaving the design in the public domain so that other manufacturers could adopt it as well. In 1988 the Society of Plastics Industries (SPI) developed the idea of assigning a number to each of nine grades of plastic and inserting those numbers inside the recycling logo. The symbol would identify what type of resin a plastic object contained. SPI then lobbied state legislatures to adopt this coding system in place of stricter laws such as bottle and can deposits or mandatory recycling laws. Over the next eight years the SPI, together with the American Plastics Council (APC), successfully fought recycling legislation in 32 states. Meanwhile the triangular logo on every container implied that they were recyclable, and hinted that perhaps they were even made of recycled materials. Consumers seeing the recycling symbol on a plastic container may assume that consuming the product is without environmental cost, and may even feel that consuming and discarding are environmentally responsible actions.

Menus

Restaurant menus are a device with potential for communicating with the public. Max Burger, a fast food chain in Sweden, uses menus to communicate with their customers. Max undertook a carbon footprint assessment in partnership with The Natural Step, which revealed that 70 percent of their carbon emissions were due to the production of beef (Becken and Hay 2012, 174). The cornerstone of their climate action program is to declare carbon emissions for their entire product range and to provide this information on their menus. Max recognized that without burgers it would have no customers, so it works to change consumer preferences by showing the carbon impacts of beef and by actively promoting vegetarian burgers.

Menus at the Australian-based Otarian, a vegetarian restaurant in London and New York, list the carbon footprints of each item on the menu, calculated using the standard Greenhouse Gas Protocol. Items on the menu are shown with their carbon footprints in kilograms alongside the carbon footprints of similar meat dishes. Since some customers do not know what saving a kilogram does, a useful addition would be a sign with a simple graphic explaining that a kilogram of carbon is about the amount released by driving a car a few miles (Strand 2010, D6).

In 2010 Thai Airways became the first airline to print carbon footprints of menu items served to passengers, expressed as carbon dioxide equivalent (CO_2e) per weight. This step was part of an initiative by the Thai government to boost competitiveness, lower energy consumption, and provide information to consumers to allow them to make informed choices (Becken and Hay 2012, 174).

The Carbon Café at the California Academy of Sciences was an exhibit from 2008 to 2012 that listed carbon emissions for a range of plant-based, meat-based, processed and packaged foods, although it reported emissions as points, not carbon quantities, so visitors could compare scores of various meals.

At the 2003 Third World Water Forum, instead of listing menu prices in dollars, the Water Footprint Network printed menus with prices shown in units of virtual water. Not only did the menus communicate about water use, visitors could see for themselves that vegetarian items required far less water than non-vegetarian ones (Hoekstra and Chapagain 2008, 13). At a 2016 planning meeting for New York City's Climate Museum, an artist on the museum's board created a menu which illustrated each meal's estimated carbon dioxide emissions per diner (Phaidon 2016).

Information Dashboards

A dashboard is a digital display of information that helps people monitor what is going on. By presenting information graphically and consolidating the graphics on a single screen, it provides an overview that can be assimilated quickly and that allows people to monitor a situation at a glance (Few 2013, 26). A dashboard supports the way human brains work, using chunking, preattentive processing, and hierarchical organization. Since we can only hold a few chunks of information in our working memory at one time, a dashboard is efficient because it gives us the ability to see everything we need in a single view, in contrast to a website or software application where we can lose sight of some information by scrolling or switching screens (ibid., 36).

Dashboards give us a sense of how we are doing in real time by making energy use and other impacts visible. Dashboards in hybrid automobiles encourage changes in driving behavior by giving drivers real-time mileage indicators. It is common for LEED-certified[1] buildings to contain dashboards which display real-time information about attributes such as heat, airflow, water use, and energy use. Dashboard screens in buildings give us feedback on our own use of resources; seeing how much we are using and when gives us incentive to modify our consumption of energy and water (Newman, Beatley, and Boyer 2009, 134).

Each dashboard is customized to monitor a particular collection of information. A dashboard screen can cover a large wall-mounted display or can be the size of a small tablet. These systems can be purchased from manufacturers who specialize in this technology. Probably the best way to begin learning the fundamental principles of dashboard design is to study the book *Information Dashboard Design* by Stephen Few (2013), a well-known advocate of excellence in graphical information design and dashboard design.

Note

1 Leadership in Energy and Environmental Design (LEED) is a rating system for buildings. LEED certification provides third-party verification that a building's design, construction, and operation will reduce greenhouse gas emissions, use water and energy efficiently, minimize environmental impact, promote social equity, and promote economic viability.

13

DIGITAL MEDIA

The world of digital media is evolving rapidly. Connection to the internet is nearly ubiquitous. Many people access the internet not from their desks but from mobile devices while moving around in the world. As with most aspects of the modern world, there are tradeoffs. The more we become captivated by digital screens, the less we see of our environment, the less real it can become, and the greater the risk that we will lose some connection with the living world around us. Access to personal electronic devices by people who can afford them increases the potential for social inequality. On the other hand, digital technology has vastly increased our collective learning and our understanding of the planet both at a global scale and in detailed particulars. Through microscopy, telescopes, digital imaging, and computer simulations it has given us access to things we wouldn't otherwise see, and it has greatly expanded our ability to connect with each other and form networks of communication and action.

Websites

The internet is a global, decentralized network that connects computers and computer networks around the world and allows them to communicate with each other. Any computer can communicate with any other computer as long as they are both connected to the internet. Technologies including email systems, social media, and the web all use the internet.

The World Wide Web, or web for short, is a part of the internet.[1] It is the system of websites and webpages that uses the internet to share information. You need a web browser to access the web. Webpages are identified by Uniform Resource Locators (URLs) and can be linked to other webpages by hypertext links, or hyperlinks.

Why have a website? It reaches the widest possible audience, connecting many people on many issues. People can look at your content whenever they choose, at times that are convenient for them. A website offers the potential for two-way communication. And unlike printed materials, it is easy to update; you can edit and update a website often.

However, the fact that you can edit a website regularly can result in information that is out of date or links that are broken, if you have linked to another website and it has changed or deleted its pages. If you put information on a website, you must commit to keeping it current. Think about how much time you can devote to maintaining and updating webpages, and consider hiring someone to maintain it for you. Your website is where many people will have their first contact with your program or organization, and it is important that the first impression be a good one.

When you make a website, the visitor's experience should be the driving factor, from how it looks to how easy it is to navigate. While you may want people to read your entire webpage, most of the time they will only glance at each new page, scan some of the text, and then click on the first link they find that resembles the thing they are looking for. So organization and clear structure are essential.

Website Organization

Organize pages in your website into logical groups in a folder system, as you would folders on your computer (Thomas et al. 2006, 104). Once you set up a file structure, try to avoid moving pages around. If you must move pages, use a redirect function from the old page so the visitor does not get an error message when they try to open a page that no longer exists. Although you may think of your content as files in folders, recognize that visitors may not perceive your structure as a file cabinet, but as something more like a conversation (Redish 2012, 3). Because webpages are linked to other pages by hyperlinks, visitors can read what they want, in whatever order they choose.

The way to organize website content for easy use is a structure journalists and technical writers call the inverted pyramid style. It is the same principle that guides the design of interpretive signage. Many readers skim headlines and just the first paragraph or two of articles, so the content that is essential to understanding comes first. Give the most important information at the top. This is the key message you want people to see, with a headline and a short, clear statement about your topic. Give background details, for those who are interested, at the bottom (Redish 2012, 138).

Navigation

Simple navigation is essential. Since our brains can consciously process only a few chunks of information at once, provide only what readers need at the moment. Organize the content into very small chunks, use lots of headings, and don't put too much information on one page. Distribute the information in a series of intuitive menus (Jacobson 2009, 287). This is similar to wayfinding design, where visible, concrete landmarks provide cues and directional signs disclose information progressively, providing it at the decisions points where it is needed. Wayfinding is a useful metaphor for thinking about navigation through websites (Lynch and Horton 2016, 207).

Build in links so that people can get more information where they need it. Many designers advise arranging the navigation so that people can get to the information they are looking for within three mouse clicks (Barnes 2011, 201). Other experts say that a smooth path is more important than the number of clicks, and that people will not notice they are clicking multiple times if they find the right amount of information at each click that keeps them going down the path (Redish 2012, 99).

Visitors use links to navigate between pages. Write the names in plain, descriptive language so visitors understand clearly where the links will take them. Give the links the same names as the pages they link to. Avoid names such as "click here" or "learn more," which are not meaningful and which are not useful for visitors with visual impairment (PLAIN 2011, 99). Use link colors for links only, and use a change in color to designate links which have been visited. Be sure to test all the links on your webpages to ensure they work correctly.

The navigation system must allow visitors to get from any page to any other page. Provide a navigation menu at the bottom or side of every webpage, in the same location on every page. Locate the primary navigation menus along the left side. Use labels that are descriptive. Provide a simple section with answers to frequently asked questions, usually labeled "FAQs," and a place to go for more detailed inquiries (ISO 2006, 12). Make contact information easy to find and in the same location on every page. And always provide a way to link back to the homepage with a single click.

For longer webpages with multiple sections, provide a short, clickable list of sections at the top of the page. These sections are known as anchors, and they provide quick access to information. They also allow the visitor a preview of the content so they can decide whether another page will contain the information they want (Usability.gov 2017, 7).

For websites with a lot of content organized hierarchically, you can include a secondary navigation tool known as breadcrumb navigation. This is an extra feature that lets visitors keep track of their locations. It appears as small and simple text links arranged horizontally at the top of the page, easy to find but not too prominent. Links to pages are separated by the "greater than" symbol (>), indicating the level of each page relative to the links beside it (Usability.gov 2017, 7).

The homepage is usually the first page a visitor will see and is typically the most important page on your website (Usability.gov 2017, 5). It introduces your project or organization and lets visitors get a sense of what your website is about. The homepage is the starting point for exploring your site and should show all the major options, including links to sub-pages. Focus on what is special or unique about your site or organization.

Website Layout and Design

Visual design, throughout the website but especially on the homepage, is the visitor's first indicator of your website's quality. If they find its initial appearance unattractive, they may leave and never see the content inside (Redish 2012, 45). Even if a site has high-quality content, visitors may decide it lacks credibility based on aesthetic first impressions alone and may go elsewhere to find the information they seek (Fogg et al. 2003).

Many of the design principles used for interpretive signage and graphic design also apply to website design (Barnes 2011, 196). Create a visual hierarchy using size, contrast, headings and subheadings. Use white space as an active design element to separate graphic elements. White space is especially important for visitors who are scanning and skimming webpages (Redish 2012, 56).

Limit the colors to two or three harmonious hues. Using too many colors gives a website an amateur, homemade look (Thomas et al. 2006, 103). So does a patterned background, which makes text hard to read (Usability.gov 2017, 11). Keep the background simple and clear, and maintain a high degree of contrast throughout (Redish 2012, 52).

Place the information you want people to focus on where they are most likely to see it: in the top third of the screen and in the middle horizontally. People are less likely to look at the screen's edges, so avoid putting anything important there (Weinschenk 2011, 14). Lay out each webpage so that people can use their normal reading pattern and won't have to bounce back and forth to different parts of the screen.

As with signage for wayfinding systems, the pages in your website should share common visual features including typography, color, images, backgrounds, layout, and navigation. Develop a visual theme and use a consistent page layout. Consistent theme and page layout reduce the effort of browsing your website because visitors become familiar with where to look. It also lets visitors recognize pages as related to each other and recognize that they have reached your site if they enter it from another page other than the homepage (Jacobson 2009, 287). Create consistent patterns of spatial composition. Align webpage elements on a grid, as in other graphic design layouts (Redish 2012, 54). If your organization has a logo, place that in a consistent location on every page.

Design pages so that they look the same on all web browsers on all types of devices. Test them to confirm that they work correctly on all browsers, operating systems, and devices.

Images

Use images to facilitate understanding. Choose images that convey information and give some benefit to visitors; avoid using images simply because they are artistic (Usability.gov 2017, 14). Label images which are clickable. Remember that some visitors have visual impairment, and include descriptive text alternatives with each image for blind and low-vision users. The World Wide Web Consortium's Web Accessibility Initiative provides extensive information, design guidelines, and tutorials (W3C 2017).

Multimedia

Use multimedia elements to support understanding. Choose them carefully and avoid inserting gadgets which are simply distractions. Animations, video, and audio can add value to a website, but only when they help to convey information. Allow animations to be user-controlled so that visitors can pause, stop, or replay them (Usability.gov 2017, 14).

Keep user software requirements to a minimum (ISO 2006, 12). Not all devices have the same plug-ins or animation technology. If you use some of these applications, provide instructions about how visitors who cannot access the feature can get the application they are missing.

Text

People use text on webpages differently than text in print. Often they do not read entire pages, but instead scan them. Research shows that on average, visitors read 18 percent of what is on one webpage (PLAIN 2011, 90). As the number of words on a webpage goes up, the percentage of the page a visitor reads goes down. People typically scan a page in an F pattern, focusing on the top left of a page, headings, and the first few words of a line. What this means is that you should keep the key message at the top of the webpage, break text into short chunks, and use headings to help visitors navigate.

When you write sentences and paragraphs for the web, use plain language, avoid jargon, use active voice, and keep sentences short. Break material into visible chunks; people often stop reading if they have to scroll through long passages of text. Lists and tables are easier to scan than paragraphs, so use them when you can. Place the most important items at the top of a list, since research shows that readers look at the first three items in a list before moving on, and tend to stop scanning a list when they come upon something relevant (Usability.gov 2017, 12). Because a bullet list is easier to read, it attracts attention and is a good way to highlight key facts (PLAIN 2011, 95). Use bulleted lists of no more than ten for related items or options, use numbered lists for instructions, and introduce each list with a heading (Redish 2012, 227). Try to start each line of a list with the same pattern syntactically; for example, start every line with a noun, or start every line with an imperative verb. Use tables to compare numbers or attributes.

Use black text on plain, light-colored backgrounds. Research has shown that on webpages with visitors who are scanning for information, people read black text on a white background up to 32 percent faster than white text on a black background (Usability.gov 2017, 11). Use familiar, sans serif typefaces with at least 12-point fonts and avoid using all capitals, which are hard to read

(Redish 2012, 61). Use a medium line length with left justification and ragged right, which gives the reader a predictable starting point for each line; do not center text, which is harder to read (ibid., 57).

Searches

Research shows that about half of visitors prefer to navigate through menus to find links to information, while the other half prefer to go directly to a search feature (Lynch and Horton 2016, 207). All visitors use both browsing and searching at some time, so it is important that you provide a functional search engine on your website. Searches entered here should be able to search the entire website and should recognize upper- and lowercase words as equivalent. Place important keywords within the content of webpages. Note that your preferred keywords may not match the ones which occur to visitors. You may need to do some user research to determine which keywords visitors are likely to use. If visitors try one or two searches and do not get usable results, they may give up and leave your website.

Search Engine Optimization

An attractive, informative website is of no use if no one can find it. So you will want to improve search engine optimization (SEO), which aims to have your website appear higher in a list of search results. Search engines such as Google use algorithms which incorporate a number of factors to rank webpages. Your goal with SEO is to make your site among the most relevant to a specific search query. Research shows that most users only look at the top 30 references from a search engine (Usability.gov 2017, 1). Search engine algorithms change frequently; check with each major search engine and in major blogs which discuss SEO to learn what the latest requirements are (Redish 2012, 7).

Websites which are linked from other sites get higher rankings in search-engine algorithms. If your website is credible, well designed, and has useful, regularly updated content, other sites are more likely to link to it (Jacobson 2009, 289). Regardless how search-engine algorithms change, the key to good search-engine ranking is to have high-quality content (Redish 2012, 7). Consider other ways to generate links, such as submitting your website to online directories, writing guest posts for other blogs, and sharing your website content on social media sites (Hyder 2016, 49).

Design the website with descriptive titles. Use title words that match keywords used by visitors to your site. Use real text in titles and headings, rather than graphic titles (Jacobson 2009, 289). Just making a title in a larger or bolder font does not attract search engines; you must code these words correctly. When you use Hypertext Markup Language, or HTML, you must code the title words using the <H1> tag (Redish 2012, 158). Search engine algorithms also consider your site's navigation structure, as well as things like hidden files or broken links (Hyder 2016, 40).

The key strategy is to identify keywords that people are likely to use when they do searches, and then to use those keywords in your website, particularly in the title. Use a search engine to help find them. When you do a search, the search engine will suggest additional keywords you may have missed, suggesting them based on keywords which have been entered by other users. At the bottom of a search engine's webpage, you will see a list of other keywords it suggests as related to your search term. These are also based on searches which have been done by other users. Save these keyword lists; you might use some of them when choosing titles and headings, and you can use them for topic ideas for new website content or social media posts.

Planning a Website

Creating a website requires the same planning process as other communication media. Before you do any designing, decide what the goals of your website are, and write them down (Jacobson 2009, 287). Identify the potential audience, develop the content, and organize it into logical groups (Barnes 2011, 196). Decide what kind of content will appear on each type of page (Redish 2012, 46). Draw a flow chart to map out how the pages will link to each other (Thomas et al. 2006, 100). Create a visual hierarchy so that the reader focuses on the elements of your webpage that are the more important (Barnes 2011, 196). Decide how many levels of headings typical pages will need, where to locate links, and what kinds of images and other non-text items to include with the text. Integrate content and design from the beginning of the planning process (Redish 2012, 46).

After you have created your website, the next stage is review and feedback. Design is an iterative process. Read through the content and revise it. Check spelling, grammar, and facts. Ask other people to review the content and the design, and think carefully about their comments. Ask them to tell you what they think your key message is (Redish 2012, 289).

In addition to qualitative evaluation, you can consider systematic usability testing in which you observe and take notes while participants try to complete typical tasks on your website. In a formal usability test you can learn whether participants are able to complete tasks successfully, what obstacles they encounter, how satisfied they are with your website, and what changes you should make to improve user experiences (Usability.gov 2017, 18).

Video

Video is a recording of moving visual images. It is easier to understand the context of an idea when you see moving images. When you look at a still photo, you can interpret it multiple ways. When you look at a video, it begins to approximate real life more closely, and it is easier to imagine yourself in the scene.

Some of the explanation for this comes from the class of nerve cells in the premotor cortex called mirror neurons, which fire not only when we perform an action, but when we watch someone else perform the action. Neurons in the primary motor cortex send signals that make our bodies move; neurons in the premotor cortex make plans to move. And when we see others move, mirror neurons in the premotor cortex allow us to enjoy a vicarious experience, essentially running simulations of their actions using a visualization of our own bodies (Ramachandran 2012, 22). By triggering mirror neurons, videos are a powerful way to help people learn and to influence behavior. For example, if you want to encourage people to use public transportation, show a video of other people using public transportation (Weinschenk 2011, 160).

Videos with captions and simple transitions can be created with relatively simple software. Multimedia software for creating animations or interactive elements does take time and energy to master, but is worth the effort if you plan to work with animations or interactive websites.

Films capture humans interacting with each other, and so they reinforce social and cultural elements (Barnes 2011, 167). Films capture wildlife, too, in ways that are profoundly valuable for our understanding of them. At the same time, they provide unreal experience. For one thing, we are separated from sensory qualities of temperature, smell, and touch. The camera zooms in closely on a particular creature, and we become separated from the larger system around it and its constant change. All cameras present subjective views by what they select and what they leave out. Yet because we see creatures moving about in their habitats, we think that we are impartial observers. The camera may show us a once-in-a-lifetime event, and we may interpret an exceptionally rare moment as normal and everyday. We may even come to believe that it is common for wild animals to return our gaze (Corbett 2006, 129).

The Academy Award-winning film documentary *An Inconvenient Truth* by Al Gore began with a slideshow that Gore presented as he traveled around the world. Often presentations filled with graphs and numbers are perceived to be uninteresting. But with the addition of video, large graphs, startling photographs of disappearing glaciers, and animations which showed what a 20-foot rise in sea level would mean in four densely populated areas, together with a narrative thread that allowed audiences to connect emotionally with the speaker as a real person, the resulting film was so compelling that it began to shift public opinion about climate change (Few 2012, xvii).

Video news releases (VNR) are subsidized information products created by government agencies and corporations. Because they are free, professionally produced videos, they greatly reduce the cost of producing television newscasts. These are videos sent free of charge to television stations and are typically aired without attribution or identification of sources. They can be produced as complete audio-video packages or they can be video footage only, so that a local station can add its own narration by reading from a script supplied with the VNR, making it nearly impossible to detect that the video was produced elsewhere (Corbett 2006, 271).

Multimedia

Multimedia combines multiple types of media, including still images, text, video, audio, and animation. Multimedia videos combine sound, vision, and movement. With multimedia, our brains receive messages through two channels, auditory and visual, so that the whole message is reinforced, and there is greater potential for understanding because the same idea has come to us through different ways (Morgan and Welton 1992, 26).

Visual moving images with sound on television, and its descendent forms on internet media, have captured viewers' attention, so that the majority of people receive their news and information from television or online. Herbert Zettl is the acknowledged pioneer of the field of media aesthetics and video production. Zettl developed a body of theory now known as applied media aesthetics which deals with the visual and auditory techniques of these media (Barnes 2011, 176). Zettl identified five fundamental elements of film, television and now, other digital media: light and color, two-dimensional (2-D) space, three-dimensional (3-D) space, time and motion, and sound (Zettl 1998, 4).

Various tools allow you to produce your own web video. Cameras in smartphones are good for shooting in natural daylight, as are point-and-shoot cameras and action cameras like GoPro; for shooting in artificial light, a traditional video camera or a digital single-lens reflex (DSLR) camera are better. If you cannot shoot in natural daylight, you need softbox lights made for recording video indoors, which diffuse light with fabric surrounding the light source. Microphones built into cameras do not give you good audio quality, so you should use an external microphone to record sound. Video editing software such as Adobe Premier or Sony Vegas allows you to edit your video recording (Hyder 2016, 175–180).

YouTube is a video-sharing website that stores billions of videos on a vast array of topics. People find your videos by doing searches, so you should add keywords that people are likely to search for. When you become a YouTube member, YouTube assigns you a channel. Your channel is like your home page on a website. Anyone can view videos on YouTube without having a channel, but you need a channel in order to upload videos. People can subscribe to channels they are interested in so that they are notified when new videos are posted. The number of subscribers to a channel determines its rank in search results (ibid., 181).

People like to get online information in a variety of formats. Blogs, articles, and reports give them material in written form, podcasts give them audio formats, and video gives them visual formats. If you offer content in all three formats, you can accommodate and appeal to people with various preferences and learning styles (ibid., 23).

Interactive Digital Media

Interactive media let audiences become participants in website graphics and interpretive exhibits. They are not just static images or animations we look at as passive observers. They respond to our actions, providing information that adapts to what we want to see and allowing us to display elements different ways in different contexts (Broda-Bahm 2012a). They allow us to select items of interest and to drill down and find more data about whatever seems important to us (Ware 2013, 345).

Unlike traditional, static graphics, interactive graphics are dynamic. Traditional graphics display everything at once; interactive graphics build based on context as we work with them. One example where interactive media are effective is a timeline. It could be a historic timeline in an interpretive exhibit, or it could be a timeline of events in a complex courtroom trial. The basic milestones can be shown in an overview. Then each milestone or time period can be expanded to provide greater detail (Broda-Bahm 2012a).

Two basic actions performed with interactive software are hovering and clicking. Hovering reveals extra information about an object when the cursor passes over it. Clicking implements a choice and often brings up menus of additional choices. Research at the Field Museum in Chicago shows that visitors to even a large exhibit will spend an average of only 20 to 30 minutes engaging with it. That means that visitors do not have time to invest in learning to play an interactive game. The game must be immediately and intuitively understandable (Suellentrop 2014).

These tools appeal in particular to digital natives[2] and to people who enjoy gaming. They can embody multiple modes with engagement techniques that appeal to different learning styles and ranges of expertise (Chicone and Kissel 2013, 78). Just as people build cognitive maps using landmarks and paths when they explore a new physical place, something similar happens as people explore data spaces (Ware 2013, 345).

At their most basic, interactive displays are electronic versions of museum exhibits where the exhibit asks a question and the visitor tries to answer, then checks to see if they were correct. Taken a step further, audiences can develop their own simulations. For example, citizens involved with community planning can explore what their community would look like and how systems would work under various planning and development scenarios.

At the Science Museum of the National Academy of Sciences, a 2011 exhibition titled "Earth Lab: Degrees of Change" let visitors experiment with their own what-if scenarios. The exhibit introduced the subject from a human perspective, using digital images to tell the story of vulnerable communities and the impacts they face in response to a warming planet. An interactive animation let visitors explore how software climate models work. The heart of the exhibit was a Mitigation Simulator, a simulation game that put visitors in the role of policymakers confronting the reality of climate change. Visitors had to establish priorities and adjust various aspects of mitigation strategies. Feedback showed them how effective each effort was, flagged conflicts between their priorities and their mitigation strategies, and suggested how to troubleshoot each issue. Each visitor could work on their own scenario, and could combine their results into a large-scale visualization. Evaluation showed that visitors spent much more time at the Mitigation Simulators than had been expected. Visitors discovered that there are many ways to approach solving the complex problem of climate change. The final section answered the question, "Now what?", and left visitors with positive, active takeaways (Second Story Interactive Studios 2012).

In the best interactive programs, every data object on the screen is capable of displaying additional information when we choose it and of disappearing when it is not needed. The purpose of interactive media is to help with the thinking process (Ware 2013, 345). Having fun leads to engagement, and engagement is a prerequisite for learning (Suellentrop 2014). These media may be entertaining, but by their nature and their ability to engage us, the real purpose is not entertainment but to provoke us to think our own thoughts and enrich the quality of our thinking.

As we know from studies in interpretive design, people are motivated by autonomy. The ancient part of the human brain which is responsible for survival likes to feel that it is in control (Weinschenk 2011, 142). People want choices about what and how much they do, and they want to do things themselves. They want to take control of their own learning and to use this control to find information that is personally relevant for them. They will spend more time, will be more engaged, and will learn more when they can interact with a program that allows them to make their own choices (Moscardo et al. 2007, 67).

It is important to let content drive the choice of medium and the design. This is true of all design and planning. But in the field of interactive media, fascination with computer graphics and the dynamic possibilities of the software can cause us to let the medium lead the way. Planning should always follow the same pattern, from general to specific, from high-level goals to implementation details: Define goals and develop a theme, select an appropriate medium to communicate those goals, then develop objectives, strategies, and detailed tactics.

Simulations

Simulations are often used in community planning. The goal of a simulation is to produce a high level of realism so that viewers can experience a simulated place in much the same way they would a real place. Simulations help lay people visualize potential changes and select among choices, translating the abstractions of scenarios, policies, and principles into 3-D models that represent actual places that would result from their implementation (Kwartler and Longo 2008, 77). Often it is not until participants see illustrations of better options that they realize the problems with conventional development patterns (Farr 2008, 80). In fact, 3-D digital simulations often attract more participants simply because they are fascinating, and they make the planning process more transparent for people who are not trained to interpret planning maps.

In visual preference surveys or community participation workshops, photographs or rendered images can be paired side by side. In the most useful pairs, a few key landmarks provide the same anchors in both images so that viewers recognize that these are options for the same spot. Captions communicate additional detail and context (Farr 2008, 69). For example, citizens can see a conventional development alongside a mixed-use, walkable neighborhood. How would a streetcar change our town's automobile-dependent main thoroughfare? What would a multiway boulevard mean for our downtown? What are the differences between a drivable suburb and a walkable neighborhood? How does a mixed-use neighborhood differ from a proposed drive-to, big-box development?

Three-dimensional simulations are used for a process called visual impact analysis. When agencies propose large-scale solar or wind turbine installations, they are sometimes met with opposition from residents concerned about visual impacts. Detailed simulations let people see how visible these elements will be from various viewing directions and distances, or choose between location options (Sullivan and Meyer 2014, 46). Simulations can be used to consider whether one big or many small installations would be a better choice.

Digital simulations can be difficult and expensive to create, and can result in large file sizes. File size increases as the level of detail increases. So planners preparing visualization tools keep two criteria in mind: How much do viewers need to know? And how close is good enough (Kwartler and Longo 2008, 19)? Rendering time can be made faster by minimizing the complexity of the objects modeled and by using digital photographs as background images rather than modeling an expanse of landscape (ibid., 56). Rendering a single building is manageable; rendering an entire city in detail would be prohibitive in terms of computer resources.

Types of Simulation

You will need to make some decisions about what to include before you begin to create a simulation or hire someone to create one. Your visualization specialist can advise you about the relative merits and tradeoffs of software approaches currently available to you.

A physical scale model of a project simulates a site, allowing the viewer to interact with it directly and to view it from various directions. People are fascinated by scale models. However, they are not able to simulate the experience of moving through the space at eye level in the same way a computer-generated model can.

A traditional approach uses the photo simulation or photomontage. Planners begin with digital images of a site, such as a city street, then use Photoshop or other image-editing software to add features such as trees, bicycle lanes, light rail, and mixed-use building fronts to help people see what changes would mean for the physical environment. Planners sometimes use this method to show incremental change, adding one feature at a time in a series of images (Snyder 2002, 99).

Image-editing applications such as Photoshop produce visual data as 2-D raster images. They can be less expensive to create. They cannot be dimensioned or queried.

Computer-aided design (CAD) applications produce 3-D, volumetric models. The complexity of 3-D models can range from simplified geometric shapes to very detailed.

Revit and other building information modeling (BIM) programs combine 3-D volumes with detailed data about every object in the model, such as cost, material source, and embodied energy. BIM is useful in green building design; it can evaluate carbon footprint, life-cycle cost, solar heat gain, passive cooling, and daylighting potential, and can analyze microclimate effects of wind, sun, and humidity in specific urban environments.

Geographic information system (GIS) programs such as ArcGIS integrate the geospatial information of maps with layers of data connected to those maps, allowing multiple types of spatial analysis. GIS stores information on layers, with each layer representing a particular theme such as demographics, soil type, or land use. It organizes these layers of information into visualizations using 2-D maps and 3-D models, providing insights into patterns and relationships. For example, a GIS program can analyze a region's progress toward Sustainable Development Goals, measure a community's water insecurity, evaluate habitat or biodiversity loss, simulate changes to a shoreline caused by rising sea level, or map climate resilience related to vulnerable communities and social equity.

BIM and GIS are typically cloud-based, so that multiple members of a team can access the model and database at the same time. Tradeoffs are high cost and a steep learning curve.

You can acquire digital information from dimensioned drawings and maps; from CAD and GIS models; or by using 3-D scanning from photography, LIDAR (Light Detection and Ranging), and other imaging technologies (Barth 2017, 56). Imagery from satellites reveals patterns and relationships that may not be visible from lower elevations, and they have played a role in our understanding of cities as complex ecological systems instead of simply assemblies of buildings (Kullman 2017, 132). Drone-based photography with high-definition cameras flying at altitudes near the surface increase the resolution of these images dramatically. Photogrammetry software creates point-cloud data from 360-degree panoramic photographs captured by drones, and is an easily accessible technology (Barth 2017, 57).

LIDAR, the most common type of 3-D scanning, is a technology for acquiring 3-D data from the air, using airplanes, helicopters, or drones, or from tripod-mounted laser scanners. Light from a pulsed laser measures ranges, or distances, from the scanner to the surface (US NOAA). While photography results in 2-D images, LIDAR generates 3-D information in what is known as a point cloud, consisting of millions or even billions of points, each of which contains data about its x, y, and z location. These scans are much more precise when you zoom in than are satellite images such as those from Google Earth. The size of data sets can be enormous. Point-cloud data can be uploaded into BIM and GIS programs. Point clouds from multiple viewing locations can be stitched together in software such as 3ds Max, a professional computer graphics program used for making models, computer games, and animation, or Agisoft PhotoScan, a program used for making measurements from digital images and for generating spatial data for GIS.

Anything that can be 3-D scanned can be 3-D printed (Barth 2017, 56). Planners sometimes use LIDAR data with 3-D printers to print perfectly scaled physical models of their cities.

Many scenes call for different conditions in the foreground, middle ground, and background (Ervin and Hasbrouck 2001, 96). If you want to simulate an urban scene, modeling all of the terrain at the same level of detail can result in enormous file sizes that can crash a computer. You may decide to make some tradeoffs. In a 3-D scanned point cloud, that can mean deleting three out of four points, which still retains adequate resolution; or it can mean deleting elements in either the distance or the foreground that are not needed, which results in the black backgrounds often associated with 3-D scanning (Barth 2017, 61).

Animations

Animations, graphics which produce the appearance of movement, show how things change over time or during a process, and they show things that we could not otherwise easily see.

Animations are fascinating to viewers. Early in the history of our species, humans evolved to be keenly aware of motion around them. Motion could mean an animal that might eat us, or it could be something we could eat (Barnes 2011, 198).

Humans are very sensitive to patterns in motion (Ware 2013, 229). We are especially sensitive to motion that is biological in origin. In fact, a series of studies showed that, when watching a pattern of moving dots produced by attaching lights to limb joints of actors in a black room, viewers identified the random dots as human motion as soon as they began moving, and could even identify the genders and the tasks being performed. In earlier studies, viewers watching animated triangles and circles attributed human characteristics to them, including motivation and emotion. The shapes were simple, implying that it was the patterns of motion, not the forms, that conveyed meaning. In studies within cultures on three continents, viewers ascribed the same motivations and emotions to moving shapes, suggesting that these reactions are probably universal and not just cultural (Ware 2013, 235). The fact that shapes do not have to be detailed or complex to be perceived as living means that even simplified animation techniques can be useful in presentations.

Animation can represent concepts in a way that is not possible with static diagrams. On the other hand, a large number of studies comparing learning outcomes in tests comparing static and animated graphics have shown that moving images are not better than still images (Ware 2013, 337). In fact, in multiple settings which tested learning about a wide range of topics including earth system processes, anatomy, physiology, geometry, mechanical systems, pedagogy design, and learning theory, learners performed as well or better with static images than they did with animations. Animation did not show an advantage over static graphics when the same information and degree of interactivity were used (Tversky, Betrancourt, and Morrison 2002, 247). One series of experiments found that static versions resulted in better retention of information and deeper understanding of the content than did animated versions (Mayer et al. 2005, 256).

For people willing to experiment, there are a range of animation programs available, from free, simple cartooning applications to expensive rendering software such as Maya and 3ds Max which have steep learning curves but produce realistic, movie-grade animations. If you want to create your own animation, the first step is to plan it by making a storyboard, which is a series of sketches of what you think the scenes will be (Ritter 2004, 242). A storyboard can use sketches of key points of view in their proper sequence. The sketches don't have to be artistic; they can be crudely drawn, with stick figures, blobs, and simple shapes to record the essence of each idea. Often, notes are written under the storyboard frames, with details about sound or details about motion indicated by large arrows (Zettl 1998, 184). Storyboard software is available to make the process easier. Some techniques used by movie directors and cinematographers are useful in animation, such as framing of camera shots, moving the viewpoints to draw attention to a series of features and to create a narrative flow, using anchors as reference landmarks in sequential frames of view, and providing an overview to a scene before a detailed view of something (Ware 2013, 340). Animation in film is a skilled art, so it is important to hire an experienced professional to design and implement an animation.

Use animations only when you have a clear purpose. When visual effects are used simply to jazz up a website they can be distracting and more annoying than helpful (Barnes 2011, 199). Elegance and simplicity are virtues in websites as they are in any other graphic design (Ware 2013, 236).

Social Media

Social media consists of platforms where people can connect and communicate (Hyder 2016, 51). We know that ideas and behaviors spread through person-to-person contact in a process known as social diffusion, and that social contacts are effective in spreading innovation and influencing sustainable behavior (Robertson 2017, 331). Social media are platforms that facilitate the spread of ideas online and magnify their impact through sheer numbers.

The original version of the web provided a one-way flow of information and is sometimes called Web 1.0. What we call Web 2.0 is the next stage of development: it is a conversation, rather than a monologue (Hyder 2016, 52). It is about sharing and is characterized by user-generated content (Lester 2011, 389). Examples of Web 2.0, or social media, include platforms such as Facebook, Twitter, Wikipedia, and YouTube.

In addition to these large-scale platforms, organizations sometimes create their own social media tools focused on specific goals. For example, New York

City created a site called "Change by Us NYC" to enable residents to post ideas for greening New York's neighborhoods, to find and connect to non-profit resources, to start their own projects to make the city greener, and to apply for neighborhood mini-grants (Ehmann et al. 2012, 188).

Ideas that spread rapidly via social media are sometimes known as memes. Genes and ideas share a similarity in that both reproduce (Flannery 2010, 18). Memes are bits of information that sometimes are replicated widely on social media. Technically, memes are stories, skills, and ways of doing things that we copy from person to person by imitation (Blackmore 2000, 53). Their replication is sometimes compared to the replication of genetic material. This ability for widespread imitation is a feature of the human species. Ideas are more likely to spread as memes when they are short, provocative, and repeatable (Duarte 2010, 152). A meme in audio format is sometimes known as a sound bite.

Twitter is a social networking site that accommodates ideas which are short, provocative, and repeatable. Originally conceived as a way to stay in touch with acquaintances, the platform is now seen as a good way to find and network with peers and to broadcast ideas or questions and answers (Kahle and Gurel-Atay, 2013, 225). Users can send messages directly to an individual using the convention of @twittername, or they can broadcast messages to larger numbers of people who are interested in a particular topic using a keyword or tag by placing a # or hash in front of a keyword (Kovacevic 2015, 14). Hashtags are also useful for keeping relevant tweets organized (Hyder 2016, 103). Tweeters[3] can use more than one hashtag in a single tweet to provide links between various issues or ideas. Tweeting is a useful tool for filtering and focusing on information of interest in a noisy world (Baron 2010, 74). As with other forms of communication, people will notice tweets more readily when they contain an image (Kovacevic 2015, 47).

A blog is a website where you share information or ideas on a regular basis, usually around a particular theme. Each entry is called a post, and entries you have written are displayed in reverse chronological order, with the most recent post appearing first. Originally, this kind of site was a web log in which someone would keep a chronological journal. The phrase "web log" was later shortened to "blog." If you use keywords in your blog and update it regularly so that it has fresh content, search engines will be more likely to display it in search results. A blog is considered a kind of social media because readers are able to comment and have discussions with other readers as well as with the author.

Maintaining a blog takes time. For it to be effective, you need to stick to a schedule and make regular posts. You need quantity. You also need quality: the content must be clear, straightforward, and useful for readers (Jacobson 2009, 296). A blog with an image is more likely to be noticed and read (Hyder 2016, 28). In addition to writing blog posts yourself, you can invite guest writers or can curate content from other sites. Use standard software such as WordPress so that your blog has the kind of appearance readers expect.

A wiki is a website that allows collaborative editing by multiple users. The name comes from the Hawaiian phrase *wiki-wiki,* meaning "quick" (Lannon and

Gurak 2017, 606). Although there is potential for inaccuracy because of multiple contributors, a well-managed wiki can become a collaborative space with a rich knowledge base with contributions by numerous content experts. Each wiki maintains a history with copies of the original and subsequent entries along with a record of what changes were made, when, and by whom.

Write and post for your audience. Think about why they come to your sites and what they are trying to do or learn. When people send you an email or post a question, what do they ask? Talk to people about what they want. Within your website, analyze its metrics to see which pages are visited the most, where visitors spend the most time, and which search terms are used most often (PLAIN 2011, 93).

Test your digital media for comprehensibility and usability. Use an iterative approach: test, revise, and re-test. Your testing can use observation, interviews, or questionnaires. Ask people to paraphrase a document or webpage, or to tell you what they think it means. Take notes, and do not correct them; you are trying to find places where people might misunderstand your message (PLAIN 2011, 102).

Give visitors incentives to stay connected. For example, offer a free white paper, a report, or a recorded webinar when they give you their email address (Hyder 2016, 22).

Social media is a robust way both to communicate and to build communities online. Encourage connections by making your content social and easy to share. For example, provide a Facebook "Like" button and a Twitter button on each page of your website, blog, or other site. Use multiple platforms. You can post intriguing short items on places like Facebook and Twitter; post intriguing longer content on blogs, online newsletters, and YouTube videos; and place high-quality, key content on your website. Use multiple types of media as well: video, audio, presentations, words, images, and others.

Make sure that everything you post online is valuable, accurate, and high quality. Use succinct, plain language. Use a consistent profile picture and background across platforms so that people begin to recognize you. Include URLs or hyperlinks to connect blog and Twitter posts to your website. Be cordial and positive, and ignore online bullies or trolls. Find like-minded people and communities you can interact with and learn from. Use social media to position yourself as a knowledgeable person within your field, and use it as an opportunity to gather knowledge about your field and beyond it.

Notes

1 Earlier in their history the words "web" and "internet" were capitalized, but modern style guides now agree that they are written in lowercase.
2 A digital native is a person who was born or grew up during the age of digital technology and so who has used digital technology from an early age.
3 A person sending a Twitter message is called a tweeter. The message being sent is called a tweet. Hashtag is a Twitter convention that means to tag a subject by placing a # symbol in front of a word, which turns the word into a searchable link. Anyone can create a hashtag.

14

MEETINGS

How to Have a Good Meeting

One way of communicating with other people is through meetings, which are structured and more formalized than conversations. A meeting is more than a single event; it is part of a system. Thus, preparation before the meeting and follow-up after the meeting are as important as work done during the meeting itself.

Meetings are used for the kind of work which requires people to interact; they should not be held just for the sake of meeting. Before planning a meeting, the first step is to define the objectives of the meeting and determine what the meeting is intended to achieve. If it is not possible to state the objectives of the meeting in a single sentence, you probably do not need a meeting. Don't hold a meeting just for the sake of meeting; if a meeting is not needed, cancel it.

Agenda

The most important meeting management tool is an agenda. "Agenda" is a Latin word which means literally "the things to be done." An agenda is a list of meeting topics. The topics are developed by first defining the goals for the meeting. If an overall project goal is large, then it should be divided into a series of smaller meeting goals. The group can make progress incrementally by achieving two or three of these meeting goals each time they come together. The agenda should be sent to participants several days in advance, and they should be invited to suggest additions or refinements.

A good agenda lists topics in a logical order, spelling out what will be discussed, the goal for each discussion, who will be presenting or discussing, and the time allotted for each. Three to six agenda items is a manageable number. It is helpful to have an agenda begin with a brief topic to bring people together, such as a check-in or an overview.

Agenda items should be framed in positive terms and presented as opportunities rather than as problems. Agenda items which are stated in negative terms can imply that a solution may not exist and so can impact a group's ability to solve problems effectively. For example, if a group is considering a climate action plan, rather than asking, "Will we be able to meet our greenhouse gas emissions goal?" the group might instead ask, "What can we do to meet this goal?"

The agenda allows members to work in a logical order. For each agenda item, work in this order: present facts, discuss, and decide. Finish one topic before going on to the next; don't jump back and forth between topics. The meeting should be brought to a close (1) when all the agenda items have been covered, (2) when the group has gone as far as it can without gathering additional information, whether or not all of the scheduled time has been used, or (3) when the time scheduled for the meeting has elapsed. Meetings should not last beyond their scheduled time unless everyone agrees to continue. A meeting should end on a positive note, which could include a summary of what was accomplished and a summary of the next steps.

Minutes

Minutes are a written record of a meeting. They serve as the group's memory, mapping its progress and making it possible to build on previous ideas and decisions. Minutes minimize confusion because everyone has the same set of notes.

In most meetings, one person is designated as the recorder at the beginning of the meeting. While in some groups a paid staff member serves as recorder, in other groups members take turns serving as recorder. Some leaders use strategies such as designating the fourth person to arrive at the meeting space as the recorder as a way of encouraging participants to arrive early. The recorder can use the agenda to make notes, recording decisions made or actions agreed next to each agenda item; they can then use these notes to compile the minutes.

The minutes summarize what was discussed, record what was decided, and list action items together with who agreed to take action, what they agreed to do, and by when. The format of the minutes is not important as long as they record actions taken, decisions made, and responsibility for actions following the meeting. Recorders should provide an objective report of what happened and should avoid inserting subjective judgments, such as "good idea" or "heated debate." Most minutes do not require the level of detail used for legal proceedings; it is not necessary to record the exact words of a discussion or the name of the person raising an issue. On the other hand, when the group is agreeing to specific language, then recording the precise wording is essential. The minutes should be sent to participants within several days, while the meeting process is still fresh in people's minds, so that they can spot any corrections or clarifications that might be needed. In some meetings, one item on the agenda is the approval of the minutes from the previous meeting.

Meeting Management

The person who organizes or chairs a meeting can be called a leader, a chair, or a convener (also spelled convenor). The leader manages the meeting process, which includes scheduling the meeting, locating a room, notifying participants, preparing the agenda, managing the meeting itself, and following up on action items after the meeting. Some groups elect to rotate the task of leading meetings.

In some situations, particularly those with complex or controversial issues to address, the group may use a facilitator in addition to the leader. A facilitator is a neutral third party, typically an individual trained in effective group facilitation methods, whose task is to guide the group process. While the leader deals with the content of the meeting, the facilitator deals with the process. A facilitator is particularly helpful at times of transformation and change, and can help a group use conflict constructively in order to maximize its collective wisdom and to produce positive outcomes with everyone's participation.

Some meeting leaders ask one person to volunteer as a timekeeper, particularly in large or complex meetings. The timekeeper watches the agenda, letting the leader know when half the time has elapsed for each agenda item and again when 2 minutes remain.

Managing a meeting includes ensuring that the group adheres to an agenda. It is important not to hold conversations about topics which are not on the agenda, and not to have side conversations. Some conveners set aside one text document or one flipchart sheet, label it the "Parking Lot," and post it off to the side of the room. Ideas which come up and which are not on the agenda can be recorded here, so that they are not forgotten and can be dealt with at a later time, but do not interrupt the main agenda topics of the meeting.

Visual Notes and Graphic Facilitation

Many meeting leaders write on flipcharts, which are large pads of paper either supported on an easel or made of self-sticking sheets which can be peeled off and stuck to walls, to help participants view and discuss the ideas generated as they work. Some meetings use equivalent electronic versions, which avoid the use of paper and are more universally accessible for people of all abilities. These tools extend the group's working short-term memory, freeing members to keep thinking and to participate more fully. For an example of how external tools improve cognition, think about multiplying numbers together without a calculator. Multiplication itself is not difficult; what is difficult is holding the partial results in memory until you can use them. Using pencil and paper for this task extends your working memory by holding the partial results outside your mind (Card et al. 1999, 2).

Graphic recording is a method of laying out an agenda or capturing a group's ideas in a nonlinear format using words, pictures, symbols, and color on flipcharts, wall-hung paper several feet long, or other media. The recorder captures the essence of ideas graphically as they are being expressed. People feel validated as their contributions are immediately captured on the chart and connected to the whole, which builds trust and increases participation. Being able to see ideas emerge makes it easier for people to build on each other's ideas, and participants are able to build a shared understanding relatively quickly. The resulting chart reflects the whole discussion, serves as an initial summary, and mirrors not only the content but the process the group went through. The visual format helps people to see not only the original ideas but the patterns and relationships among them as individual participants' ideas are woven together into a composite whole. Graphic meeting facilitation emerged in the 1970s through the work of graphic designer David Sibbet (2010). A number of books and organizations now offer training in the graphic method of taking notes and thinking with pictures. Several approaches appear under various names, including idea mapping, concept mapping, mind maps, graphic recording, and graphic facilitation.

Group Process Techniques

Having an agenda does not guarantee that a meeting will be productive. You need to decide not only what the group will discuss, but how you will discuss it. For each topic on the agenda you need a process for generating ideas, evaluating those ideas, and making decisions.

Differences of opinion are a normal part of working together. Depending on the group, you might want to establish ground rules as a group about appropriate meeting behavior to help promote positive interactions. Rules could include focusing on issues not individuals, listening respectfully, no name calling or accusatory statements, and so forth.

Group processes are not a way to eliminate conflict; they are a way to manage conflict. Differences of opinion and even conflict are a natural part of working together, and an absence of conflict usually means that a diversity of viewpoints has been excluded from the decision-making process. Conflict can be seen as a resource, a positive force for information exchange, learning, and dynamic change (Leach 2013, 237). Disagreement helps to broaden and enrich the range of options available within a group. Humans, as members of a species which depends upon social interaction, instinctively try to reduce conflicts as quickly as they can. A skilled facilitator can help a group instead work through these conflicts, make them visible, and use them to result in a stronger, more productive group which generates better solutions.

You will accomplish two broad types of activity using group processes: generating ideas and evaluating ideas. Leaders and participants need to be clear that these are two different activities. Once you have generated and evaluated ideas, then you can make decisions as a group, using approaches such as majority voting or consensus.

Generating Ideas

Brainstorming is a group process for generating ideas. Effective brainstorming has a specific set of ground rules that are different from general meeting protocol. A brainstorming session should begin with the facilitator or leader reminding the group about these unique ground rules:

1   No evaluation of ideas, positive or negative, is permitted.
2   The primary goal is to generate a large quantity of ideas; the more, the better.
3   Wild ideas are encouraged; the wackier, the better.
4   Hitchhiking, or building on previously offered ideas, is encouraged.

Research has shown that the first fifteen or twenty ideas generated are usually already known or tried, and the truly creative ideas only appear once the obvious ideas have been offered. Truly wild ideas may not themselves become the solution, but many times they spark a related idea and spur a group to find a connection which does become the solution. Brainstorming works well with participants who do not normally interact with each other. In fact, the more diverse the group, the better.

Some steps in problem-solving are best approached through independent thinking. Other steps benefit from the synergy that occurs during social interaction and the free exchange of ideas. Effective meetings provide room for both. A process known as Nominal Group Process or Nominal Group Technique is a process for generating and evaluating ideas which defines when people should be working individually and when they should work as a group.

In the Nominal Group Process, each participant silently and anonymously writes as many ideas as they can about a particular issue, writing one idea per sticky note or index card. During this period people are able to organize their thoughts without influence from others, and less assertive members have equal input to more vocal members. After five or ten minutes the ideas are shared without discussion or evaluation. The facilitator goes around the room, asking each person in turn to read one idea, recording each idea on a flipchart and repeating until all ideas have been recorded. (The practice of going around a room one person at a time, usually in a circle, is known in meeting management as "round-robin.") Or, to preserve anonymity, the facilitator can collect the cards, then post each, one at a time. Once all the ideas have been posted, members discuss the ideas, one at a time. They then take a preliminary vote on the relative importance or priority of each idea. In some groups this is done anonymously, with members ranking each idea on a scale of 1 to 5. The group discusses the vote, possibly votes again, discusses again, and then conducts a final vote.

Several variations of Nominal Group Process are used in meetings. In the process known as Gallery or Gallery Walk, sometimes also referred to as Museum Tour, people sit at small tables in clusters of four to eight. Each table is given a flipchart and easel or self-stick flipchart sheets, on which they write, draw, or diagram as many ideas as they can. Or, members can write individual ideas on sticky notes, which they post on flipcharts. After a few minutes, the facilitator asks the groups to rotate clockwise to the next table, where they discuss the ideas at that station. The process is repeated until everyone has toured every station. Participants return to their own tables to make modifications and additions, as idea hitchhiking occurs.

In a variation of Gallery, each subgroup is assigned to explore a different perspective on the topic. Each table generates and displays their ideas, as described above. When the facilitator asks the groups to rotate to the next table, one member of each group remains at their original table to act as an expert. Once group members complete their tours, they can take the place of the members acting as experts, so that every person has an opportunity to see and discuss every chart.

In the process known as Brain Writing, sometimes called Pin Card or Silent Brainstorm, each person silently writes three ideas on a sticky note or piece of paper. After one or two minutes, each person passes their ideas to the person on their right. That person adds three new ideas or adds to the ideas already on the sheet. Using sticky notes allows ideas to be connected together and passed in chains. The passing continues for several more rounds as members add ideas and improvements to the original ideas. A participant always has the option to "pass" if they can't think of anything to add.

A simpler variation of Brain Writing is to have each person contribute just one idea each time and then pass the paper. In this version, the process moves more quickly and doesn't bog down as people try to think of multiple ideas. This simpler process is helpful toward the end of Brain Writing, when it becomes more difficult for each person to think of three new ideas.

In the process known as Crawford Slip Writing, each person is given from five to fifty sticky notes or slips of paper. Each person silently writes their ideas, one per sticky note or slip. At the end of five or ten minutes, the sticky notes or slips are collected and the facilitator or another group organizes and evaluates them. The Crawford Slip method is an effective way for large groups to generate and organize ideas.

Evaluating Ideas

Affinity Diagramming is a synthesizing step that can be used to organize and evaluate ideas which have been generated by a group. It can be used following a brainstorming session or can be used by itself. Some facilitators recommend limiting affinity diagrams to groups of five to fifteen people, while others use this process in groups of up to thirty people. First, each person is given a large number of sticky notes and a marker, so that the writing is bold and so that everyone's format is similar. As in Nominal Group Process, participants silently and anonymously generate as many ideas as they can, as fast as possible. Each person writes one idea on each sticky note. At the end of five or ten minutes, members post their notes on a wall or other surface. As an alternative, people may use index cards instead of sticky notes, and arrange them on a table or on a large display board using pushpins.

To create an affinity diagram, now members look for ideas that may be related and begin organizing the notes into related groups. Depending on the group and the subject being worked upon, a facilitator may suggest that one person at a time try categorizing, or they may suggest working as a group. Some facilitators believe that the sorting should be done in silence, and others suggest that members discuss what they are doing. A variation of this process is to determine several grouping categories in advance while also allowing for the emergence of new ones as ideas are evaluated.

It is permissible to move notes multiple times. If an idea keeps moving between two categories, participants may want to make a duplicate of the note and post the idea in more than one category. If a note is moved many times, it can be placed to the side by itself. After groupings seem to be stable, members discuss their thoughts and select a heading for each group. The groupings and their titles should be recorded. A digital camera is a useful tool for preserving a backup record of details in these kinds of processes.

The Affinity Diagram process is sometimes known as Snow Card or Snowball. Each individual card containing an idea is called a snow card. When the cards are grouped by theme, they produce clusters of cards, or snowballs.

The Delphi method uses multiple rounds of questionnaires to help a group converge toward a common idea. A questionnaire is sent to participants, who send them back to a facilitator by a given date. The facilitator tabulates the responses, then sends the anonymous results along with a new questionnaire to members, asking them to evaluate and rank the responses. Sometimes these questionnaires ask participants also to include written statements about their positions. The surveys are returned again and the facilitator tabulates the ratings and summarizes the arguments anonymously. Another survey is sent, and members revise their responses based on information from other participants. The process continues until consensus is reached or no new information is generated. The Delphi method can be conducted online, with results compiled by computer.

A weighted criteria chart is a numerical method for evaluating ideas relative to each other in order to reach a decision. Because this method analyzes multiple alternatives against multiple selection criteria, it is also known as Multiattribute Decision Analysis. It can be done manually or using specialized decision software. First, the group generates a list of options it is considering. Participants then develop a list of criteria they will use for evaluating each of the choices.

The facilitator sets up a table, with one alternative in each column and one criterion in each row. The group assigns a relative weight to each criterion, depending upon how important each one is. Some groups assign a number from 1 to 10, with 10 being the most important and 1 the least important; others assign a number from 1 to 3 or from 1 to 5. Other groups assign a percentage of the total to each by assigning decimal numbers to signify the relative weight, with the total weights adding up to 1. For each alternative, the group assigns a number from 1 to 10 for each criterion, indicating how well that alternative satisfies that criterion. Each number is then multiplied by the weighting factor for that criterion. Finally, the totals are added up for each alternative. The alternative with the highest total score is the preferred alternative. Participants discuss the results to be sure they make sense.

A number of software products are available for developing concept maps or mind maps, many of them at low or no cost. Some groups display concept mapping software and then a facilitator modifies it as the group discusses topics and how to organize them. The group continues discussing and watching concept map changes on the screen until they reach consensus.

Making Decisions

As your group works toward decision points, you may want to get a sense of whether there is agreement and whether there are in fact disagreements. For that, you can use a straw poll, which is an unofficial, nonbinding vote that can be used to help bring potential conflicts out into the open. You can take straw polls more than once as the team works on an issue to help build consensus.

If your group is facing a long list of items and is having difficulty making decisions, you can use multi-voting to shorten the list and set priorities. One way to do this is to vote with peel-off file folder sticker dots. Count the number of items on the list, and give each person one-third that many dots. For example, if there are 18 items, each person receives six dots. Then each participant places a dot on every item they want to be treated as a high priority. Some facilitators say that each person can distribute the votes however they want; others do not allow placing multiple dots on one item. As an alternative, you can give participants votes, rather than dots, and conduct voting by a show of hands or by placing tally marks next to items on the list. In another method of multi-voting, you can give each person points to distribute, typically 10 or 100 points. Participants write numbers of votes or make tally marks beside items on the list.

Using any of these multi-voting methods, if the votes appear unanimous, then the top vote-getting items become the high-priority list. If they are not unanimous, then the bottom third to half of the items is eliminated, and another vote is taken. In the second round of voting, each member has fewer votes to distribute. Repeat the voting until the desired number of items remains.

Multi-voting is a democratic process which avoids one of the problems inherent in standard majority voting: situations in which there are only two sides. When a majority vote is taken, the result is that some members are winners and some are losers. Multi-voting distributes power equally. And since most participants will see at least one of the items that they voted for near the top of the priority list, the feeling of winners and losers is avoided.

The two basic ways of making a group decision are voting and consensus. Reaching consensus usually involves a lot of listening and exchanging of ideas.

The word "consensus" means agreement; it comes from the Latin word *consentire,* "to feel or perceive together." Consensus is reached after all the participants have had the opportunity to voice their opinions, each person's concerns have been heard and understood, and the group working together has developed a solution that everyone agrees is the best solution given all the factors. Consensus does not mean that people are in 100 percent agreement. It means that the members of the group have together generated a decision that all of them can live with.

Public Participation

At the community scale, the process of people working together to solve community problems or plan for the community's future is called public participation or community participation. Common projects which can involve public participation include city climate plans, regional land use plans, transportation planning, community visioning, and design of public spaces such as parks, street systems, city halls, and schools. Community participation is a bottom-up planning approach for exchanging information, finding creative solutions, and empowering citizens, including disenfranchised citizens, beginning early in the process.

Communication can go in one direction as one-way communication. This is what happens when an organization distributes information, such as issuing a report or making a presentation to a group. Two-way communication happens when people exchange information and ideas. In participatory decision making, people not only exchange information, they actually collaborate, and those who will be affected are able to give feedback and influence the outcome (ISO 2006, v).

Real participation occurs when people who will be affected by planning are empowered to influence the actions that will be taken. Or as some disability rights advocates say, "Nothing about us without us" (Sanchez and Brenman 2008, 115). Participation means that people work together to define their own objectives and find their own solutions. This process is not a one-way communication from leaders to citizens; it is a collaboration in which everyone who affects or is affected by an issue works together, interacting and influencing one another, learning together, and developing a shared vision. In the process social capital grows and the web of multiple, sometimes divergent interests co-evolve. It is a process of community building.

When innovative solutions actually come from members of a community, the solutions are far more likely to be implemented and to remain durable elements of community life. Real sustainability gains from an initiative depend a lot upon how people actually live in their homes and communities.

Participation involves stakeholders. A stakeholder is anyone who has a stake in the problem and in the outcomes of the group process, any individual or group who is affected by the problem or by the actions of other stakeholders, or who can affect other stakeholders. There are different kinds of stakeholders and also different kinds of experts. Citizens and users are experts in the places where they live or work, bringing detailed local knowledge that is helpful in identifying problems and evaluating alternatives. Professionals, such as ecologists, architects, or planners, have technical expertise they can contribute to complex problem-solving. Working out the best solutions requires both.

This is not easy work. Democracy is messy. People disagree. Stakeholders come from different backgrounds, from a range of cultures, customs, education, and economic circumstances, and each brings their own needs, wants, beliefs, and ideas, and often they appear to be in conflict. Participation at the community scale requires courage and commitment, but it may be worth the effort when one considers the alternative scenarios.

Social research in public participation has shown that the main source of user satisfaction is not the degree to which a person's needs have been met, but their feeling of having influenced the decisions (Sanoff 2000, 12). When the goal is to collect public input, large meetings with presentations, question-and-answer sessions, and public comment are the least effective method. While these sessions may be one way to present information to an audience, they do not provide an opportunity to work together and to find common ground.

The International Association for Public Participation (IAP2) defines five levels of involvement: The first, and least participatory, is to *inform.* The second level is to *consult,* that is, to tell people what is being planned for them and to collect public feedback. Gathering feedback is important, but it is not genuine participation. A more active level is to *involve* the public, working directly with people and developing alternatives which reflect their goals. An even more participative level is *collaboration,* in which participants work as partners. The most participative approach is to *empower,* with participants making decisions and controlling the outcomes (IAP2 2004).

Community participation includes a need to identify problems and opportunities. One approach to doing this is known as SWOT analysis (pronounced like the word "swat"), which stands for Strengths, Weaknesses, Opportunities, and Threats. Strengths and weaknesses are typically internal elements inherent in an organization, community, or situation. Opportunities and threats are typically current or future external elements in the environment. A similar approach is known as PARK analysis (Sanoff 2000, 40). The letters stand for Preserve (what we have now that is positive), Add (what we do not have that is positive), Remove (what we have that is negative), and Keep out (what we do not have that is negative). Many of the group process techniques discussed above can be used to identify and organize SWOT or PARK ideas.

Conferences and Workshops

One of the ways people working in sustainability communicate ideas and collaborate with others is through the planning of conferences, workshops, and other events. Bringing a range of interested people together to discuss ideas can be very productive and can help people reach consensus on high-priority issues (ISO 2006, 15). Sustainability principles can be applied to these events. Known as a "sustainable event" or "green meeting," such an event is organized and implemented in ways that minimize environmental impact, add value to the local economy, and leave a positive social legacy for the host community. Sustainable events have ripple effects, leading by example and inspiring change as they raise awareness among participants, staff, vendors, and the local community.

Before moving onto other planning steps, the first step is to consider whether a meeting is really needed. It might be possible to conduct meeting activities electronically, for example through email or teleconferencing, or it might be possible to conduct several smaller regional meetings to minimize travel and consumption of resources. If it is determined that a face-to-face meeting is needed, then careful planning is required in order to minimize impacts (UNEP and ICLEI 2012, 14). Be aware that successful workshops and conferences entail large numbers of details of many types and are time-consuming to organize.

Planning an Event

The steps in planning a sustainable event are similar to the planning steps for other sustainability initiatives. One person should be given responsibility for "greening" the event, together with participation by a team (ibid.). Together, the team develops an action plan which identifies goals, objectives, deadlines, vendor selection criteria, and performance indicators, and identifies who is responsible for each element. Some organizations begin by crafting a sustainable event policy or green meeting policy to serve as a formal guiding framework. Once a team is organized and a plan is in place, organizers take steps to reduce greenhouse gas emissions, minimize consumption of energy and natural resources, avoid toxic substances, minimize waste generation, and foster social and economic benefits.

Social and economic factors are considered in addition to minimizing environmental impact. An event can foster social equity through promoting respect for diversity, inclusion of underrepresented groups, universal accessibility for people of all abilities and, where appropriate, use of Fair Trade certified products. An event can promote economic benefits through a transparent, public procurement and contracting process, supporting local employment, sharing leftover food with a local food bank, and looking for other ways to give back to the local community (UNEP and ICLEI 2012, 2).

When selecting a venue, caterer, and other supply vendors, it is standard practice to issue a request for proposal (RFP). An RFP and subsequent contracts should include sustainability performance criteria for vendors. If possible, catering staff and vendors should be considered stakeholders and should be included in the event planning.

Location

Minimizing the environmental impact of a meeting begins with selecting a location. For small and regional meetings within driving distance, organizers can arrange carpooling. If distances are so great that attendees must fly, organizers should look for a host city with an airport that maximizes the number of direct flights and minimizes the number of connecting flights. Participants should be able to travel easily to and from the airport, hotel, and meeting site by public transit, bicycle, or foot. The meeting site and hotel venues should be near public transportation or within walking and bicycling distance of each other. In some locations, event organizers may need to consider providing shuttle service. Organizers should do everything they can to make public transportation easy and attractive, first by selecting appropriate locations and then by publishing information about transportation options—including maps, schedules, and instructions—in registration materials, via email updates, and in a central location at the event itself.

Lodging

When selecting a hotel venue, sustainable event organizers often provide a checklist or questionnaire which respondents return with their proposals, with preference given to hotels with higher scores. Preference is also given to hotels which already have green policies or environmental management systems in place (UNEP and ICLEI 2012, 24). Venues should be able to demonstrate water- and energy-efficient practices. Examples include providing at least some lighting from natural daylight, strategies for minimizing use of air conditioning, recycling and composting programs, minimal or no use of disposable products, no use of polystyrene cups, use of nontoxic cleaning products, and allowing guests to reuse sheets and towels for multiple days. Organizers should visit hotel and conference sites to verify that their green-event criteria can be met.

Food

Organizers should work with caterers and food vendors to plan meals and snacks, using local, organically produced food in season as much as possible to reduce greenhouse gas emissions from transportation, require less synthetic fertilizers and pesticides, and benefit the local economy. For food and beverage that must be imported, look for Fair Trade certification. Reduce environmental impact by offering vegetarian options, which require many times less land and water and produce many times fewer emissions than meat. Provide condiments in bulk, and use washable, reusable dishes and cups. Avoid disposable items such as plastic flatware, coffee stirrers, straws, paper doilies, and polystyrene cups. If disposable items are used, ensure that they are chlorine-free and compostable, and work with catering and venue staff to set up a composting system for food scraps and paper.

Food provides an opportunity to communicate with and educate attendees. Place signs or place cards next to foods that describe where and by whom the food was produced, any certifications, and other details about why this food was chosen. Provide recycling, composting and, if appropriate, landfill receptacles in convenient locations, and label them clearly using colors and pictures.

Have strategies in place to minimize food waste. Using attendee head count, work with the caterer to estimate quantities carefully. A more formal system could ask attendees to indicate meal preferences ahead of time, either within the registration form or in a separate questionnaire. Set up a program to donate leftover food to a local food bank or homeless shelter, if the caterer does not already have such a program in place.

Event Material

Minimize paper consumption beginning with registration. Send announcements, 'save the date' information, and registration materials via email and websites, and conduct all event registration online. Make all agendas, programs, handouts, and proceedings available online. Provide printed materials by request only, and if provided, use recycled-content or hemp paper, vegetable-based ink, and double-sided printing. Use recyclable name badges and reusable badge holders, avoid the use of extra ribbons on badge holders, and provide convenient badge-recycling receptacles. If the event requires decorations, artwork, signs, posters, or banners, create reusable versions without dates. Consider packaging type, content, and quantity when making conference or meeting purchases.

For conferences which include trade shows and exhibits, communicate with exhibitors early. Event organizers can include requirements for sustainable practices in exhibitor agreements; since these may be new to some exhibitors, constructive and clear communication is important. Require exhibitors to reuse or take back discarded materials at their own cost. Encourage them to minimize promotional materials. For both exhibitors and other meeting events, eliminate or reduce gifts and favors; if used, encourage gifts that are locally made using sustainable materials.

Climate Neutrality

Travel, lodging, food, and various event materials all carry climate impacts. Reduce carbon emissions in every way possible. Calculate the remaining carbon emissions of the event that could not be avoided, then purchase offsets to bring the event's net emissions to zero. Some organizers offer attendees ways to purchase offsets for travel individually, although there is disagreement over the effectiveness of such purchases.

Monitoring and Reporting

As with all sustainability activities, measurement is essential both to verify that sustainability goals were met and to provide a baseline for improvement in future meetings. Organizers should collect data on greenhouse gas emissions, energy and water consumption, recycling and waste management, and economic impact in the local community. Metrics should also include basic data such as number of attendees and number of days (UNEP and ICLEI 2012, 59). In addition to technical measurement, provide a questionnaire or survey to attendees to gage level of satisfaction and to uncover observations and suggestions which might not have occurred to organizers. Be sure to share both successes and lessons learned with attendees, vendors, and the public.

Event Communication

Planning and implementing a green event is an opportunity to educate and raise awareness for vendors, organizers, attendees, and the local community (UNEP and ICLEI 2012, 15). Begin by sharing sustainability concepts, goals, and strategies in event announcements and registration materials sent to participants and in bid invitations and contract materials sent to vendors. Communicate participants' own roles in contributing toward a green event, helping them understand the choices they can make and the implications of those choices. Include information about sustainability concepts, goals, and strategies in the conference program, and provide additional, preferably reusable, informational signage in food service areas and throughout the event. Help participants understand what you are doing and why.

Monitor and collect data throughout the event, and after the event share this information with vendors, participants, and the community. Consider including data such as tons of greenhouse gas emissions avoided, pounds or tons of paper use avoided, number of trees saved as a result of reduced paper usage, pounds or tons of recyclables and composted material diverted from landfills, and quantities of water and energy used and conserved relative to a known baseline. Describe sustainability goals for the event and whether they were met, and discuss lessons learned. Publicize steps that vendors, caterers, and venues took to become more sustainable; consider giving them certificates of appreciation, and recognize their efforts publicly. Show how the successes of the event were the result of everyone, working together.

Planning Tools

Concept Maps

Concept maps are visual representations of a set of ideas. These diagrams can be as simple as circles or boxes connected by lines. They are useful in helping you recognize relationships, such as between steps in a process, indicators in a monitoring program, elements in an ecosystem, or problems and potential solutions.

These simple diagrams are visual tools for thinking (Ware 2013, 316). Because they engage a different part of the brain than do verbal communication and information, they allow us to think in new ways (Cunningham 2010, 11). Unlike words, which must be read sequentially in a linear way, a concept map lets you see an overall system and its relationships all at once. Thinking visually on big pieces of paper is often a process of pattern finding. You may be able to speak or write about a concept with words that still remain ambiguous, both to you and to the people receiving the message. The act of drawing a diagram, however, forces you to clarify your ideas and really think about how things work (Thomas et al. 2006, 51).

Concept maps serve multiple purposes. You can create concept maps as part of a brainstorming process, where they both provide a framework and are helpful in generating new ideas and connections. You can use them as a way to take notes and summarize ideas in a meeting, where they are tools for building a common understanding (Ware 2013, 317). And you can use them to communicate with others. Concept mapping can be done as a group exercise and is often used as part of a planning process, such as when a team is developing a climate action plan or designing an interpretive exhibit. When a group has collected a lot of information about a subject but has not yet put it together, that is a good time to begin focusing on finding patterns (Sibbet 2010, 154).

There is no definite way to draw concept maps. You simply represent a set of ideas visually, in whatever way shows the concepts and their relationships. You can use boxes, circles, and connecting lines, supplemented by labels and more detailed captions as needed. Your diagrams do not need to be artistic. In fact, if they look too finished, a polished appearance can discourage stakeholders from questioning ideas or proposing changes (McKenna-Cress and Kamien 2010, 226).

After your group has created a concept map, if it is on paper then put it in a location where people can study it, make notes, and add ideas. Some teams call this a "butcher paper conversation." Using sticky notes in your concept-mapping process makes it possible to rearrange ideas. In addition to old-fashioned paper and sticky notes, a number of software tools are available which are designed for creating and modifying diagrams. If you have created a concept map electronically, make it available to everyone and allow participants to comment and make changes. Be sure you include a way to save earlier versions as well.

Scenario Planning

Scenario planning is a method that asks "what-if" questions to imagine possible futures. First used by military planners after World War II, then used by Royal Dutch Shell during the 1973 oil crisis, this approach is now used by the Intergovernmental Panel on Climate Change (IPCC), the United Nations (UN), the International Energy Agency (IEA) in its *World Energy Outlook*, and many corporations, cities, and sustainability planners (Schwartz 1996, 7). Scenarios are plausible what-if stories. They are short, evidence-based fictional narratives about the future that enable an organization to make decisions that will be sound for all plausible futures (Hopkins and Zapata 2007, 84).

The process begins by brainstorming and identifying driving forces that could impact the future. Participants use group processes to cluster the driving forces, typically sorting driving forces into five categories: environmental, economic, social, political, and technological. Then they rank the driving forces, finding the factors with the greatest impact and the factors with the greatest uncertainty. If some forces are contrasting, they might become axes or ends of a spectrum.

Once the driving forces have been grouped, teams create four to six very different but plausible stories about the future. The more diverse the teams, the richer the scenarios will be. Participants try to describe each plausible future in as much detail as possible as if it had already come to pass, giving each one a vivid, memorable name (Hopkins and Zapata 2007, 247). They flesh out these scenarios, thinking about how the world might get from the present to there and what events would need to occur to make a particular scenario plausible. They develop a set of indicators, small details to watch for that might indicate a particular future is possible.

After considering several varied stories of equally plausible futures, an organization can think about its vision—what it wants to become—and what it would take to achieve that vision under each of the possible futures. Teams can identify the future they most desire and the future with the greatest potential risk, working backward to identify ways to make their most cherished future more likely and their least preferred future less likely.

15

COMMUNICATION TOOLS

Written Documents

Types of Written Documents

Written documents include reports, policies, brochures, and letters. A report gives you an opportunity to address multiple issues in depth, and is a way to build trust and create transparency. Be aware that a report does take effort and time to prepare, and may be difficult to update frequently. Keep in mind that this document is not primarily a marketing document; it is a report of facts. A factual report includes both successes and failures, opportunities and challenges (ISO 2006, 12).

If you develop a comprehensive report, you should also write a summary. For example, every few years the Intergovernmental Panel on Climate Change (IPCC) issues a highly detailed assessment report that describes in precise detail over thousands of pages the current scientific understanding about climate change (IPCC 2014). Each edition of the assessment reports includes a document titled *Synthesis Report: Summary for Policymakers,* which organizes the key ideas in a few pages using headings, subheadings, color, and white space, illustrated with clear graphics.

An executive summary is a stand-alone document that synthesizes the key points of the report, including a summary of any recommendations your report makes. People read the executive summary to understand the overall content and can then turn to the full report for details that help them implement the recommendations. To write the summary, read the entire report and take notes of important facts and conclusions as you read. Then use your notes to write your summary. The length of an executive summary should generally be no more than 10 percent that of the original document (USC 2018).

Brochures and flyers are generally one-page paper documents, although they sometimes have multiple pages. They often have both words and images, and are good for summarizing a lot of information in a compact space. They have the advantage of being objects that people can take with them and can look at again weeks or months later. You can place them on a table or rack, and you can leave them with audiences after a presentation or a meeting to reinforce key ideas and to help people remember your conversation. Since some brochures are saved and subjected to folding and refolding, use quality paper and good print quality.

A brochure is folded, typically as a trifold in which two folds create three panels, with one panel overlapping another. Two folds can also produce an accordion fold or z-fold, so called because the end view of the brochure makes a Z shape; this layout is useful if you have a single graphic that spans the entire width of all three panels. Other brochure folds are possible: the simplest is a bifold, folded once; a gate fold is folded twice, with two outside panels that open like swinging gates which cover a large middle section; a larger sheet like a map can receive a half-fold and then a tri-fold.

The effectiveness of a brochure depends on its attractiveness, clarity, and good content (Jacobson 2009, 324). Provide a short, thematic title. Include graphics. Make your illustration interesting by showing something happening. Try mocking up a layout and evaluating how the images and information appear once it is folded. Think about whether the layout captures a reader's attention and conveys the message efficiently (Caputo et al. 2008, 75).

A newsletter is a document that provides a periodic update. It can be printed or can be electronic, and is a way to maintain a connection with people who have interest in your work or topic, either internally or externally or both (ISO 2006, 12). Consistency is an important element if you plan to release newsletters more than once. Your readers want to become familiar with your layout and know where to look to find certain types of information including the date, the table of contents, the lead story, and contact information (Caputo et al. 2008, 69).

A newsletter can use full color and can contain multiple pages. The front page should contain a summary of the newsletter's content; the bottom of the last page should contain contact information and a reference list, if needed. Visual elements should be used to help explain concepts. Grids, with an odd number of columns, are effective for laying out pages. For example, you could use a general pattern of three columns, then allow text boxes and visual elements to take up more than one column width in places for contrast and emphasis without compromising the overall layout (Thomas et al. 2006, 87).

A poster is a printed sheet designed to be posted on a wall or other vertical surface. Posters are intended to catch viewers' attention; they are usually larger than standard printer paper and are printed on thick stock. Many conferences include an event known as a poster session, in which a number of presenters each stand next to a poster they have prepared; conference participants circulate through the room, stopping to look at and discuss poster topics that are of interest to them. If you participate in a poster session, consider making a handout with the poster title, a brief summary, one or two graphics, and your contact information. Another way to produce a handout is to print a letter-size version of your poster. If it has been well designed, it should still be readable at this size (Thomas et al. 2006, 85). When you are still in the draft stage of designing a poster, print a draft on letter-size paper and evaluate it with a critical eye. Can you read the type? Do the colors and the spatial balance look right? Do the main points stand out clearly?

Design Guidelines for Brochures, Newsletters, and Posters

Many of the guidelines for designing effective interpretive signs and exhibits apply to brochures, posters, and newsletters. Help the reader navigate your document by giving it attributes that support what we know about visual perception (Few 2012, 61).

Begin with the title, which communicates your theme or main message. Make it as short as possible. For brochures, the title may be two or three words. Newsletters and posters can use a short question or a theme statement written in active voice. Some designers write the title in sentence case, which is more readable than title case or all capitals. Use a large, clear font. For posters, which must be read from 30 feet away, use a bold font at least 72 points or one inch in height.

Use graphic elements with color to explain your theme and reinforce your message. Use small amounts of text to support the graphics. Use a clear typeface. For posters, use a font 18 to 24 points in height. Avoid big blocks of text. Chunk the information, keep paragraphs short, and use short sentences. Break up the elements with white space, a hierarchy of headings, subheadings, images, and captions. Provide a caption for each image. Many designers choose a sans serif typeface for the title and headings and a serif typeface for the body text for maximum readability.

Use a light-colored, neutral background with dark text for contrast. Use a plain background; photographs or patterns as backgrounds occasionally work, but usually they simply distract and impede communication. Use two or three subtle main colors throughout. Use additional color or contrast as highlights so that readers notice elements preattentively (Baron 2010, 191).

Use desktop publishing software such as Adobe InDesign to lay out pages for brochures, newsletters, and posters. This kind of software makes it possible to locate elements in a flexible way, and it saves files with a CMYK color format, appropriate for printing. Try to avoid using presentation software such as PowerPoint, if possible, which is designed for on-screen presentations; it uses RGB light-based color format, which causes surprises when printing ink-based CMYK color (Thomas et al. 2006, 79). Give your printer a high-resolution PDF file of your poster or document. When you give your desktop-publishing file to a printer, be aware that graphics are linked and not embedded, which means that any image files linked to your document must be in the same folder as the document file itself.

You might find it helpful to sketch a very rough layout by hand first to help determine where main graphic, text, and title elements will be located, to help you plan the flow of information, and to help you find a balance between text and images. Locate the most important information near the top left corner. Arrange the elements so information flows top to bottom and left to right. Keep the sequence obvious and well organized.

The Process of Writing

Writing will be easier if you approach it methodically. Start by writing a short and simple theme statement that answers the question, "What is this about?" Try to reduce the main idea of your writing project to one sentence. This statement does not usually become part of your written document; it is just a tool for you to help you stay on task. So, for example, depending upon your topic, a theme statement might say, "Geothermal power uses volcanic heat," or "Hurricanes are increasing in intensity," or "With passive solar heating, the building *is* the system."

Conduct research. Figure out what information you will need, then start collecting it.

Take notes. You can use pieces of paper, sticky notes, index cards, or documents in your computer. Make sure you keep track of which notes came from which sources so you can verify details or cite them later.

Organize your notes. Sift through the notes you collected. See if you can sort them by category. You could color code or number code each piece of paper, or stack pages in labeled piles, or split electronic files into separate documents or even separate folders.

Make an outline. You might want to begin by simply jotting down a summary of the main points, what some writers call a "jot outline" (Hart 2006a, 36). Don't worry about headings and subheadings; just make a quick list. Then develop a more detailed outline, expanding your outline as you discover more material. You can also use the main headings in your outline later to help you write a table of contents, if your document is long enough to benefit from one (Garner 2013, 152).

Write a draft. Some writers advise that you stay loose and write fast at this stage, aiming just to get what is in your notes onto the page in rough form without slowing down to worry over details (Hart 2006a, 38). Other writers aim to get the vocabulary, phrasing, and syntax right from the beginning.

Now you can raise your standards and fine-tune the details. Polish your draft. Think about wording, check grammar and spelling, check facts for accuracy, look for things that might not make sense and try to say them more clearly. Use a style guide for consistency. A number of style guides are in use, and they disagree on many points. The important thing is to pick one and then use that one consistently.

Include a feedback step when you write. Write a draft and read it yourself. Allow yourself enough time that you can let it rest for a while before you come back and re-read it. Ask other people to read what you have written, and pay attention to what they say. Ask them what they think your key message is, and see whether it aligns with what you think your theme is (Redish 2012, 289).

A Few Guidelines for Writing

The one quality that distinguishes good writers from bad writers is this: Good writers have empathy for their readers (Garner 2013, 171). Good writing makes the reader's job easy. A reader should be able to understand something that is well written with a single reading, and should not need to go back and re-read or puzzle through phrases in order to understand it (LaRocque 2003, 6).

Think about writing sentences the way you would speak them. Although written communication does tend to be more formal than spoken communication, your readers will connect with your writing more readily if it feels more like a conversation. Check your writing by reading it out loud and see whether it feels comfortable and whether the words are easy to say.

Use active, not passive, voice (Garner 2013, 53). Active voice means that the subject is the doer of the action. Passive voice means that the subject is the receiver of the action; it consists of a form of the verb "to be" and the past participle of a verb, usually with the preposition "by" (Hart 2006a, 85). For example, the sentence "people eat vegetables" is in active voice; the sentence "vegetables are eaten by people" is in passive voice. "Loggers cut the trees" is in active voice; "the trees were cut by loggers" is in passive voice. People tend to use active voice when speaking aloud to each other (Moscardo et al. 2007, 62). Passive voice is less direct, and overuse of passive voice can feel dull and wordy. You can use passive voice occasionally, however, to bring some variety to your writing, and you can use it when you want to focus attention on the thing receiving the action. For example, if you wanted to focus on state laws, you could use the active voice: "Most states have laws regulating water pollution." But if you wanted to focus on pollution, passive voice would be more appropriate: "Water pollution is regulated by law in most states" (Millward 1980, 239).

Use active, vivid verbs, and use the simplest form of a verb. The simplest and strongest form of a verb is present tense (Garner 2013, 53). When you use present tense, your writing is more direct, more immediate, and less complicated (PLAIN 2011, 22). The use of future tense is less direct and makes your readers work harder. Use tenses other than the present tense only if they are needed for accuracy (Garner 2013, 38).

Use verbs instead of nouns or adjectives derived from verbs (Moscardo et al. 2007, 62). Avoid hidden verbs (PLAIN 2011, 22). For example, instead of saying, "we need to carry out a review," say, "we need to review." Instead of saying, "you must make an application in writing," say, "you must apply in writing."

Omit unnecessary words. For example, instead of "a sufficient number of," say, "enough." Instead of "on a monthly basis," say, "monthly." Avoid the use of empty or meaningless words and phrases, known in writing as expletives.

Examples of expletives to avoid include "there are" and "it is necessary that." Commit to what you are saying and minimize the use of qualifiers such as "somewhat" or "rather" (Hart 2006a, 91). Minimize the use of intensifiers. Most of the time, using a word such as "very" or "really" does not improve the meaning (Garner 2013, 44). Watch for redundant pairs, such as "final outcome," "future plans," and "completely overhaul." An outcome, by definition, is final; a plan always means something in the future; and overhaul, by definition, means to rework something completely (Bruno 2012).

Use plain language. That is, speak the audience's language. When you have a choice between words, choose a familiar or frequently used word over an unusual word. Choose a concrete word over an abstract word (LaRocque 2003, 22). Choose a short word over a long word (PLAIN 2011, 36). You can still occasionally use words that are more complex when they are needed, and to provide contrast and variety (Moscardo et al. 2007, 60). Plain language is not dull language. It is robust and direct, the opposite of gaudy and pretentious (Garner 2013, xiv). Use it by choosing the simplest and most straightforward way of expressing an idea. Straightforward writing is typically interesting to read.

Avoid jargon. Jargon is technical language used for a specialized audience that is not generally understood by people outside that specialty. It can be the clearest way to communicate within a specialized group. If you do need to use technical terms to communicate precisely, and sometimes you do, then make sure that your other language is as clear as possible. Often, however, jargon is unnecessarily complicated and is used to impress rather than to inform your audience (PLAIN 2011, 46). Academics talk or write amongst themselves using words like "discourse" and "contested" and "heuristic." But these words are not useful for communicating with others outside the group. You can use these words to show that you are a scholar who can write about scholarly things, but when your goal is communication with people outside your specialized academic group, such words are not useful and they make your writing opaque. Write to communicate, rather than to impress. Translate specialized terms into plain English for lay audiences and use plain, everyday language instead of jargon whenever possible (ibid.).

Use shorter sentences and simpler sentences, on average. Express one main idea in each sentence. Short sentences break the information into smaller cognitive chunks that are easier to process (ibid., 50). You don't need every sentence to be short as long as the average length is short, around 20 words. Include a mix of short, medium, and long sentences to give your readers variety and help them stay interested (LaRocque 2003, 5).

Sentences can include subordinate ideas, as long as each carries only one main idea. Limit the number of qualifying phrases and dependent clauses.[1] The main idea can get lost in a forest of words when the essential parts of sentences are separated by collections of dependent clauses. Instead, try to keep subjects and objects close to their verbs (PLAIN 2011, 60). If you want to engage your readers' attention, get right to the point.

Use a positive message and focus on solutions, rather than problems. Use positive language and say what something is, rather than what it is not (Moscardo et al. 2007, 62).

Treat communication as a conversation between you and the audience. Even though your document may be read by many people, you are speaking to one person at a time who is reading your document. Write as if you are addressing one person, rather than a group. Use pronouns such as *you* and *we* to speak directly to the reader (Garner 2013, 135). Speaking directly to readers with pronouns such as *you* pulls them in, makes the content relevant to them, and helps them to picture themselves in the text (Garner 1995, 643).

Policies

Policy is a tool used in managing many organizations, from small nonprofit groups to governments at all levels. A policy is a formal statement of principles, a set of guidelines or rules that guide decision-making, activities, and conduct (Campbell 1998, 1). Policies provide consistency and continuity. With policies in place, everyone has a common understanding, can refer to the same framework for decisions, and the framework remains in place even if personnel change. Policies provide a written record that is accessible to everyone, reducing the potential for conflict or misunderstanding. Once issues are discussed and policies agreed upon, decision-making is more efficient since people do not need to keep discussing the same issues again.

People who work in sustainability are often called upon to write or collaborate on the writing of policies. The basic approach to writing a policy is to identify the topic of focus, collect examples of similar policies from other organizations, write and distribute a draft, collect and integrate feedback, revise as needed, finalize, approve, draft procedures for implementing, and schedule regular reviews.

As in any problem-solving process, the first step is to define the problem or identify the issue to be addressed (ibid., 26). Sometimes a single issue is what prompts a particular policy to be written. In other cases an organization decides to work methodically to develop a collection of multiple policies, and thus the first activities are planning sessions by stakeholders to identify collaboratively which policies are needed and in what priority. As with all planning and management work, the development of policies is built upon the organization's mission, goals, and objectives.

Once a particular topic of concern is identified as the subject of a policy that needs to be written, participants begin by gathering information and conducting research. Often the most productive activity is to search for policies written by similar organizations on similar topics, from which to compile a list of elements to consider for inclusion. For example, if a sustainability team at a university needed to develop a policy on green cleaning methods, they could search for existing green cleaning policies at other universities. Although care must be taken not to copy someone else's policy, this kind of benchmarking is very helpful in providing a framework. Other resources can include professional organizations, technical experts, and relevant laws and regulations, as well as conversations with people who have experience with or who are impacted by this issue, a process which can include both formal surveys and informal conversations.

An individual or small team is then selected to do the writing of a first draft. In general, policy writing should not be done in committee meetings, as there is the potential both to get hung up on insignificant details and to have difficulty getting started with crafting language in the first place. It is easier for a committee to work when participants have an existing document to which to respond. The policy should be written as clearly as possible in straightforward, jargon-free language and should be no more than one page in length. Bullet points are often used to make the layout easy to use. The document should avoid using brand names, names of people, dates, and any other information that can become outdated.

The first draft is then distributed to stakeholders for comment. Feedback can be collected and discussed verbally in meetings; however, it is more efficient if participants first make comments directly on electronic documents, using either a different-colored font or the markup feature of word-processing software, so that those marked-up versions can be distributed and read by participants in advance before coming together for discussion.

The process of meeting to review feedback, agreeing on and incorporating revisions, and circulating a revised draft is continued as needed until a final draft is agreed upon by the group. The final draft is then presented to the approving body in the organization for ratification, which might be an administrator, a management committee, or a board of trustees or directors. Once ratified, the final approval date is added to the policy, and the policy can be communicated to others and then implemented.

Every policy within an organization should follow the same format for consistency. A typical policy contains the title; a brief statement of purpose; a description of scope, that is, where or to whom the policy will apply; the policy narrative itself; the approval date, date of most recent revision, and date of next review; the responsible party with contact information; reference to relevant statute, regulation, or governing authority, if appropriate; reference to related procedure; and definitions of any uncommon or specialized terms or words that can have different meanings in different contexts, listed in alphabetical order.

A written policy is implemented through written procedures. A policy is a statement of guiding principles; it describes 'what' and 'why.' A procedure provides instructions for carrying out the policy; it describes 'how.' A procedure describes the specific action steps to be done, how they will be done, and by whom.

Every policy should be reviewed on a regular basis to determine whether it is understandable as written and whether it is working as intended (Campbell 1998, 343). This is the standard feedback step that is essential to all planning and management activities. As with the original drafting of a policy, review and evaluation should be done collaboratively (Info Entrepreneurs 2014). The policy is adapted and revised as needed and, unless changes are minor, presented to the approving body in the organization for re-approval.

News Media

The term news media includes sources from the internet, television, radio, magazines, and newspapers which present news, as distinct from art or entertainment. News reports operate within cultural frames. Reports must include some facts and ignore others, so the result is not a reflection of objective reality but a constructed version of a social reality. For example, if a news story reports that a cougar was found in a suburban garage, the framing indicates that it was the cougar who was trespassing and not the humans (Corbett 2006, 215).

Both new and traditional news media offer efficient ways to communicate with large numbers of people. The more media types you use, the more audiences you can reach. Print media, such as magazines and newspapers, are good for communicating complex ideas about subjects like social equity, ecological restoration, or climate change, because readers are able to go at their own speed and to re-read sections as they choose. Radio is a conversational medium that allows listeners to experience a more personal connection with speakers. Television, film, and the internet are visual, and so make information more accessible and emotionally meaningful to viewers. And while some critics argue that electronic media disconnect us from nature, these media also can show us dimensions of the living world that we would not otherwise have access to and so can result in fundamental shifts in thinking and behavior (Reist 2014).

Radio producers sometimes say that radio is a visual medium. What they mean is that they use sound to create a vivid mental image and help the listener visualize. Christopher Joyce, science correspondent for National Public Radio, advises that if you are interviewed on radio you should use short sentences, simple language, metaphors and analogies, and personal anecdotes. Perhaps describe what you see and try to create a sense of place for listeners (Baron 2010, 146). Questions are part of most interviews, so see whether you can talk with the interviewer or get a list of questions in advance.

Print media options include articles, letters to the editor, and opinion pieces known as op-eds. The term "op-ed" refers to a position in a newspaper and is short for "opposite the editorial page" (Baron 2010, 162). An op-ed is a place where you can make a strong, passionate argument about a significant issue. An op-ed is focused, consisting of around 700 to 800 words. It has a clearly defined topic and a theme, which is the big idea of the column. It needs an engaging first line and a strong ending. Most op-ed columns are conversational in tone. When considering whether to run an op-ed, editors look for topics that are currently in the news. When you submit a column for consideration electronically, make it easier for editors by pasting it into your email message in addition to sending it as an attachment (Baron 2010, 164).

If you would like a newspaper to write an article about something you are working on, you first need to find the reporter who focuses on that kind of topic and make a pitch to them. Journalists have deadlines. Make their work easier by giving them a quick overview of your story, including a general idea of how widely the story applies and why their audience should care about it (Baron 2010, 30).

While reporters constantly search for story ideas themselves, many of their story ideas come from news tips from outside sources. A news tip amounts to an information subsidy which saves the journalist time and money (Corbett 2006, 221). The more effective your organization is at supplying these tips, the more likely you are to affect which stories get reported. Most news is driven by events, and timeliness is a critical criterion. A journalist is a gatekeeper who lets in some stories and not others. They rely on known sources, people they believe to be experts with some level of economic or political power. So part of your effort should go toward building relationships and gradually establishing yourself as an expert with intellectual authority to speak on a particular topic.

Many organizations send out news releases. Writing a news release does not mean that your story will get covered. Coverage depends upon what is currently happening in the news and what competing stories arrive at the news desk, together with your group's reputation for high-quality information, its prestige, and the social environment into which your story must fit. Reporters sometimes ignore press releases but respond to individual pitches if the pitch comes from someone with credibility and the story is timely.

Email is a good way to pitch a story if you send it to the appropriate recipient, not only because you can compose your thoughts carefully, but also because it allows busy reporters the flexibility to read it and reply when it is most convenient for them after other deadlines have been met (Baron 2010, 156). Be specific in the subject line, get to the point in the first line or two of the message, provide additional details that are brief, and tell them who you are and why your perspective on the story is interesting.

News is driven by daily events, not long-range stories, so stories about slower, omnipresent, more complex social or environmental issues do not always compete well. Your issue is more likely to get covered if reporters have a specific event to tie it to (Jacobson 2009, 29). A story that is connected to a specific event, particularly if the narrative involves people or ideas in conflict, increases your chances to be noticed. So does a story that is visually compelling or one that offers a local angle on a national or international issue. Most journalism textbooks tell students that the basic news values are proximity, pocketbook, prominent people and places, human interest and drama, unusualness, trends, impact, importance, and currency (Corbett 2006, 227).

Journalists are professional storytellers. They tell stories with a human dimension that involve characters, challenges, and plot twists. They look for stories that contain something new or surprising and stories that activate readers' emotions (Baron 2010, 43).

Most news stories are written in a form known as an inverted pyramid, designed for transmitting information quickly and easily (LaRocque 2003, 99). The most important elements are presented at the beginning of the story where they draw in the reader. Then details are added in subsequent paragraphs in decreasing order of importance. The reason for writing in this way is that most newspaper readers skim. They read headlines and subheadings as they decide which articles to read. Then they may read the first paragraph of a story as they decide whether to continue reading. Most readers do not read all the way to the end of many stories.

Personal Communication Tools

Emails

"Email" is a contraction of the words "electronic mail." Earlier in its history the word was spelled with a hyphen, but modern style guides now agree that it is written as a single unhyphenated word.

Email is the primary way people send messages and information in professional settings. This method of communicating has advantages: It is fast and easy to use, can reach many people at once, and is an effective way to communicate with diverse people on different schedules or in different time zones. Busy recipients can choose when to open emails at times that are convenient for them.

Email is an easy way to send documents, even long ones, as attachments to other people. Messages can be saved and used to track steps in a conversation or to provide written documentation if needed for legal purposes. They are easy to forward to other people. That's an advantage, but it also means the sender has no control over who sees a message they have sent. Be aware that when multiple people are discussing a topic, relevant information may be scattered across multiple messages, and every message may not contain all of the conversation threads.

All email software programs have fields for the sender's address, recipients' addresses, and a subject line. There is also a field labeled "cc," which is short for "carbon copy," for recipients to whom you want to send a copy as a courtesy, and a field labeled "bc," short for "blind copy," for recipients whose addresses you want to hide. Some email programs label the subject line "Re," which is short for "in reference to," instead of "Subject."

The subject line is important. People are flooded with information, including emails, and generally do not read every message. The subject line is how a recipient decides whether to delete a message, to read it, or to file it for later. State the purpose of the message as clearly as you can in the subject line. For example, if you have conducted a greenhouse gas inventory and have a draft report you want people to see, instead of simply writing the word "Report" as the subject, write "Draft GHG inventory report: please review and comment."

Opinions differ on whether to use sentence case or title case in the subject line of an email. Subject lines which use sentence case can feel more conversational and accessible and can be easier to read. Subject lines which use title case can appear more authoritative and professional. A one-year study of 115 million emails found that 54.3 percent of messages with title-case subject lines were opened, but the number fell to 47.6 percent of messages with sentence-case subject lines opened (Levine 2016).

If you use "Reply" or "Reply All" to an email as a convenient way to send a message to recipients without needing to look up their addresses again, be sure that the subject line reflects the content of the message. If it does not, take a moment to write an accurate subject line.

Because people are flooded with information, email messages must be succinct. If you need to communicate information in greater detail, use attachments or website links which the reader can go to if they need more information. Get to the point in the first sentence, explain supporting details clearly, and end with a brief conclusion. Use short bullet lists, headings, and white space between paragraphs to help readers quickly grasp the organization and main points. Limit the message to one main point. If you have a second topic, send that in a separate email. Often the conclusion says what action the sender is requesting, for example, "please send comments to me by March 1." A signature block at the end gives contact information so that readers know how to contact the sender.

People do use texting and instant messaging to exchange short messages quickly. However, this is not an appropriate medium when you need to compose and edit a message carefully, and it does not keep a written record in the same way that emails do.

Memos

The word "memo" is short for "memorandum," a Latin word meaning "a thing to be remembered." The plural of this word is "memoranda," although in common usage many people say either "memorandums" or simply "memos." A memorandum signals that this is a formal communication. It can be printed, sent as an attachment, or can be the body of an email itself.

What distinguishes a memo from a letter is the heading format, which has slots for the sender, recipients, date, and subject. This consistent format allows readers to digest the contents quickly. Memos are typically sent only to people within the same organization. Memos in many workplaces do not include a salutation or greeting; they just get right to the main point of the memo, and the message often gets to the point more quickly and directly than happens in letters. As with emails, it is important that the subject line be descriptive and that the body of the message be succinct and easy to grasp.

Both letters and memos provide a distribution list of people who will receive copies as a courtesy to recipients. The list is at the bottom of the memo or letter, after any signature block. It lets readers know who else will be reading the message and who might be asking them about it, and also confirms that people who should receive this information have received it. For example, some people such as managers or officials simply need to know that the memo was sent but do not need to read or act on its content.

Letters

Letters are more formal documents than memos or emails. Use them when you want an official record of something. They are addressed to a specific person or people and so are personal and individualized. Begin composing a letter by thinking about your reader. Who are they, what is your relationship to them, and what level of formality do they expect? What action do you want them to take after they read your letter? (Lannon and Gurak 2017, 338).

The typical format of a letter includes elements in this order: the sender's address and date at the top, then the recipient's name and address, a salutation, the body of the message, and a complimentary closing followed by four blank lines for the signature and ending with the sender's name and title. The salutation says "Dear" followed by the recipient's name or title and a colon. If you do not know the recipient's name or you are sending a letter to multiple people, an alternative is to replace the salutation with a line beginning with the word "Attention:" followed by the name of the position or the name of the department. Subject lines are typically used in memos but not in letters; however, if the recipient is not expecting the letter, a subject line placed below the sender's address or below an attention line helps the reader focus on what the letter is about. Words that can be used in the complimentary closing include yours truly, sincerely, respectfully, best wishes, or best regards.

If you are enclosing documents, write the word "Enclosure:" below the signature and either state how many documents are enclosed or list them by name. If you are sending copies to other people, provide a distribution list labeled either "copy:" or "cc:" followed by names or positions.

Begin the text of your letter with a brief introductory paragraph that includes the main point of the letter, follow that with explanation and details, and end with a concluding paragraph that summarizes and requests an action, where appropriate. Use moderately short paragraphs of about eight lines or fewer to help your reader grasp content easily. If a paragraph becomes overly long, consider using lists or bullet points to make reading easier for readers.

The first rule of clear writing is to write for your audience. Think about who they are, what they already know, what they need to know, and what questions they might have. Tell them why the material in your letter is important to them. Write the letter with your reader's perspective in mind and convey what this subject means for them, rather than how it affects you (ibid., 346). Use plain language, even if your letter is formal and even if it deals with legal matters (Garner 2013, 2). Plain language is a reflection of clear thinking and it lets your readers understand and use what they read.

When you send materials to someone, such as a set of drawings, a long report, or a proposal, accompany the materials by a transmittal memo or a letter of transmittal. This signals to the recipient that you are sending material, describes what is enclosed, and provides a legal, written record of what was sent. Depending on the project, a letter of transmittal sometimes gives the names of people who contributed to the work.

Presentations

A presentation is a way to communicate with a group and can be used to build a working relationship with a group (ISO 2006, 16). An illustrated presentation, often done by projecting words and images on a screen, builds on the visual nature of human perception and cognition. As we have seen, 40 percent of the human brain's resources are dedicated to seeing and interpreting what we see (Werner et al. 2007, 92). Research shows that images and words in combination are often more effective than either words or images alone (Ware 2013, 332). Keep in mind a key finding of cognitive psychology, that associations play a fundamental role in thinking, learning, and remembering (Few 2012, 67). New information is more meaningful and more relevant when it elicits associations from long-term memory, and that happens when you place it in a context that audiences already recognize and understand (Ham 2002, 170).

Organize Your Presentation

Like all communication, an effective presentation has a clear structure. Provide your audience an organizational framework so that they can process incoming information quickly. If you give them a framework to help them structure the content, they are more likely to find the content meaningful and memorable and more likely to continue paying attention through the end of the presentation. If the content consists of separate bits of information and the structure is not clear to them, they must work harder to hold onto ideas and to try to fit them into some sort of pattern (Ham 2002, 165). If the effort is too great, they will give up and let their attention wander.

Organize your presentation around a unifying theme. The theme is the simple, big idea you want your audience to think about that will enable them to make their own meaningful connections (Larsen 2001, 1). It allows your audience to understand and remember the central message without great effort (Jacobson 2009, 310). After the presentation, if someone were to ask an audience member what the program was about, they should respond with the theme or an idea related to the theme. State the theme in the introduction and again in the conclusion (Ham 2013, 180).

The introduction, although short, gives the audience a mental road map and plays a key role in the rest of your presentation. This is where audiences learn what the theme is, how the presentation is organized, and some clues about how to chunk the information they are going to receive. The introduction sets the stage for the conclusion by saying or showing something that you return to at the conclusion. Try offering a key phrase or sentence in the introduction, then repeating it with emphasis in the conclusion. Or tell the beginning of a story in the introduction, and come back to finish it in the conclusion (Ham 2013, 176). It is so important to how the audience processes the rest of the presentation that you should write the introduction last, after you have developed the body and conclusion. Try introducing your theme with something that affects the audience directly. For example, if your presentation is about stormwater management, you might say, "We all drink water from the Bull Run watershed, but do you know where the water has been?" (Jacobson 2009, 331).

The body of the presentation gives the audience facts and experiences that support the theme. Since we know that humans only hold three to five chunks of information in their working memory at one time, organize your main points into no more than five perceptual chunks. Use stories, anecdotes, analogies, and examples to help the audience connect to the facts and ideas you present. Like interpretive exhibits and talks, an effective presentation has a theme, is organized, is relevant, and is enjoyable (Ham 2013, 14).

A transition is a connector that alerts the audience that the focus is about to change. Use transitions to connect one idea with an idea that will follow. For example, you could say, "Now that we know why temperature causes sea level to rise, let's see how that might affect life in this Alaskan village."

The primary purpose of any conclusion is to reinforce the theme. If you showed a memorable image in the introduction, you can show it again in the conclusion. If you said a key phrase at the beginning, you can reemphasize it here. If you told an unfinished story in the introduction, you can tell the rest of the story here. You can summarize the main points, suggest what the theme might mean within a larger context, or suggest what the audience can do now with their new information (Ham 2013, 175). The conclusion can be short.

Plan your presentation by writing a detailed outline of the body of the presentation. Include details such as where to foreshadow, where to use transitions, where to add intangible, universal concepts, and where to insert personal anecdotes (Ham 2013, 193). Once you have developed the body of the presentation, go on to the conclusion. Finally, lay out the introduction once you know how the body and conclusion will flow. Now your presentation has a clear beginning, middle, and end.

An engaging presentation has a story line (Roam 2014, 30). Thus it is different from a report, which is factual, organized by topic, and relatively exhaustive (Duarte 2010, 26). As you plan your presentation, make the information more vivid and personal by transforming it into a story (Jacobson 2009, 329). Just as a movie director creates storyboards before actually filming a scene, you should plan the story of your presentation. Translate facts into stories of personal situations and use descriptive detail to let audiences feel as though they are part of the scene. Nancy Duarte, whose firm designed presentations for

Michael Pollan, author of *Omnivore's Dilemma,* and developed the compelling graphics in Al Gore's film about climate change, *An Inconvenient Truth,* explains that "A report primarily conveys information; stories produce an experience" (Duarte 2010, 27). Successful presenters at TED Talks usually start not with facts but with a personal story. Storytelling activates multiple regions of the brain and breaks down walls between presenters and the audiences they want to reach (Gallo 2014, 45).

A story has a hero who faces a challenge or conflict that is resolved at the end. In a compelling presentation, the audience is the hero in the story (Duarte 2010, 34). Your presentation can describe a problem and take the audience to the threshold of solving it, at which point they can choose whether to cross it or not. Duarte's approach is to begin with a concise description of what everyone agrees is true, showing an audience what is, and then to conclude with what could be (ibid., 38). That is, show a clear contrast between who your audience is in their ordinary world and who they could be when they leave your presentation, as if crossing a threshold into a special world. Point out the gaps between what is and what could be, the forces that your audience-heroes must contend with in order to resolve the conflict. "What is" might be your organization's low recycling rate, or its greenhouse gas emissions that contribute to an existential climate-change crisis in the world. "What could be" might be a closed-loop system that eliminates waste, or a net-zero energy program that is part of a healthy, regenerative world.

Human brains cannot ignore novelty. In our evolutionary past, something that stood out could mean something delicious or something dangerous, so our sensory systems evolved in a way that makes us sensitive to differences (Few 2012, 79). This is why the use of contrast is so effective in graphic design. And it is why including something surprising in a presentation, or presenting something in a novel way, makes the experience vivid and memorable and prompts the audience to care (Todd 2013, 142). Think about how you can reveal information that is completely new to your audience, or how you can present familiar information in a way that is unexpected.

Use novelty and difference to break up the flow of slides. If every slide is the same, with yet another list of bullet points or another in a string of charts, audiences' attention will drift. If you need to communicate data, deliver one statistic or theme per slide, break up the sameness by interspersing slides with images, and bring the facts to life for your audience by telling personal stories about people behind the data (Gallo 2014, 219).

Slide Design

Presentation software such as PowerPoint uses slides which are projected onto a screen. Use a consistent slide background, color scheme, typeface, and layout between slides so that audiences do not have to reorient themselves each time a new slide appears. You want the audience to focus on the content, not the tools.

Use dark-colored text on a light-colored background (Moscardo et al. 2007, 51). It is more readable and easier to look at for long periods of time than dark letters on light backgrounds[2] (Usability.gov 2017, 11).

Use less saturated colors, including colors found in nature, for most of the slide, with saturated colors used only to provide contrast and highlight certain information. Saturated colors, especially bright, warm colors, are hard on the eyes when projected on a screen (Caputo et al. 2008, 67). It takes time to find designs and color schemes you think are effective. So once you create a good slide design and format, save it as part of a library of slides you can turn to.

Images on Slides

Choose images with enough resolution to be clear when projected on a large screen. Choose images that clearly illustrate an idea and avoid generic illustrations that do not add meaning. Include humans in some of the images; people respond to images that contain other people. Consider extending your images all the way to the edges of a slide. Or consider placing a vertical image over half a slide, with a title and brief text on the other side (Finkelstein 2012, 74). Occasionally cover an entire slide with one image.

Images have impact. They can be beautiful or surprising or troubling. High-quality images, particularly if they are surprising, trigger what neuroscientists call emotionally charged events. These images connect the visual cortex and the amygdala, the region of the brain responsible for tagging the emotional importance of things, so that they arouse our emotional responses and cause us to perceive information more vividly and to remember it more clearly (Todd 2013, 142).

You can use a sequence of images to develop an idea, such as neighborhood transformation, a changing ecosystem, or an evolving climate system. Or you can begin with a simple base image and use a sequence of images to add details progressively. Revealing information one piece at a time allows audiences to focus on the first piece, then build understanding through association as subsequent pieces are added (Ritter 2004, 136).

You don't have to limit your graphics to photographs or professional illustrations. Depending upon the audience and the topic, in some cases using crude, hand-drawn images can be inviting and can help establish a personal connection (Roam 2010, 23).

Text on Slides

Your audience will be viewing your presentation on a screen from a distance, so font size for slide titles must be big. Use sans serif typefaces, which are easier to read from a distance (Thomas et al. 2006, 95).

Slides should contain relatively little text. When a slide contains words, audiences will read them before they begin listening to you (Thomas et al. 2006, 89).

People cannot read and study an image at the same time, but they can listen to spoken words while studying an image (Ware 2013, 333). Spoken, not printed, words should accompany images. Slides are not the sole focus of the message. It is you, rather than the slides, who delivers the message (Duarte 2010, 178). You can then provide electronic or printed handouts so that audiences have a record of what was said.

Slide Layout

Limit each slide to a single idea. Each slide must be vivid and uncluttered if it is to communicate clearly (Baron 2010, 129). You will confuse your audience or lose their attention if a slide contains multiple ideas, a list of bullet points, or a lot of text. Where you can, include only a title in large font, an image that explains the title, and a brief caption. Changing visuals frequently helps audiences to stay engaged. Placing only one idea on each slide means you will have more slides in a presentation than is traditional, and occasionally you may even need to explain to workshop planners that having many slides does not mean your presentation will be long.

Align elements on a slide with each other, both horizontally and vertically where possible. Unaligned elements give a jumbled, random appearance and require more effort for the viewer to comprehend. If elements on a slide appear disconnected, consider using a thin line to connect them or to guide the viewer's eye. Or consider placing a band of color across the entire slide, behind the text and image, to tie elements together (Finkelstein 2012, 60).

Slides can be laid out on grids, just as other graphic design layouts are. For example, you can use the rule of thirds. Divide the slide into thirds, both vertically and horizontally. Put important content at the intersection of those imaginary grid lines, or put content along one or more of the lines. If you are using PowerPoint, the software offers guides that you can place at whatever locations you choose. If you place them in your slide master (the master slide), they will be visible on every slide.

Elements that are centered and symmetrical can appear static; using the rule of thirds allows a more dynamic layout. Diagonals also feel dynamic, even when they are subtle. Look for diagonals in your images. Or, since we read from top to bottom and left to right, place text in the upper left and an image in the lower right of a slide (Finkelstein 2012, 82).

Avoid special effects: animations that zoom in, sound effects, and animated backgrounds. The audience's focus should be on the content, not tool.

Practice

People who give high-quality presentations have one trait in common: they take this task seriously and prepare carefully, every time (Baron 2010, 225). A good presentation doesn't happen on its own; it takes planning and practice. The more you practice, the better you will know the material and the more confident you will be. Then, instead of worrying about how you look or what you should say, you can focus on connecting with your audience (Roam 2014, 246).

If you can find people willing to help you, practice in front of other people. Ask them for feedback.

Record yourself and watch the recording. Look for filler words and verbal tics, such as "um" or "you know," for gestures that are distracting, and for lack of movement or lack of eye contact (Gallo 2014, 78). You are the only person who will see the recording; use it to improve your presentation.

Do at least one practice in the room where you will be presenting, or one similar to it. Set up your equipment like it will be when you present. Make sure everything works. Then practice your presentation more than once. Practice walking onstage or stepping to the podium, look at your imaginary audience, and go through your entire presentation, word for word, image by image.

Delivering a Presentation

Use words on the slides as cues to prompt you for key points you want to make in your talk. Your goal is to connect with the audience so, if you can, avoid memorizing a speech or reading from a script. Having said that, if you are new to presenting and feeling uncertain, then using written outline notes or a verbatim script can get you through your first few presentations until you begin to feel more comfortable with the process.

Practicing will help you evaluate your speaking speed. If your speed is too slow, you will sound unnatural. If your speed is too fast, your message may be hard for listeners to absorb. The ideal rate of speech used to record audio books is about 150 to 160 words per minute. Tests show this is the rate at which most listeners can comfortably listen, understand, and remember (Williams 1998, 1447). You can speak slightly faster because visual inputs of facial expressions, movement, and eye contact add meaning for audiences. Many successful presenters at TED Talks deliver messages at a rate of about 189 words per minute (Gallo 2014, 84). The ideal pace is the rate you would use in normal conversation. Think of your speech not as a presentation you deliver, but as a conversation you have with the audience.

Use body language to connect with your audience. The style that social scientists have found to be persuasive is known as eager nonverbal. This style of effective speakers includes animated, open movements, hand movements that open and project outwards, and body position that leans forward (Fennis and Stel 2011, 806). Aim for natural movement. Physical tics such as tapping, shoving your hands into pockets, or fidgeting with objects make you look nervous and uncertain. Staying motionless in one spot makes you appear bored and unengaged, and can have the same effect on your audience. Do some moving and even walking to appear natural and to engage your audience (Gallo 2014, 102).

It is normal to feel nervous before a presentation. Even well-known speakers and actors get nervous before going onstage. If you have practiced, you will be familiar with your material. Then, what makes a strong delivery is the passion you feel for your topic. Think about what it is you care about, and why you want your audience to know about it and to care, too. Then have a conversation with them, with the passion inside you providing the underlying energy.

Handouts

Give your audiences handouts, either on paper or online. Weeks or months later, people can look back at these handouts and be reminded of your key points. If you meet with policymakers, you should give them a one-page leave-behind sheet to make it easy for them to recall your conversation. If you present at a workshop or conference, you can make the pages available to download as PDFs. Some conference organizers also ask you to make your presentation slides available for download, but these do not take the place of a one- or two-page summary sheet. Use a takeaway handout to reinforce your main points and increase the longevity of your message (Thomas et al. 2006, 85). Include a summary of the presentation's main points and your contact information. Place the main point at the beginning, rather than starting with background material. Break information into chunks and use headings, contrast, and white space so that people can read your key message at a glance (Baron 2010, 191).

Communication Plans

To make your communication successful, approach it methodically—with a plan. A communication plan is the way an organization provides information, acquires information, and engages in dialog with people inside or outside the organization to encourage a shared understanding (ISO 2006, 1). Your plan will include a range of options. People learn and communicate in different ways; the more your communication plan provides a variety of media, the more you can support a diversity of people and their diverse approaches.

Developing a Plan

First, decide what you intend to achieve with your communication activity (ISO 2006, 8). Define your overall goals and a time frame. Understand the situation; look at all the issues that could affect your communication initiative: social, cultural, economic, legal, environmental, political, and technical (UNEP 2005, 16). Define not only what information you want to give but what information you hope to gain (ISO 2006, 21).

Identify the audiences you want to reach (Jacobson 2009, 56). Think about them before you begin planning or developing content (PLAIN 2011, i). Conduct audience research. How are they connected to the issue about which you are communicating? What is their level of knowledge and experience? What motivates them? Who can influence them? What actions do you want them to take? Develop a profile of your audiences. For larger communication initiatives, use research tools including focus groups or surveys (UNEP 2005, 16). Your communication plan should include a range of potential target groups, not just those who are supportive of your work or who have the resources to organize and express themselves (ISO 2006, 8). Be open to including a range of communication approaches, depending upon the needs and interests of your target audiences (ISO 2006, 20).

Set objectives that are realistic, achievable, and measurable. Define what changes will indicate that you have met your objectives (UNEP 2005, 17). Define what you will use as quantifiable indicators of progress toward your objective. Identify separate, measurable objectives for each target audience (Jacobson 2009, 56).

Develop a clear message. Create a central message that will run through the various elements of your communication materials, including things like logo, color theme, and style. Then tailor the message to different audiences (UNEP 2005, 17). Develop key messages for each piece of content (Redish 2012, 38). Have conversations with stakeholders as you develop your communication.

Define communication channels and the media you will use. Identify the ways your audience prefers to receive information. Choose a variety of formats so that materials are appropriate and accessible for a range of target groups (ISO 2006, 10). Include social networks so that your message is delivered by real people (UNEP 2005, 17). Determine what social media you will use, how you will use them, and whether you will form groups within some of them.

Plan how you will manage and implement the communication campaign as it progresses. Define roles and responsibilities, both because that is good planning practice and so that you can coordinate between the people who gather and formulate information to be communicated and the people who are responsible for communicating and conducting outreach (ISO 2006, 17). Name a project leader or coordinator to be responsible for managing day-to-day details and maintaining the content. In smaller organizations, all these tasks may be assigned to one individual. Depending on the size of your project, set up a steering committee and include people with expertise in communications, policy, and sustainability issues. Identify who will design, write, edit, illustrate, produce, and maintain various communication components, identify who will be in charge of monitoring and maintaining websites and social media, and determine what skills are needed by each of these people (Redish 2012, 39). Or consider whether to use an outside consultant to produce communication materials.

Designate people who can serve as spokespeople. Provide them with speaker training or media training (ISO 2006, 20). Have a person who is the face of your campaign, someone who is trustworthy and sympathetic (UNEP 2005, 18).

Develop a project plan with a timeline and a budget, and define who will be responsible for certain tasks. Plan what to do if deadlines are missed or if something else goes wrong (UNEP 2005, 18). For your timeline, develop a schedule, with a list of tasks and who is responsible; begin with your target date, estimate the time required for each action item, and work backwards to milestones with dates (Hayward 2015). When you plan the timeline, think about outside factors in timing: what external events or internal business cycles might you want to synchronize with and when will stakeholders be available? If your communication is carried out by communication professionals, consider training for others in your organization on both communication techniques and on the issues to be communicated (ISO 2006, 17).

As part of the implementation, provide advance notice of publication so that interested parties have a chance to review and provide feedback (ISO 2006, 20).

After you plan the content, coordinate, and implement a communication plan, you need to manage and maintain it and then review it regularly.

What to Include

Brainstorm with stakeholders and planning teams about what kinds of components to use as part of your communication plan. Some of your choices will depend on whether you are only sharing information with recipients or whether you envision a multiway conversation.

Examples of communication tools for sharing information include articles in news media, op-ed columns, letters to the editor, printed or electronic newsletters, brochures, one-page flyers, fact sheets including contact information, and process sheets describing timelines and the process itself. Examples of communication tools for collecting information or for conducting conversations include survey forms, written notes or letters sent through the mail by participants, and "butcher paper conversations" with large pieces of paper and markers in public locations.

Examples of online communication tools include social media tools, blogs, online discussion forums, online feedback forms and surveys, slides or graphics which people can download for general information or as an introduction to a later forum, live-streamed forums with websites where participants can submit questions and comments, as well as websites that provide answers to frequently asked questions (FAQs), links to reports, articles, glossaries, and other websites.

Examples of face-to-face communication include focus groups, surveys, personal interviews with prepared questions, community groups, drop-in chats, scheduled conversations such as coffee talks or brownbag lunches, and facilitated group discussions or forums.

Each of these elements can use a different mix of text, images, and video which can be expressed in different styles (Redish 2012, 40). Each of these choices should be deliberate, and a consistent central theme should run through them.

Guidelines

Be sure your communication plan is readily accessible to everyone involved in planning or communicating. When changes occur, update the plan and communicate the changes to team members and stakeholders. Provide regular updates to both team members and stakeholders. And ask stakeholders for feedback on whether the level of information and the frequency of updates are helpful (UNEP 2005, 19).

Provide some sort of document management system for organizing and maintaining the materials you collect so that people can find what they need quickly and easily (ISO 2006, 19).

If you include multiple types of components and formats in your communication plan, maintain consistent style, color scheme, typefaces, and formatting. This links the components to each other visually, gives your information consistency and allows your audiences to get oriented quickly (Thomas et al. 2006, 15). Develop or adopt style guidelines. Develop additional guidelines for posting or commenting on social media (Redish 2012, 43). Put all these guidelines in writing.

Be on a constant lookout for ideas. Look for examples of websites, newsletters, posters, or other communication tools. Look for what works and what doesn't work. Look for elements you like and elements you would avoid (Caputo et al. 2008, 19). This doesn't mean you should directly copy other people's work, but you can use other examples to stimulate ideas. You can use a certain color palette, layout, or typeface as long as it is not trademarked or copyrighted. You can find examples everywhere, not just in sustainability work. Take pictures and notes, and keep an idea file of color combinations, designs, word choice, and other strategies.

Evaluation

Measure and evaluate your communication so that you learn whether your communication plan worked as intended and how it could be improved (Jacobson 2009, 18). If a program does not reach your target audience, or they misunderstand a message, or you aim for the wrong behavior change, the result can be negative impact or actual damage. You will not know this unless you evaluate. And if a communication plan is effective, you will not know what specific factors made it successful unless you evaluate (ibid., 394). Document the evaluation.

Evaluate two dimensions of your communication plan: the process and the results. Measure the process by assessing what was communicated, how often, where, and to how many people. Measure outcomes by evaluating changes in awareness, attitudes, and behaviors (UNEP 2005, 18). You can do this with before and after surveys, interviews, direct observations, and other measures such as number of new members joining or amount of donations (Jacobson 2009, 407).

Conduct before and after surveys to measure outcomes of your communication: Evaluate the quality and appropriateness of the information you communicated, whether the approach was transparent, and whether it fostered meaningful dialog with your target audiences. Evaluate whether your target audiences' needs were met and whether your objectives were reached (ISO 2006, 21). Note outcomes that met your objectives as well as unintended outcomes, both negative and positive (Caputo et al. 2008, 92). Determine how people responded, what was the impact, and what changes occurred in people's awareness, attitudes, and behaviors (UNEP 2005, 18).

Get feedback from your audiences. Evaluate whether they knew they were heard, whether they were informed how their input was to be used, and whether there was appropriate follow-up for any issues raised by your audiences (ISO 2006, 21).

You can also evaluate a communication plan using pilot tests before you commit to implementing it fully. To do this, use conversations with focus groups or surveys, either people you know or representatives of your target audience selected at random. Or do a portfolio test: put printed materials or illustrations in a folder, either one at a time or with alternatives, and ask people for their reactions (Jacobson 2009, 67). You can ask open-ended questions such as, "What does this set of colors make you think of?" or "what word or phrase would you use to describe the personality of this typeface?" (Caputo et al. 2008, 23). Because implications or conclusions that are obvious to you may be invisible to your audiences, you should test draft materials not with people you know but with a sample of your target audience (Morgan and Welton 1992, 141).

Always provide a way for people to give feedback so that people feel heard and so that you can make continuous improvement. In a presentation, that means leaving time for questions. In a written document, that means providing contact information. In a website, that means providing an online form or contact link (Thomas et al. 2006, 14). Actively promote and respond to feedback (ISO 2006, 20). You may or may not choose to make changes based on feedback, but people who give you input need to be assured that they have been heard (ISO 2006, 21).

Notes

1 A clause is a sequence of words that contains a subject and a verb phrase. An independent clause can form a complete sentence; a dependent clause cannot (Millward 1980, 12).
2 Not all designers agree on whether dark-colored or light-colored backgrounds are more legible on projected slides.

BIBLIOGRAPHY

Anthropocene Working Group, Subcommission on Quaternary Stratigraphy, International Commission on Stratigraphy. Updated February 23, 2016. http://quaternary.stratigraphy.org/workinggroups/anthropocene/

Appleton, Jay. *The Experience of Landscape.* New York: Wiley, 1975, 48–73.

Arnheim, Rudolf. *Visual Thinking.* Berkeley: University of California Press, 1969; reprinted 1997.

Arthur, Paul and Romedi Passini. *Wayfinding: People, Signs, and Architecture.* New York: McGraw-Hill, 1992.

AtKisson, Alan. *The Sustainability Transformation: How to Accelerate Positive Change in Challenging Times.* London: Earthscan, 2011.

Aveni, Anthony F. *Between the Lines: The Mystery of the Giant Ground Drawings of Ancient Nasca, Peru.* Austin: University of Texas Press, 2000.

Baddeley, Alan D. "The Magical Number Seven: Still Magic after All These Years?" *Psychological Review* 101 (1994): 353–356.

Barlett, Peggy F. and Geoffrey W. Chase, eds. *Sustainability on Campus: Stories and Strategies for Change.* Cambridge, MA: MIT Press, 2004.

Barnes, Susan B. *An Introduction to Visual Communication.* New York: Peter Lang, 2011.

Baron, Nancy. *Escape from the Ivory Tower: A Guide to Making Your Science Matter.* Washington, DC: Island Press, 2010.

Barth, Brian. "Infinite Mapping: 3-D Scanning and the Holographic Landscape." *Landscape Architecture Magazine* 107 no. 1 (January 2017): 56–62.

Becken, Susanne and John E. Hay. *Climate Change and Tourism: From Policy to Practice.* London: Routledge, 2012.

Beckley, Janet A. "Scientists Calculate Total Amount of Plastics Ever Produced." *UGA Today,* July 19, 2017.

Bejan, Adrian. "The Golden Ratio Predicted: Vision Cognition and Locomotion as a Single Design in Nature." *International Journal of Design & Nature and Ecodynamics* 4 no. 2 (2009): 97–104.

Bell, Simon and Stephen Morse. *Measuring Sustainability: Learning from Doing.* Sterling, VA: Earthscan, 2003.

———. *Sustainability Indicators: Measuring the Immeasurable?* Sterling, VA: Earthscan, 2008.

Berger, Craig. "The Image of the City." *segdDESIGN* No. 26 (2009).

Biggar, Hugh. "Honoring the Bay's Original Shorelines." *The Cardinal Inquirer*, February 5, 2004.

Blackmore, Susan. "The Power of Memes." *Scientific American* 283 no. 4 (October 2000): 52–61.

Bosley, Deborah. "International Graphics: A Search for Neutral Territory." *INTER-COM*, August/September 1996: 4–7.

Braasch, Gary. "Climate Change: Is Seeing Believing?" *Bulletin of the Atomic Scientists* 69 no. 6 (November/December 2013): 33–41. doi:10.1177/0096340213508628

Brochu, Lisa. *Interpretive Planning: The 5-M Model for Successful Planning Projects.* Fort Collins, CO: National Association for Interpretation, 2003.

Broda-Bahm, Ken. "Don't Just Display Graphics, Interact with Them." *Persuasive Litigator*, February 16, 2012a. www.persuasivelitigator.com/2012/02/dont-just-display-graphics-interact-with-them.html

———. "Learn from Memes." *Persuasive Litigator*, December 24, 2012b. www.persuasive litigator.com/2012/12/learn-from-memes.html

Brown, Robert D. *Design with Microclimate: The Secret to Comfortable Outdoor Space.* Washington, DC: Island Press, 2010.

Bruno, Crystle. "Expletive Words and Phrases." San José State University Writing Center, 2012. www.sjsu.edu/writingcenter/

Butler, Katy. "Winning Words." *Sierra Magazine* 89 no. 4 (July/August 2004): 54.

Calori, Chris. *Signage and Wayfinding Design: A Complete Guide to Creating Environmental Graphic Design Systems.* New York: John Wiley, 2007.

Campbell, Joseph. *The Hero with a Thousand Faces.* New York: Pantheon Books, 1949.

Campbell, Nancy J. *Writing Effective Policies and Procedures: A Step-by-Step Resource for Clear Communication.* New York: AMACOM, 1998.

Campoli, Julie and Alex S. MacLean. *Visualizing Density.* Cambridge, MA: Lincoln Institute of Land Policy, 2007.

Caputo, Paul, Shea Lewis, and Lisa Brochu. *Interpretation by Design: Graphic Design Basics for Heritage Interpreters.* Fort Collins, CO: InterpPress, 2008.

Card, Stuart K., Jock D. Mackinlay, and Ben Shneiderman. *Readings in Information Visualization: Using Vision to Think.* San Francisco, CA: Morgan Kaufmann, 1999.

Carey, Alison. Personal interview. Ashland, OR: Oregon Shakespeare Festival, August 11, 2016.

Chen, Chaomei. *Mapping Scientific Frontiers: The Quest for Knowledge Visualization.* London: Springer-Verlag, 2002.

Chicone, Sarah J. and Richard A. Kissel. *Dinosaurs and Dioramas: Creating Natural History Exhibitions.* Walnut Creek, CA: Left Coast Press, 2013.

Corbett, Julia B. *Communicating Nature: How We Create and Understand Environmental Messages.* Washington, DC: Island Press, 2006.

Corner, James. "A Discourse on Theory I: 'Sounding the Depths'—Origins, Theory, and Representation." *Landscape Journal* 17, special issue (1998): 61–78.

Crutzen, Paul J. "Geology of Mankind." *Nature* 415 (January 2002): 23.

Cunningham, William P. and Mary Ann Cunningham. *Environmental Science: A Global Concern*, 11th ed. New York: McGraw-Hill, 2010.

Deans, Emily. "Dopamine Primer." *Psychology Today*, May 13, 2011. https://www.psychologytoday.com/blog/evolutionary-psychiatry/201105/dopamine-primer

Dederer, Claire. "Looking for Inspiration in the Melting Ice." *New York Times*, September 23, 2007.

Dobbs, David. "The Quest of Christof Koch." *Scientific American Mind* 16 no. 2 (2005): 32–37.

Dreiseitl, Herbert, Dieter Grau, and Karl H.C. Ludwig, eds. *Waterscapes: Planning, Building and Designing with Water*. Basel: Birkhäuser, 2001.

Duarte, Nancy. *Resonate: Present Visual Stories that Transform Audiences*. New York: John Wiley, 2010.

Earthjustice. *Re: Green – The Ecological Roadmap*. San Francisco, CA: Earthjustice, 2008.

Edwards, Andrés R. *The Sustainability Revolution: Portrait of a Paradigm Shift*. Gabriola Island, BC: New Society Publishers, 2005.

Ehmann, Sven, Stephan Bohle, and Robert Klanten, eds. *Cause and Effect: Visualizing Sustainability*. Berlin: Gestalten, 2012.

Ehrenfeld, John R. *Sustainability by Design*. New Haven, CT: Yale University Press, 2008.

Elkins, James. *The Domain of Images*. Ithaca, NY: Cornell University Press, 1999.

Engelman, Robert. "Beyond Sustainababble." In Worldwatch Institute. *State of the World 2013: Is Sustainability Still Possible?* Washington, DC: Island Press, 2013, 4–16.

Ervin, Stephen M. and Hasbrouck, Hope H. *Landscape Modeling: Digital Techniques for Landscape Visualization*. New York: McGraw-Hill, 2001.

Ewing, B., D. Moore, S. Goldfinger, A. Oursler, A. Reed, and M. Wackernagel. *The Ecological Footprint Atlas 2010*. Oakland, CA: Global Footprint Network, 2010.

Fahey, Anna. "Got Policy Solutions? Think: Brownies." Sightline Institute, February 5, 2015. www.sightline.org/2015/02/05/got-policy-solutions-think-brownies/

Falk, John H. and Lynn D. Dierking. *The Museum Experience*. London: Routledge, 2016.

———, and Susan Foutz, eds. *In Principle, In Practice: Museums as Learning Institutions*. New York: Altamira Press, 2007.

Farr, Douglas. *Sustainable Urbanism: Urban Design with Nature*. New York: John Wiley, 2008.

Fennis, Bob M. and Marielle Stel. "The Pantomime of Persuasion: Fit Between Non Verbal Communication and Influence Strategies." *Journal of Experimental Social Psychology* 47 (2011): 806–811.

Few, Stephen. *Now You See It: Simple Visualization Techniques for Quantitative Analysis*. Oakland, CA: Analytics Press, 2009.

———. *Show Me the Numbers: Designing Tables and Graphs to Enlighten*, 2nd ed. Burlingame, CA: Analytics Press, 2012.

———. *Information Dashboard Design: Displaying Data for At-a-Glance Monitoring*, 2nd ed. Burlingame, CA: Analytics Press, 2013.

Field, Syd. *Screenplay: The Foundations of Screenwriting*. New York: Delta, 2005.

Fiksel, Joseph. *Design for Environment*, 2nd ed. New York: McGraw-Hill, 2009.

Finke, Gail Deibler. *City Signs: Innovative Urban Graphics*. New York: Madison Square Press, 1994.

Finkelstein, Ellen. *Slide Design for Non-Designers*. Fairfield, IA: Rainbow Resources, 2012.

Fisher, Anna V., K.E. Godwin, and H. Seltman. "Visual Environment, Attention Allocation, and Learning: When Too Much of a Good Thing May Be Bad." *Psychological Science* 25 no. 7 (2014): 1362–1370.

Flannery, Tim. *Here on Earth: A Natural History of the Planet*. New York: Atlantic Monthly Press, 2010.

Fogg, B.J., C. Soohoo, D.R. Danielson, L. Marable, J. Stanford, and E.R. Tauber. *How Do Users Evaluate the Credibility of Web Sites? A Study with over 2,500 Participants*. Proceedings of DUX2003, Designing for User Experiences Conference. Stanford University Persuasive Technology Lab, 2003.

Foley, Jonathan. "Boundaries for a Healthy Planet." *Scientific American*, April 2010, 54–57.

Folke, Carl. "Respecting Planetary Boundaries and Reconnecting to the Biosphere." In Worldwatch Institute. *State of the World 2013: Is Sustainability Still Possible?* Washington, DC: Island Press, 2013, 19–27.

Foster, John. "Making Sense of Stewardship: Metaphorical Thinking and the Environment." *Environmental Education Research* 11 no. 1 (February 2005): 25–36. doi:10.1080/1350462042000328721

Frankel, Felice C. and Angela H. DePace. *Visual Strategies: A Practical Guide to Graphics for Scientists & Engineers.* New Haven, CT: Yale University Press, 2012.

Gallant, Joanna, Samuel H. Solomon, and John P. Esser, eds. *The Science of Courtroom Litigation: Jury Research and Analytical Graphics.* New York: ALM Publishing, 2008.

Galli, Alessandro, Thomas Wiedmann, Ertug Ercin, Doris Knoblauch, Brad Ewing, and Stefan Giljum. "Integrating Ecological, Carbon and Water Footprint into a 'Footprint Family' of Indicators: Definition and Role in Tracking Human Pressure on the Planet." *Ecological Indicators* 16 (2012): 100–112.

Gallo, Carmine. *Talk Like TED: The 9 Public-Speaking Secrets of the World's Top Minds.* New York: St. Martin's Griffin, 2014.

Galloway, Stephen. "'An Inconvenient Truth,' 10 Years Later." *The Hollywood Reporter*, issue 16 (May 27, 2016).

Gallup. *Gallup News: Environment*, March 27, 2017. http://news.gallup.com/poll/1615/environment.aspx

Gardner, Howard. *Multiple Intelligences: The Theory in Practice.* New York: Basic Books, 1993.

Garner, Bryan A. *A Dictionary of Modern Legal Usage*, 2nd ed. New York: Oxford University Press, 1995.

———. *Legal Writing in Plain English,* 2nd ed. Chicago, IL: University of Chicago Press, 2013.

Geyer, Roland, Jenna R. Jambeck, and Kara Lavender Law. "Production, Use, and Fate of All Plastics Ever Made." *Science Advances* 3 no. 7 (July 19, 2017). doi:10.1126/sciadv.1700782

Gibson, James J. *The Perception of the Visual World.* Cambridge, MA: Riverside Press, 1950.

Gilding, Paul. *The Great Disruption.* New York: Bloomsbury Press, 2011.

Goffman, Erving. *Frame Analysis: An Essay on the Organization of Experience.* Boston, MA: Northeastern University Press, 1986.

Goodman-Khasani, Julie. *15 Essential Tips to Sharpen Your Graphic Design.* Webinar. Washington, DC: American Society of Landscape Architects, March 4, 2014.

Goodstein, David L. "Richard P. Feynman, Teacher." *Physics Today* 42 (1989):70–75.

Griswold, Mac. "Damaged and Healed Landscapes: The Landfill's Progress." *Landscape Architecture Magazine* 83 no. 10 (October 1993): 78–81.

Groffman, Peter M. et al. "Restarting the Conversation: Challenges at the Interface between Ecology and Society." *Frontiers in Ecology and the Environment* 8 no. 6 (August 2010): 284–291. doi:10.1890/090160

Gross, Michael, Ron Zimmerman, and Jim Buchholz. *Signs, Trails, and Wayside Exhibits: Connecting People and Places,* 3rd ed. Stevens Point, WI: UW-SP Foundation Press, 2006.

Hall, Edward T. *The Hidden Dimension.* Garden City, NY: Doubleday, 1969.

Hall, Sean. *This Means This, That Means That: A User's Guide to Semiotics.* London: Laurence King, 2007.

Ham, Sam H. "Cognitive Psychology and Interpretation." In Eilean Hooper-Greenhill, ed. *The Educational Role of the Museum,* 2nd ed. London: Routledge, 2002, 161–171.

————. "Foreword." In Doug Knapp, *Applied Interpretation: Putting Research into Practice.* Fort Collins, CO: InterpPress, 2007.

————. *Interpretation: Making a Difference on Purpose.* Golden, CO: Fulcrum Publishing, 2013.

Hamre, Emily. "3 Tips for Becoming a Better Design Communicator." AIGA, The Professional Association for Design. 2017. www.aiga.org/better-design-communicator

Harris, Robert L. *Information Graphics: A Comprehensive Illustrated Reference.* Atlanta, GA: Management Graphics, 1996.

Hart, Jack. *A Writer's Coach: The Complete Guide to Writing Strategies that Work.* New York: Anchor Books, 2006a.

Hart, Maureen. *Guide to Sustainable Community Indicators.* 2nd ed. West Hartford, CT: Sustainable Measures, 2006b.

Hayward, Jennifer. *Project Management.* Eugene, OR: Lane Community College Sustainability Systems Seminar, May 11, 2015.

Heath, Chip and Dan Heath. *Made to Stick: Why Some Ideas Survive and Others Die.* New York: Random House, 2007.

Heinberg, Richard. *The End of Growth: Adapting to Our New Economic Reality.* Gabriola Island, BC: New Society Publishers, 2011.

Helphand, Kenneth. "Interpretive Interventions." *Cultural Resource Management* 18 no. 5 (1995): 13–17.

Hicks, Wilson. *Words and Pictures: An Introduction to Photojournalism.* New York: Harper & Brothers, 1952.

Hitchcock, Darcy and Marsha Willard. *The Step-by-Step Guide to Sustainability Planning.* Sterling, VA: Earthscan, 2008.

Hoekstra, Arjen Y. and Ashok K. Chapagain. *Globalization of Water: Sharing the Planet's Freshwater Resources.* Oxford: Blackwell, 2008.

————, M. Maite Aldaya, and Mesfin M. Mekonnen. *The Water Footprint Assessment Manual: Setting the Global Standard.* London: Earthscan, 2011.

Hogben, Susan. "It's (Not) Easy Being Green: Unpacking Visual Rhetoric and Environmental Claims in Car, Energy and Utility Advertisements in the UK (2007–08)." *Language & Ecology* 3 no.1 (2009).

Hopkins, Lewis D. and Marisa A. Zapata, eds. *Engaging the Future: Forecasts, Scenarios, Plans, and Projects.* Cambridge, MA: Lincoln Institute of Land Policy, 2007.

Hosein, Neesha. "Apollo Astronaut Shares Story of NASA's Earthrise." Houston, TX: Johnson Space Center, March 29, 2012. www.nasa.gov/centers/johnson/home/earthrise.html

Hu, H., E. Real, K. Takamiya, M.G. Kang, J. Ledoux, Richard L. Huganir, and Roberto Malinow. "Emotion Enhances Learning via Norepinephrine Regulation of AMPA-Receptor Trafficking." *Cell* 131 no. 1 (October 5, 2007): 160–173.

Hyder, Shama. *The Zen of Social Media Marketing,* 4th ed. Dallas, TX: Benbella Books, 2016.

Info Entrepreneurs. "How to Write an Environmental Policy." Chambre de Commerce du Montréal Métropolitain. 2014. www.infoentrepreneurs.org/en/guides/how-to-write-an-environmental-policy/

International Association for Public Participation (IAP2). *IAP2 Public Participation Spectrum.* 2004. www.iap2.org/

IPCC. *Climate Change 2014: Synthesis Report. Contribution of Working Groups I, II and III to the Fifth Assessment Report of the Intergovernmental Panel on Climate Change.* (Core Writing Team, R.K. Pachauri and L.A. Meyer, eds.). Geneva, Switzerland: IPCC, 2014.

ISO. *ISO 14063: Environmental Management – Environmental Communication – Guidelines and Examples.* Geneva: International Organization for Standardization, 2006. https://www.iso.org/standard/34676.html

Jacobson, Susan K. *Communication Skills for Conservation Professionals,* 2nd ed. Washington, DC: Island Press, 2009.

James, Rachel. *Promoting Sustainable Behavior: A Guide to Successful Communication.* Berkeley: University of California Press, 2010.

Johns Hopkins Medical Institutions. "Why Emotionally Charged Events Are So Memorable." *Science Daily,* October 7, 2007. www.sciencedaily.com/releases/2007/10/071004121045.htm

Johnson, Jeff. *Designing with the Mind in Mind,* 2nd ed. Waltham, MA: Morgan Kaufmann, 2014.

Jones, Van. *The Green Collar Economy.* New York: HarperOne, 2009.

Jordan, Chris. *Running the Numbers II: Portraits of Global Mass Culture.* 2015. www.chris-jordan.com/gallery/rtn2/

Kahle, Lynn R. and Eda Gurel-Atay, eds. *Communicating Sustainability for the Green Economy.* Armonk, NY: M.E. Sharpe, 2013.

Kandel, Eric R. *The Age of Insight: The Quest to Understand the Unconscious in Art, Mind and Brain from Vienna 1900 to the Present.* New York: Random House, 2012.

Kaplan, Rachel, Stephen Kaplan, and Robert L. Ryan. *With People in Mind: Design and Management of Everyday Nature.* Washington, DC: Island Press, 1998.

Kemp, Martin. *Visualizations: The Nature Book of Art and Science.* Berkeley: University of California Press, 2000.

Kibert, Charles J. *Sustainable Construction: Green Building Design and Delivery,* 3rd ed. New York: John Wiley, 2012.

Knapp, Doug. *Applied Interpretation: Putting Research into Practice.* Fort Collins, CO: InterpPress, 2007.

Knight, Carolyn and Jessica Glaser. *Diagrams: Innovative Solutions for Graphic Designers.* Mies, Switzerland: RotoVision, 2009.

Kovacevic, Michelle. "How to Tweet about Science and Sustainability." FutureEarth: Pop-up Webinars. September 9, 2015. http://futureearth.org/blog/pop-webinars

Kullmann, Karl. "High Fidelity: Drone Mapping Fills a Missing Link in Site Representation." *Landscape Architecture Magazine* 107 no. 5 (May 2017): 132–139.

Kunkle, Kristen and Martha Monroe. "Misconceptions and Psychological Mechanisms of Climate Change Communication." Chapter 8 in Monroe, Martha C. and Marianne E. Krasny, eds. *Across the Spectrum: Resources for Environmental Educators,* 2nd ed. Washington, DC: North American Association for Environmental Education, 2015.

Kwartler, Michael and Gianni Longo. *Visioning and Visualization: People, Pixels, and Plans.* Cambridge, MA: Lincoln Institute of Land Policy, 2008.

Lake Champlain Basin Program. *Lake Champlain Wayside Exhibit Manual,* 2nd ed. Grand Island, VT: Lake Champlain Basin Program, 2004.

Lakoff, George. "Why It Matters How We Frame the Environment." *Environmental Communication: A Journal of Nature and Culture* 4 no. 1 (March 2010): 70–81.

—— and Mark Johnson. *Metaphors We Live By.* Chicago, IL: University of Chicago Press, 2003.

Langer, Susanne K. *Philosophy in a New Key: A Study in the Symbolism of Reason, Rite, and Art,* 3rd ed. Cambridge, MA: Harvard University Press, 1979.

Lannon, John M. and Laura J. Gurak. *Technical Communication,* 14th ed. New York: Pearson, 2017.

LaRocque, Paula. *The Book on Writing: The Ultimate Guide to Writing Well.* Arlington, TX: Grey and Guvnor Press, 2003.

Larsen, David L. *Interpretive Themes.* Washington, DC: National Park Service, 2001.

————, ed. *Meaningful Interpretation—How to Connect Hearts and Minds to Places, Objects and Other Resources.* Fort Washington, PA: US National Park Service, Eastern National, 2003.

Leach, Melissa. "Pathways to Sustainability: Building Political Strategies." In Worldwatch Institute. *State of the World 2013: Is Sustainability Still Possible?* Washington, DC: Island Press, 2013, 234–243.

Leiserowitz, Anthony, Edward Maibach, and Connie Roser-Renouf. *Global Warming's Six Americas 2009: An Audience Segmentation Analysis.* Yale University and George Mason University. New Haven, CT: Yale Program on Climate Change Communication, 2009.

Lester, Paul Martin. *Visual Communication: Images with Messages,* 5th ed. Boston, MA: Wadsworth, 2011.

Levine, Ronn. "New Subject Line Study Reveals 4 Ways to Increase Open Rates." Software & Information Industry Association (SIIA). August 9, 2016. www.siia.net/blog/index/Post/67946/New-Subject-Line-Study-Reveals-4-Ways-to-Increase-Open-Rates

Lewis, Karen. *Storytelling for a Cause.* Seattle, WA: Association of Writers and Writing Programs (AWP), February 28, 2014.

Lin, Maya. *What Is Missing?* 2012. https://whatismissing.net/

Loewenstein, George. *Exotic Preferences: Behavioral Economics and Human Motivation.* Oxford: Oxford University Press, 2007.

Lovins, Amory B. *Reinventing Fire.* White River Junction, VT: Chelsea Green Publishing, 2011.

Lynch, Kevin. *The Image of the City.* Cambridge, MA: MIT Press, 1964.

Lynch, Patrick J. and Sarah Horton. *Web Style Guide: Foundations of User Experience Design,* 4th ed. New Haven, CT: Yale University Press, 2016.

McKee, Robert. *Story: Substance, Structure, Style and the Principles of Screenwriting.* New York: HarperCollins, 1997.

McKenna-Cress, Polly and Janet A. Kamien. *Creating Exhibitions: Collaboration in the Planning, Development, and Design of Innovative Experiences.* New York: John Wiley, 2010.

McKenzie-Mohr, Doug and William Smith. *Fostering Sustainable Behavior.* Gabriola Island, BC: New Society Publishers, 1999.

McNall, Scott G. and George Basile. "How to Create a New Narrative for Sustainability that Will Work: and Why It Matters." *Sustainability: The Journal of Record* 6 no. 6 (December 2013): 297–301.

Maczulak, Anne. *Waste Treatment: Reducing Global Waste.* New York: Facts On File, 2010.

Makower, Joel. *Strategies for the Green Economy.* New York: McGraw-Hill, 2009.

————. "Earth Day and the Polling of America 2015." *Greenbiz,* April 6, 2015. www.greenbiz.com/article/earth-day-and-polling-america-2015

Marshall, George. *Don't Even Think about It: Why Our Brains Are Wired to Ignore Climate Change.* London: Bloomsbury, 2014.

Maslow, Abraham H. "A Theory of Human Motivation." *Psychological Review* 50 (1943): 370–396.

————. *Motivation and Personality,* 2nd ed. New York: Harper & Row, 1970.

Mayer, Richard. *Multimedia Learning,* 2nd ed. New York: Cambridge University Press, 2009.

Mayer, R.E., M. Hegarty, S. Mayer, and J. Campbell. "When Static Media Promote Active Learning: Annotated Illustrations Versus Narrated Animations in Multimedia Instruction." *Journal of Experimental Psychology: Applied* 11 no. 4 (2005): 256–265. http://dx.doi.org/10.1037/1076-898X.11.4.256

Mayo, Corky and David Larsen. *Foundations of Interpretation Competency Narrative.* Bloomington, IN: Eppley Institute for Parks & Public Lands, 2009.

Meister, Michael. Personal interview. New York: American Museum of Natural History, March 25, 2015.

Mijksenaar, Paul. *Visual Function: An Introduction to Information Design.* New York: Princeton Architectural Press, 1997.

Miller, G.A. "The Magical Number Seven, Plus or Minus Two: Some Limits on Our Capacity for Processing Information." *Psychological Review* 63 no. 2 (1956): 81–97.

Miller, G. Tyler, Jr. and Scott E. Spoolman. *Living in the Environment: Concepts, Connections, and Solutions,* 16th ed. Belmont, CA: Brooks/Cole, 2009.

Millward, Celia. *Handbook for Writers.* New York: Holt, Rinehart and Winston, 1980.

Monroe, Martha C. and Marianne E. Krasny, eds. *Across the Spectrum: Resources for Environmental Educators,* 2nd ed. Washington, DC: North American Association for Environmental Education, 2015.

Morgan, John and Peter Welton. *See What I Mean? An Introduction to Visual Communication,* 2nd ed. London: Arnold, 1992.

Moscardo, Gianna. *Making Visitors Mindful: Principles for Creating Sustainable Visitor Experiences through Effective Communication.* Champaign, IL: Sagamore, 1999.

———, Roy Ballantyne, and Karen Hughes. *Designing Interpretive Signs: Principles in Practice.* Golden, CO: Fulcrum, 2007.

Muir, John. "The National Parks and Forest Reservations." *Sierra Club Bulletin* 1 no. 7 (1896): 271–284.

National Association for Interpretation (NAI). *Definitions Project.* Fort Collins, CO: NAI, January 2007.

Nattrass, Brian and Mary Altomare. *The Natural Step for Business: Wealth, Ecology & the Evolutionary Corporation.* Gabriola Island, BC: New Society Publishers, 1999.

———. *Dancing with the Tiger: Learning Sustainability Step by Natural Step.* Gabriola Island, BC: New Society Publishers, 2002.

Newman, Peter, Timothy Beatley, and Heather Boyer. *Resilient Cities: Responding to Peak Oil and Climate Change.* Washington, DC: Island Press, 2009.

Newman, Scott and Sara Urizar. "Facilities Planning in the New Economy." Baltimore, MD: American Alliance of Museums. Annual Meeting, 2013.

Nisbet, Matthew C. "Communicating Climate Change: Why Frames Matter for Public Engagement." *Environment* 51 (2009): 12–23.

——— and Todd P. Newman. "Framing, the Media, and Environmental Communication." Chapter 28 in Anders Hansen and Robert Cox, eds. *The Routledge Handbook of Environment and Communication.* London: Routledge, 2015.

Norman, Donald A. *Emotional Design: Why We Love (or Hate) Everyday Things.* New York: Basic Books, 2004.

———. *The Design of Everyday Things,* rev. ed. New York: Basic Books, 2013.

OECD. *OECD Environmental Outlook to 2050: The Consequences of Inaction.* Paris: OECD Publishing, 2012. www.oecd-ilibrary.org/environment/oecd-environmental-outlook-to-2050_9789264122246-en

On the Cutting Edge. "Teaching Geoscience with Visualizations: Using Images, Animations, and Models Effectively." Workshop: On the Cutting Edge. February 26–28, 2004. Carleton College, Northfield, MN.

O'Neill, Saffron J., Maxwell Boykoff, Simon Niemeyer, and Sophie A. Day. "On the Use of Imagery for Climate Change Engagement." *Global Environmental Change* 23 (2013): 413–421.

Orr, David W. "Reassembling the Pieces: Ecological Design and the Liberal Arts." Chapter 12 in Gregory A. Smith and Dilafruz R. Williams, eds. *Ecological Education in Action: On Weaving Education, Culture, and the Environment*. Albany: State University of New York Press, 1998.

Parker Pearson, Michael. *Stonehenge: A New Understanding*. New York: The Experiment, 2014.

Parman, Alice and Jeffrey Jane Flowers. *Exhibit Makeovers: A Do-It-Yourself Workbook for Small Museums*. New York: Altamira Press, 2008.

Pascal, Blaise. *The Provincial Letters*. 1656. Translated by A.J. Krallsheimer. New York: Penguin Classics, 1982.

Passini, Romedi. *Wayfinding in Architecture*. New York: Van Nostrand Reinhold, 1984.

Patterson, Steve. "The 27 PPI Web Resolution Myth." *Photoshop Essentials*. 2017. www.photoshopessentials.com/essentials/the-72-ppi-web-resolution-myth/

Pelletier, Tom C. "Word of the Day: Thigmotaxis." *Ask a Naturalist*. June 15, 2010. http://askanaturalist.com/word-of-the-day-thigmotaxis/

Phaidon. "Olafur Eliasson Puts Carbon on the Menu." *Phaidon Agenda,* September 7, 2016.

Plain Language Action and Information Network (PLAIN). *Federal Plain Language Guidelines*. Washington, DC: PlainLanguage.gov, 2011.

Poole, Robert. *Earthrise: How Man First Saw the Earth*. New Haven, CT: Yale University Press, 2010.

Ramachandran, Vilayanur S. *The Tell-Tale Brain: A Neuroscientist's Quest*. New York: W.W. Norton, 2012.

Raphael, David. *Wayfinding: Principles and Practice,* 2nd ed. Landscape Architecture Technical Information Series. Washington, DC: American Society of Landscape Architects, 2013.

Redish, Janice. *Letting Go of the Words: Writing Web Content that Works*, 2nd ed. San Francisco, CA: Morgan Kaufmann, 2012.

Rees, William E. "The Way Forward: Survival 2100." In Robert Costanza and Ida Kubiszewski, eds. *Creating a Sustainable and Desirable Future*. Singapore: World Scientific, 2014.

Regnier, Kathleen, Michael Gross, and Ron Zimmerman. *The Interpreter's Guidebook: Techniques for Programs and Presentations*. Stevens Point, WI: UW-SP Foundation Press, 1994.

Reist, Sami. *Environmental Media*. Thematic essay. Routledge Sustainability Hub, 2014.

Ritter, G. Christopher. *Creating Winning Trial Strategies and Graphics*. Chicago, IL: American Bar Association, 2004.

Roam, Dan. *The Back of the Napkin,* expanded edition. New York: Portfolio/Penguin, 2010.

———. *Show and Tell: How Everybody Can Make Extraordinary Presentations*. New York: Portfolio/Penguin, 2014.

Robertson, Margaret. *Sustainability Principles and Practice,* 2nd ed. London: Routledge, 2017.

Rogers, Elizabeth Barlow. *Landscape Design: A Cultural and Architectural History*. New York: Harry N. Abrams, 2001.

Rogers, Heather. *Gone Tomorrow: The Hidden Life of Garbage*. New York: The New Press, 2005.

Roper-Starch. *NEETF Environmental Attitudes and Knowledge Survey*. New York: Roper-Starch Worldwide, 1996.

Roser-Renouf, Connie, Neil Stenhouse, Justin Rolfe-Redding, Edward Maibach, and Anthony Leiserowitz. "Engaging Diverse Audiences with Climate Change: Message Strategies for Global Warming's Six Americas." Chapter 31 in Anders Hansen and Robert Cox, eds. *The Routledge Handbook of Environment and Communication*. London: Routledge, 2015.

Ryan, Charlotte and Kimberly Freeman Brown. "To Act in Concert: Environmental Communication from a Social Movement Lens." Chapter 10 in Anders Hansen and Robert Cox, eds. *The Routledge Handbook of Environment and Communication*. London: Routledge, 2015.

Sagan, Carl. *The Demon-Haunted World: Science as a Candle in the Dark*. New York: Random House, 1995.

Sanchez, Thomas W. and Marc Brenman. *The Right to Transportation: Moving to Equity*. Chicago, IL: APA Planners Press, 2008.

Sanoff, Henry. *Community Participation Methods in Design and Planning*. New York: John Wiley, 2000.

Scherbaum, Peggy Ann. *Handles: Helping Visitors to Grasp Resource Meanings*. Washington, DC: National Park Service Interpretive Development Program, 2006.

Schuller, Gerlinde. "Information Design = Complexity + Interdisciplinarity + Experiment." AIGA, The Professional Association for Design. March 14, 2007. www.aiga. org/complexity-plus-interdisciplinarity-plus-experiment

Schwartz, Peter. *The Art of the Long View*. New York: Currency Doubleday, 1996.

Second Story Interactive Studios. "Case Study: Earth Lab: Degrees of Change." AIGA, The Professional Association for Design. October 4, 2012. www.aiga.org/ justified-2012--case-study--earth-lab

SEGD (Society for Experiential Graphic Design). "What Is Information Design?" 2014. https://segd.org/what-information-design

Shepard, Paul. *Man in the Landscape*. Athens: University of Georgia Press, 2002.

Shermer, Michael. "Turn Me On, Dead Man." *Scientific American* 292 no. 5 (May 2005): 37.

Sibbet, David. *Visual Meetings: How Graphics, Sticky Notes and Idea Mapping Can Transform Group Productivity*. New York: John Wiley, 2010.

Simons, Daniel J. and Christopher F. Chabris. "Gorillas in Our Midst: Sustained Inattentional Blindness for Dynamic Events." *Perception* 28 no. 9 (September 1999): 1059–1074.

Smith, Brooke, Nancy Baron, Chad English, Heather Galindo, Erica Goldman, Karen McLeod, Meghan Miner, and Elizabeth Neely. "COMPASS: Navigating the Rules of Scientific Engagement." *PLoS Biol* 11 no. 4 (April 2013): e1001552. https://doi. org/10.1371/journal.pbio.1001552

Snyder, Ken. "Tools for Community Design and Decision-making." Chapter 6 in Stan Geertman and John Charles, *Planning Support Systems in Practice*. Berlin: Springer, 2002.

Steffen, Will. "Connecting the Solution to the Problem." *Solutions* 5 no. 4 (July–August 2014): 1.

———, Paul J. Crutzen, and John R. McNeill. "The Anthropocene: Are Humans Now Overwhelming the Great Forces of Nature?" *Ambio* 36 no. 8 (December 2007): 614–621.

Stendhal. Letter to Honoré de Balzac, October 16, 1840. Quoted in Louis Dupré, *The Quest of the Absolute: Birth and Decline of European Romanticism*. Notre Dame, IN: University of Notre Dame Press, 2013.

Stevenson, Burton. *Macmillan Book of Proverbs, Maxims and Famous Phrases*, 5th ed. New York: Macmillan, 1965.

Stibbe, Arran, ed. *The Handbook of Sustainability Literacy: Skills for a Changing World*. Totnes, Devon: Green Books, 2009.

Strand, Oliver. "Otarian." *New York Times*, June 9, 2010, D6.

Strang, Gary. "Infrastructure as Landscape." *Places* 10 no. 3 (Summer 1996): 8–15.

Suellentrop, Chris. "At Play in Skies of Cretaceous Era." *New York Times,* March 20, 2014, F4.

Sullivan, Robert and Mark Meyer. *Guide to Evaluating Visual Impact Assessments for Renewable Energy Projects.* Denver, CO: National Park Service, 2014.

Sussman, Ann and Justin B. Hollander. *Cognitive Architecture: Designing for How We Respond to the Built Environment.* New York: Routledge, 2015.

Thayer, Robert L., Jr. "Increasingly Invisible Infrastructure." *Landscape Architecture* 85 no. 6 (June 1995).

Thomas, J.E., T.A. Saxby, A.B. Jones, T.J.B. Carruthers, E.G. Abal, and W.C. Dennison. *Communicating Science Effectively: A Practical Handbook for Integrating Visual Elements.* London: IWA Publishing, 2006.

Thompson, Catharine Ward and Penny Travlou. *Open Space People Space.* London: Taylor & Francis, 2007.

Tilden, F. *Interpreting Our Heritage.* Chapel Hill: University of North Carolina Press, 1957.

———. *Interpreting Our Heritage,* 3rd ed. Chapel Hill: University of North Carolina Press, 1977.

Todd, Rebecca M. "Remembering 9/11 and Forgetting Your Keys." Interview by Carmine Gallo, February 25, 2013. Quoted in Carmine Gallo, *Talk Like TED: The 9 Public-Speaking Secrets of the World's Top Minds.* New York: St. Martin's Griffin, 2014.

———, D. Talmi, T.W. Schmitz, J. Susskind, and A.K. Anderson. "Psychophysical and Neural Evidence for Emotion-Enhanced Perceptual Vividness." *Journal of Neuroscience* 32 no. 33 (2012): 11201–11212. doi:10.1523/JNEUROSCI.0155-12.2012

Toomey, Diane. "Maya Lin's Memorial to Vanishing Nature." *Yale Environment 360,* June 25, 2012. http://e360.yale.edu/features/maya_lin_a_memorial_to_a_vanishing_natural_world

Tufte, Edward R. *Envisioning Information.* Cheshire, CT: Graphics Press, 1990.

———. *Visual Explanations.* Cheshire, CT: Graphics Press, 1997.

———. *The Visual Display of Quantitative Information,* 2nd ed. Cheshire, CT: Graphics Press, 2001.

Tulving, Endel. "Episodic and Semantic Memory." In E. Tulving and W. Donaldson, eds. *Organization of Memory.* New York: Academic Press, 1972.

———. *Elements of Episodic Memory.* New York: Oxford University Press, 1983.

Turnbull, David. *Maps Are Territories: Science Is an Atlas.* Chicago, IL: University of Chicago Press, 1994.

Tversky, Barbara, M. Betrancourt, and J.B. Morrison. "Animation: Does It Facilitate Learning?" *International Journal of Human-Computer Studies* 57 (2002): 247–262.

United Nations. *The Future We Want.* New York: UN, 2012.

United Nations Environment Programme (UNEP). *Communicating Sustainability: How to Produce Effective Public Campaigns.* Nairobi: UNEP, 2005.

——— and ICLEI: Local Governments for Sustainability. International Annual Meeting on Language Arrangements, Documentation and Publications (IAMLADP). *Sustainable Events Guide.* Nairobi: UNEP, 2012.

University of Southern California (USC). *Research Guides: Executive Summary.* USC Libraries, January 2018. http://libguides.usc.edu/writingguide/executivesummary

US EPA. *Greenhouse Gas Equivalencies Calculator.* 2017. https://www.epa.gov/energy/greenhouse-gas-equivalencies-calculator

US National Oceanic and Atmospheric Administration (NOAA). *What Is LIDAR?* https://oceanservice.noaa.gov/facts/lidar.html

Usability.gov. *Usability Guidelines.* US Department of Health & Human Services, 2017. https://www.usability.gov/

Wackernagel, Mathis and William Rees. *Our Ecological Footprint: Reducing Human Impact on the Earth.* Gabriola Island, BC: New Society Publishers, 1995.

Ware, Colin. "Visual Queries: The Foundation of Visual Thinking." In Sigmar-Olaf Tergan and Tanja Keller, eds. *Knowledge and Information Visualization.* Berlin: Springer-Verlag, 2005.

———. *Information Visualization: Perception for Design,* 3rd ed. Waltham, MA: Morgan Kaufmann, 2013.

Weiler, Betty and Liam Smith. "Does More Interpretation Lead to Greater Outcomes? An Assessment of the Impacts of Multiple Layers of Interpretation in a Zoo Context." *Journal of Sustainable Tourism* 17 no. 1 (January 2009): 91–105.

Weinschenk, Susan M. *100 Things Every Designer Needs to Know about People.* Berkeley, CA: New Riders, 2011.

Weiss, Allen S. *Unnatural Horizons: Paradox & Contradiction in Landscape Architecture.* New York: Princeton Architectural Press, 1998.

Werblin, Frank and Botond Roska. "The Movies in Our Eyes." *Scientific American* 296 no. 4 (April 2007): 73–79.

Werner, John S., Baingio Pinna and Lothar Spillmann. "Illusory Color & the Brain." *Scientific American* 296 no. 3 (March 2007): 90–95.

White, Alexander W. *The Elements of Graphic Design: Space, Unity, Page Architecture, and Type.* New York: Allworth Press, 2002.

White, Jan V. *Using Charts and Graphs.* New York: R.R. Bowker Company, 1984.

White, Mark A. "Sustainability: I Know It When I See It." *Ecological Economics* 86 (2013): 213–217.

Wijkman, Anders and Johan Rockström. *Bankrupting Nature: Denying Our Planetary Boundaries.* London: Routledge, 2012.

Willcox, Jessica. "OMSI Green Exhibit Certification: A Cost-saving Tool for the Exhibition Field." *Exhibitionist,* Spring 2009, 14–20.

Williams, James R. "Guidelines for the Use of Multimedia in Instruction." *Proceedings of the Human Factors and Ergonomics Society 42nd Annual Meeting* 42 no. 20 (1998): 1447–1451.

Williams, Kimber. "Maps for the *Times.*" *Oregon Quarterly* 89 no. 4 (Summer 2010): 36–40.

Wilson, Edward O. *The Future of Life.* London: Abacus, 2002.

World Wide Web Consortium (W3C). *Web Accessibility Initiative (WAI).* 2017. https://www.w3.org/WAI/

Wurman, Richard S. *Information Anxiety.* New York: Doubleday, 1989.

Yau, Nathan. *Visualize This.* Indianapolis, IN: Wiley, 2011.

Zeisel, John. *Inquiry by Design: Environment/Behavior/Neuroscience in Architecture, Interiors, Landscape, and Planning,* rev. ed. New York: W.W. Norton, 2006.

Zeki, Semir. "The Visual Image in Mind and Brain." *Scientific American,* September 1992, 69–76.

Zettl, Herbert. *Sight, Sound, Motion: Applied Media Aesthetics,* 3rd ed. Belmont, CA: Wadsworth, 1998.

INDEX

3-D printing 149
3ds Max 150

absolute versus relative 15, 99
accessibility 58
active voice 62, 173
Adobe software 117
aerial perspective 16
Aesop's fables 37
affective 17, 38
Affinity Diagrams 158–9
agenda 153–4
albedo 35
all capitals 102, 104, 140
American Museum of Natural History 51
Americans with Disabilities Act 80
amoeba graph 122
amygdala 17
analogies 34, 51, 57, 62, 86
analogous colors 99
anchor, website 138
anchor points 77
animation 143, 149–50; websites and 140
Anthropocene epoch 4
anthropocentric 8
Apollo 8 28
Apollo 17 28
ArcGIS 148
area 87
area graphs 122
Aristotle 23, 34, 40
arrows on signs 79
art 64–5

associations 12, 18–19, 33, 51, 75, 182
asymmetry, in design 106
AtKisson, Alan 42
atmospheric perspective 16
Attenborough, David 47
attention, selective see selective attention
attentive processing 126
audiences 188; empathy for 24
audience research 188–9
automobile, weight of 87
autonomy 52, 146
axis mundi 36

background 15–16, 74–5; patterned 104, 139, 171; websites and 139
background color, text and 104, 140, 171, 185, 192
bar graph 121
Beethoven, Ludwig von 27
benchmark 129
billboards 90
biophilia 114
bird's-eye view 82
bleeds 107
blind men and elephant 36
blind users, websites and 140
blogs 144, 151–2
blue color 100, 126; sensitivity 13
Blue Marble 28
body language 187
border cells 74
Braille 64
Brain Writing process 158

brain, development of 17
brainstem 17
brainstorming 157
breadcrumb navigation 138
bread-crumb trail 78
Bretz, J. Harlan 54
brevity 27
brightness 98
brochures 170–1
brownie-mix analogy 26
bubble chart 122
building information modeling 148
buildings 92–3
bullets 25, 140

California Academy of Sciences 134
Campbell, Joseph 41
canonical silhouettes 112–13
capitalization *see* all capitals
car, weight of 87
Carbon Café 134
carbon footprint 132
cause and effect 4, 38, 49, 53, 55, 113
centered text 141
cerebellum 17
Challenger see Space Shuttle Challenger
charts 119–20
Chinese gardens 93
choice 52 *see also* autonomy
choice 57
chroma 98
chunking 25–7, 79, 106, 126, 135, 171, 183;
    cognitive 19; handouts and 188; websites
    and 140
chunks: cognitive 75; seven 19; in text 104;
    three to five 25, 120, 126, 183
circular economy 35, 36n2
clauses 174, 192
clicking 145
climate change 6–11, 21–2, 42, 52, 64–5, 86;
    graphs and 121, 125; images and 111–14;
    Inconvenient Truth and 143; Science
    Museum and 145–6
Climate Museum 134
clip art 113
closed-loop system 35, 36n2
closing, complimentary 181
closure 14–15
cloud-based applications 148
CMYK 99, 171
cognition 18–22
cognitive maps 73, 78–9, 81; digital media
    and 145
cognitive psychology 18

coherence 39, 76–7
collective learning 136
color 13, 16, 98–101; in documents
    171; information graphics and 126;
    in presentations 185; on signage 63;
    websites and 139
color blindness 101
color coding 79–80
color constancy 16
color space 98
color wheel 99
Columbia River Gorge 54
common fate 14–15
communication plans 68, 188–92
community participation 146; *see also* public
    participation
community planning 129, 145–6
comparison 33
complementary colors 99
complexity 76–7; visual 114
complimentary closing *see* complimentary
    closing
composition 104–8
computer-aided design 148
concept maps 160, 166–7
conclusion 183
concrete representation 85–90
cones 13–14
conferences *see* event planning
confirmation bias 7, 18, 91
conflict 156
connectedness 14–15
consensus 160–1
constellations 36
constructivist theory 24
Container Corporation of America 133
continuity 14–15
contours 16
contrast 15, 16, 33, 50, 75, 100, 104–5;
    color and 126; edges and 16; in graphs
    and diagrams 125; handouts and 188;
    hierarchy and 105; landmarks and 74; on
    signage 63
cool colors 100
copyright 117
cortex 17
courtrooms 41–2
Crawford Slip Writing 158
Creative Commons 118
criteria chart, weighted *see* weighted
    criteria chart
critical path method chart 123
cultural differences, images and 114–15
curiosity 39

dark versus light background *see*
    background color, text and
dashboard 93, 135
Dawkins, Richard 111
deduction 55
deficit model 7, 21
democracy 3
density and urban planning 112
depth of field 115
design, wayfinding 77–8
desktop publishing 109, 171
diagonals 115, 186
diagrams 120, 123–4; design of 125–6
diffusion *see* social diffusion
digital divide 11
digital media 136–52
digital natives 145, 152
diorama, forest 84–5
directional signs 78–9
distinctiveness 77
districts 74
document management system 191
dopamine 17, 50, 76
dots per inch 116
draft, writing of 172
drama 42
drones 148
Duarte, Nancy 183–4

eager nonverbal 187
Earthrise 28
EcoArts 64
ecocentric 8
eco-labels 133
ecological footprint 87, 132
Ecological Roadmap 9
ecosystem services 35, 36n1
edges 16, 74, 77
efficacy 11, 111
electromagnetic radiation *see*
    electromagnetic waves
electromagnetic waves 13, 98
elephant: blind men and 36; weight of 87
email 178–80
embedded files 171
emotion 17–18, 21, 55; stories and 38
emotionally charged event 17, 185
empathy for audience 24–5
endorphins 50
energy efficiency 86–7
enjoyability 49
environment, protection of 22, 35
environment-behavior 70
environmental communication 77

environmental graphic design 71
environmental management system 129
episodic memory 20, 49, 54, 57
EPS files 117
ethos 23
evaluation 68–70, 191–2
event planning 162–6
examples 62
executive summary 169
exhibit: definition of 55; design 55–8
expletives 173–4
exploration 53, 75–6

Facebook 150, 152
faces, recognizing 112–14
facilitator 155
familiarity 51–53
feedback 68, 142, 176, 190–2;
    communication and 23; dashboards
    and 135; gages and 93; participation
    and 161–2; policies and 175–6; writing
    process and 172; *see also* evaluation
Feynman, Richard 25, 85–6
Fibonacci numbers 108
field, depth of *see* depth of field
Field Museum 51, 145
fifth great turning 5
fighting mind 26
figures 15, 75
figure/ground 14–15, 75
file management 118
file structure: SEO and 141; websites
    and 137
fill patterns: graphs and 126; *see also*
    background, patterned
films 143, 177
Fisher Museum 84–5
Flesch readability scale 62
flipcharts 155
flood markers 89
flowchart 123
flush left 104
flyers 170–1
focus groups 69–70, 189–90, 192
font 101
food, visualizing content of 89–90
football field, area of 87, 93
football stadium, volume and 87 88
footprints 132
forest diorama *see* Fisher Museum
Forest Stewardship Council 133
forms *see* shapes
formative evaluation 69
fossil fuels *see* petroleum

fovea 13–14
frames 20–22, 90
frameworks 131; mental 8
frequency 13
frequently asked questions 138
front-end evaluation 68–9
Fry test 62
Fuller, R. Buckminster 35
fusiform gyrus 113

Gallery Walk process 157
gaming 145
Gantt chart 123
Gardner, Howard 20
gateways 77
geographic information systems 148
geological time scale 5
Gestalt 14–15
Global Reporting Initiative 131
goals 66
golden rectangle and field of vision 108
golden section 108
Google 141
Gore, Al 143
gorilla *see* invisible gorilla study
graphic design 97–109; websites and 139
graphic facilitation 155–6
graphs 121–3; design of 125–6
Great Acceleration 5
green: color 100, 126; dramaturgy 42;
    exhibits 58–9; infrastructure 91–2;
    rooms 100
greenhouse effect 35
Greenhouse Gas Equivalencies
    Calculator 86
Greenhouse Gas Protocol 134
grid cells 74
grids 107–8, 139, 186
grotto 36
group process 156–61
guardrails 35

Ham, Sam 45
handouts 170–1, 186, 188
hands-on 49, 57, 85
hashtags 151–2
hatch patterns *see* fill patterns
headings 105–6; handouts and 188
heads-up orientation 82
hero's journey 41; presentations and 184
hierarchical organization 135
hierarchy, visual 51, 75–6, 104–6, 125, 139,
    142, 171
hierarchy of needs *see* Maslow's hierarchy
    of needs

hippocampus 71, 74
Hobbit, The 41
hockey-stick graph 121
Holocene epoch 5
homepage 138–9
Homer 38
hovering 145
hue 98
hyperlinks 136–8; social media and 152
hypertext 136
Hypertext Markup Language 141

Ice Age Floods 54
icons 29, 79–80
identifier signs 78–9
illustration software 116
Illustrator 117
image-editing software 147
images 110–18; choosing 113–15; impact of
    110; in presentations 185; processing of
    27; on signage 62–3; on websites 139–40
inattention blindness 18
inciting incident 40
Inconvenient Truth 143
InDesign 117
Index Color 99
indicators 128–31
indigenous maps 124
induction 55
infographics 119
information-gap perspective 39
information design 119
information graphics 119–20; design of
    125–6
information overload 6–7
information visualization 126–7
infrastructure 90–1; green *see* green
    infrastructure
instant messaging 180
instruction manual 35
intangibles 47–9
intellectual property 117
intensifiers 174
interactive: exhibits 57; media 143–6
International Association for Public
    Participation 162
International Commission on Stratigraphy 4
internet 136, 177; capitalization of 152
interpretation 3, 44–54; definition of 45–6
interpretive signage: websites and 137, 139;
    see signage, interpretive
interviews 69–70
introduction 182–3
Inuit wooden maps 124
inverted pyramid 21, 179; websites and 137

invisible gorilla study 18
ISO 133; 14020 133; 14063 64
iterative process: design as 142; testing
    and 152

jargon 25, 174
journalism, visual *see* visual journalism
journalism, writing style in 21
journalists 178
JPEG files 116
justification 104, 141

Keeling Curve 121
keywords 141–2

labels 132–4
labyrinth 73
lagging indicators 130
landmarks 15, 50, 73–7, 79, 81–2; in text
    104; websites and 138
leading 103
leading indicators 130
LEED-certified buildings 135
left-to-right reading 107; diagonals and 115
legibility 73–5
letter height, on signs 103
letters 180–2
LIDAR 148
life-cycle assessment 133
light 13, 22n1
light versus dark background *see*
    background color, text and
lighting 115; signage and 64; for video 144
limbic system 17, 21, 71
Lin, Maya 65
line 97, 114; graph 121; length 104;
    spacing 103
linear perspective 16
linguistics 115
linked files 171
links *see* hyperlinks
lists 25
litigation 41–2
Living Building 93
logos 29
logos 23
long letter versus short letter 27
long-term memory 49
low vision: websites and 139–40; *see also*
    visual impairment
lowercase 102, 104
Lynch, Kevin 73–4, 83

magazines 177
maintenance 64, 78

Manhattan 89
maps 78–83, 123–4; orientation of 82
Marshall Islands 124
Maslow's hierarchy of needs 72, 74
Max Burger 134
Maya 150
meat diet, impact of 90
media aesthetics 144
meetings 153–68
memes 111, 151
memory: episodic *see* episodic memory;
    formation of 17; long-term *see* long-
    term memory; semantic *see* semantic
    memory; short-term *see* short-term
    memory; working *see* working memory
memos 180–1
menus: food 134; website 138
messaging 180
metamerism 100
metaphors 18, 22, 33–6, 51, 57, 62
metonym 33
microphones 144
milestones 190
Minard map 124
mind maps 160
mindfulness 46, 50, 53, 60
miniatures 84
minutes 154
mirror neurons 39, 142–3
mixed-use neighborhood 147
models 79, 83–5, 147
monochromatic color scheme 99
Mont Ventoux 28
motion: in photographs 115; *see also*
    movement
movement 13, 16, 63, 142–3, 149
Muir, John 44
Multiattribute Decision Analysis 159
multimedia 144; websites and 140
multiple intelligences 20
multi-voting 160
Museum Tour process 157
mystery 39–40, 50, 75–7

Napoleon, Minard map and 124
narrative structure 40–1
National Academy of Sciences 145
natural capital 35
Natural Color System 100
Natural Step *see* The Natural Step
navigation, in websites 137–8
negative approach 8, 26
neocortex 17
neurons 17
neurotransmitters 76

New York Harbor 89
news: media 177–9; releases 178
newsletters 170–1
newspapers 177–8
Newton, Sir Isaac 99
nodes 74
noise 23
Nominal Group Process 157
nonpersonal interpretation 45
norepinephrine 17
normalized data 130
Norman, Donald 58
novelty 50, 184

objectives 189
observation 70
Odysseus 38
op-ed 177
optic nerve 13
Oregon Convention Center Rain
    Garden 92
organic certification 133
organization: exhibits and 55–6;
    interpretation and 48
organizational chart 123
orphans 104
Otarian 134
outline 172
overlap 16

Pantone 100
paper consumption 87
PARK analysis 162
participation see public participation
Pascal, Blaise 27
passive voice 62, 173
path 74
pathos 23
pattern: recognition 19; -seeking 12, 14–15,
    18–19, 75, 105
patterned background see background,
    patterned
patterns: perception of in concept maps 167;
    perception of in graphics 119, 121, 125
PDF 117
percept 12
perception 12; visual 12–18; visual, and
    diagrams 123
peripheral vision 14
personal: connection 51–53; interpretation
    45, 59–60; pronouns see pronouns
perspective 16
PERT chart 123
Petrarch 28

petroleum, meat diet and 90
Pharos Project 132–3
phi 108
photogrammetry 148
photographs: composition of 115; use
    of 112
photons 22n1
Photoshop 117, 147
pica 102
picture is worth a thousand words 29
pie chart 122
Pin Card process 158
pixelated 116
pixels 116; per inch 116
place cells 74
plain language 25, 61–2, 174, 181; social
    media and 152; websites and 138, 140
plan: communication see communication
    plan; sign see sign plan; view 82
planetary boundaries 35, 122
planning 146; of communication see
    communication plans; of events
    163; interpretation and 65–70; of
    presentations 183; tools for 166–7;
    wayfinding 77–8
plastic waste 87–9
plot point 41
PNG files 116–17
podcasts 144
point size 102
point-cloud data 148
policies 175–7
Pollan, Michael 90
Polynesian navigation maps 124
position 16
positive approach 8, 26
poster 170–1; session 170
Potsdamer Platz 91–2
PowerPoint 171, 184, 186
practice, presentations and 186–7
preattentive processing 16, 126, 135
presentations 182–92; software 171
primary colors 99
problem approach 8, 26
procedures 176
process chart 123
project plan 189
pronouns 62, 175
prototypes 67–9, 80–1
provocation 46–7, 55–7, 59–60, 146
proximity 14–15
public domain 117
public participation 161–2
pyramid 36

radar graph 122
radial graph 122–3
radio 177
ragged right 104
rain garden 92
raster images 116
rational brain 17
recorder 154
recycling 88; symbol 28, 133–4
red color 100, 126; sensitivity 13
redundancy 22, 26, 54, 77, 101
relative size *see* size, relative
relative versus absolute 15, 99
relevance, interpretation and 48–9
repeat photography 111
repetition 20, 49
reports 169, 183
reptilian brain 17
request for proposal 163
resolution: of images 116; of storyline 40
resolution
retina 13
Revit 148
RGB 98, 171
Rhetoric 23
rods 13–14
route strategy, for wayfinding 73
roving interpretation 59
rule of thirds 107–8; photographs and 115

saccades 14
safe operating space 122
Sagan, Carl 47
salutation 181
sans serif typefaces 101–3, 140, 171, 185
satellite imagery 148
saturation 98
scale 50–1; diagrams and 120, 123–4; exaggerated 49–51; models and 83–5
scenario planning 167–8
scenarios, climate change and 145
schema 20
schemata 20
schools 92–3
Science Museum 145
search 141–2; engines 141–2; engine optimization 141–2
seating 58
Seattle 129, 131
secondary colors 99
segmentation 9–11
selective: attention 7, 18; perception 18
semantic memory 20, 49, 54
senses 40, 57, 60

sensitivity to colors 13
sentence length 174
sequential order versus simultaneous 120–1
serif typefaces 101–3, 171
seven cognitive chunks *see* chunks, seven
shade, of color 98
Shakespeare, William, metaphors and 34
shapes 13, 97, 126
short letter 27
short-term memory 49
show don't tell 40, 123
sight lines 77
sign: fabrication 64, 78; inventory 78; location 63–4, 79; plan 68, 78; *see also* signage
signage 78–81; interpretive 60–4; installation of 63
silhouettes, canonical *see* canonical silhouettes
similarity 14–15
simile 34
simplicity 27
simulations 145–9
simultaneous versus sequential order 120–1
Six Americas 9–10
size: relative 16; of type *see* type size
slide: design 184–6; master 186
Snow Card process 159
Snowball process 159
soccer field, area of 87
social: capital 11; diffusion 150; equity 11; factors 8–11; inequality, digital technology and 136; media 150–2; media, SEO and 141
Society for Experiential Graphic Design 80
Society of Plastics Industries 133
Socrates 24
soil exhibit 51, 84
solar power, visual impact and 147
solution approach 8, 26
sound bites 151
South Bronx 38
Space Shuttle Challenger 85–6
spatial planning 77
specialization 7
spectrophotometer 100
speech, rate of 187
speed *see* speech, rate of
spider graph 122
squid, giant 42
stakeholder 161
star graph 122
Star Wars 41
Stendhal 24

stewards 35
stick navigation charts 124
stock photos 113
stories 10, 18, 22, 37–43, 53–4, 57;
    interpretation and 49; in presentations
    183–4; see also storytelling
stormwater 91–2
story arc 37, 41
storyboard 150, 183; software 150
storytelling 8, 37; images and 113;
    journalists and 178
straight lines 114
straw poll 160
streakers 56
strollers 56
structure 105; presentations and 182
studiers 56
style guides 172
subway map 124
summative evaluation 69–70
survey knowledge strategy, for
    wayfinding73
surveys 69–70, 189, 191–2
sustainability 4
Sustainability Tracking, Assessment and
    Rating System 131
Sustainable Development Goals 129
Sustainable Seattle 129, 131
SWOT analysis 162
symbols 22, 28–9, 33, 79–80
symmetry 14–15, 36, 97; in design 106, 186
synecdoche 33–4
System 1 and System 2 17

table of contents 26, 172
tables 120–1, 140; design of 125–6
tactile maps, Inuit 124
tangibles 47–9
TED Talks 184
television 177
tertiary colors 99
text: color and background see background
    color, text and; height 61; in
    presentations 185; on signage 61; size see
    type size; on websites 140–1
texting 180
texture 16
Thai Airways 134
The Natural Step 131–2
theater 42
theme 47, 49, 51, 55–7, 66–7; presentations
    and 182–3; statement 172; visual 139
therapeutic garden design 77
thigmotaxis 71
third-party verification 133, 135

thirds, rule of see rule of thirds
Thorne Miniature Rooms 84
thought listing 69
three cognitive chunks see chunks, three
    to five
TIFF files 116
Tilden, Freeman 27, 45
timekeeper 155
timeline 145; project planning and
    189–90
timescale, exaggerated 51
tint 98
title 171
TORE: acronym in interpretation 47;
    presentations and 183
track-up orientation 82
trailblazer signs 78–9
transformation stories 41
transition 5, 183
transmittal letters 182
trial lawyers 41–2
triangular coordinate graph 122
trimtab 35
triple bottom line 131
Tulving, Endel 20, 49
turning point 40–1
Twain, Mark 27
tweeting 151–2
Twitter 150–2
type size 103, 171
typeface 101–3
typography 101–3
Tyson, Neil deGrasse 47

Uniform Resource Locators 136
unity 106
universal concepts 48
uppercase 102, 104
urban: heat islands 35; planning 112
usability testing 142, 152

value 98
vanishing point 16
variety 50, 63
vector images 116
verbs 173
video 142–3; editing software 144; news
    releases 143–4; production 144; websites
    and 140
virtual water 132
visibility, low vision and 80
visible light 13, 22n1, 98
visual: communication 27–9; cortex 13, 17;
    field 13; hierarchy see hierarchy, visual;
    impact analysis 147; impairment 80, 83;

impairment and websites 139–40;
journalism 27; perception *see* perception,
visual; preference surveys 146–7;
processing 27
vividness 18, 49
voting 160

walkable neighborhood 147
walking: circle 81; tour 53
walks: guided 60; self-guided 60
wall-hugging 71
warm colors 100
waste: audit 88; visualizing 87–9
water: footprint 132; level, visualizing 89;
volume 87
watershed models 85
waves 13
wavelengths 13, 22n1, 98
wayfinding 15, 53, 71–83; definition of
71; process 72–4; websites and
138–9
web 136; browsers 136, 139; capitalization
of 152
Web 2.0 150
Web Accessibility Initiative 140

websites 136–9; organization of 137;
planning of 142
weighted criteria chart 159
white space 105–7, 139, 171; graphs and
126; handouts and 188
wicked problems 5
widows 104
wiki 151–2
Wikipedia 150
wind: power and visual impact 147; rose 122
Wizard of Oz, The Wonderful 41
wooden maps, Inuit 124
word clouds 127
WordPress 151
working memory 120, 125–6
workshops *see* event planning
World Wide Web 136; Consortium 140
worldview 8–9
writing: guidelines for 173–5; process
172–3

you are here 81
YouTube 144, 150, 152

Zettl, Herbert 144

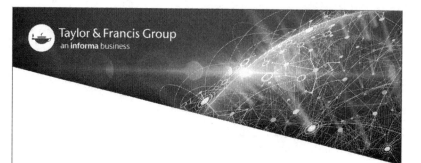